LUST

and Other Uses for Spare Hormones

Also by Jerry Scott and Jim Borgman

Zits: Sketchbook 1
Growth Spurt: Zits Sketchbook 2
Don't Roll Your Eyes at Me, Young Man!: Zits Sketchbook 3
Are We an "Us"?: Zits Sketchbook 4
Zits Unzipped: Zits Sketchbook 5
Busted!: Zits Sketchbook 6
Road Trip: Zits Sketchbook 7
Teenage Tales: Zits Sketchbook No. 8
Thrashed: Zits Sketchbook No. 9
Pimp My Lunch: Zits Sketchbook No. 10
Are We Out of the Driveway Yet?: Zits Sketchbook No. 11
Rude, Crude, and Tattooed: Zits Sketchbook No. 12
Jeremy and Mom
Pierced

Treasuries

Humongous Zits
Big Honkin' Zits
Zits: Supersized
Random Zits
Crack of Noon
Alternative Zits
My Bad

LUST

and Other Uses for Spare Hormones

WITHDRAWN

A **ZITS**® Look at Relationships
by Jerry Scott and Jim Borgman

**Andrews McMeel
Publishing, LLC**

Kansas City • Sydney • London

Zits® is syndicated internationally by King Features Syndicate, Inc. For information, write King Features Syndicate, Inc., 300 West Fifty-Seventh Street, New York, New York 10019.

09 10 11 12 13 RR2 10 9 8 7 6 5 4 3 2 1

ISBN-13: 978-0-7407-8544-3
ISBN-10: 0-7407-8544-3

Library of Congress Control Number: 2009924139

Zits® may be viewed online at
www.kingfeatures.com.

www.andrewsmcmeel.com

──────── **ATTENTION: SCHOOLS AND BUSINESSES** ────────

Andrews McMeel books are available at quantity discounts with bulk purchase for educational, business, or sales promotional use. For information, please write to: Special Sales Department, Andrews McMeel Publishing, LLC, 1130 Walnut Street, Kansas City, Missouri 64106.

NOW DON'T KISS ME BACK THIS TIME, JEREMY.
DON'T KISS ME, I'LL KISS YOU... DON'T KISS ME, I'LL KISS YOU...
©2009 ZITS Partnership. Distributed by King Features Syndicate.
6/18
WHAT DID I JUST SAY??
I WAS ONLY TRYING TO HELP!
SCOTT and BORGMAN

Introduction

Lust? On the funny pages?

In the quaint paper-and-ink world of the newspaper comic strip, certain rules and behaviors still apply. The main one being that humorous comic strip characters don't think, say, or do anything that's too sexy. Easy to accomplish in *Garfield* or *Ziggy* (in fact, disturbing to think otherwise), but a little trickier if you happen to do a present-day comic strip featuring a teenage boy.

Hormones pulse through a teenager's body like bubbles through a lava lamp. We've learned to suggest, hint, and imply That Which Must Not Be Said on the comics page. We still get in trouble for using "sucks" unless a Hoover is involved. But doing a comic strip about a teenager without mentioning sex is like writing a biography of Neil Armstrong without mentioning the Moon. They're inseparable.

In *Zits*, the trick has been to imply romantic feelings and actions, and then let the reader's imagination do the rest of the work . . . with a few exceptions. For example, it's not too hard to understand that Rich's tongue sliding out of Amy's ear and wrapping around her body like a python means that they're fond of each other.

The strips in this book are some of our favorite examples of sweet infatuations, passionate encounters, wishful fantasies, and (most often) awkward romantic moments between the characters in *Zits*, including Jeremy and Sara, Pierce and D'ijon, Richandamy, and even Mom and Dad.

Mom and Dad? Ewwwwwwwwwwww! We might as well have said Ziggy and Garfield.

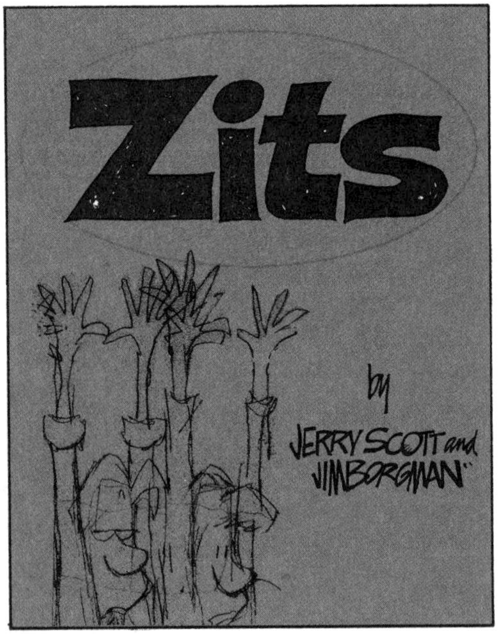
Zits
by
JERRY SCOTT and
JIM BORGMAN

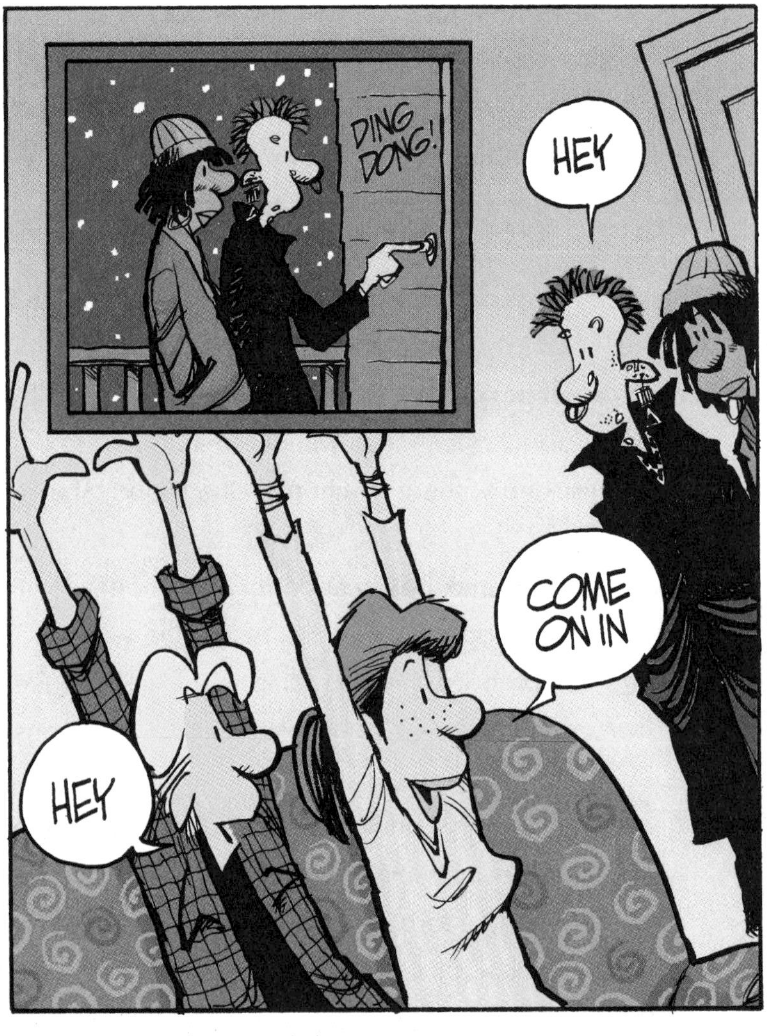
DING DONG!
HEY
COME ON IN
HEY

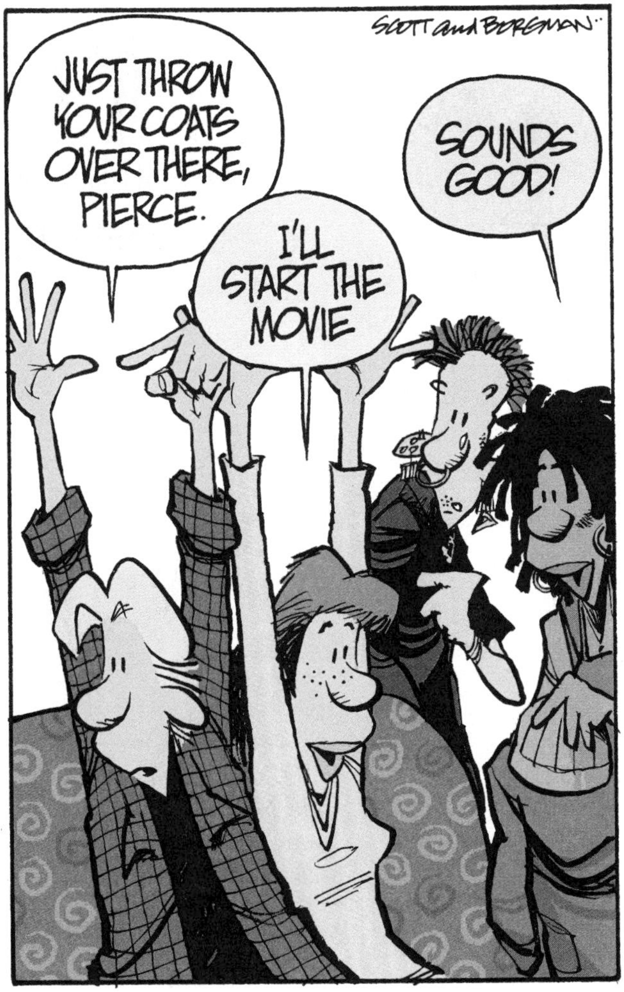
SCOTT and BORGMAN
JUST THROW YOUR COATS OVER THERE, PIERCE.
I'LL START THE MOVIE
SOUNDS GOOD!

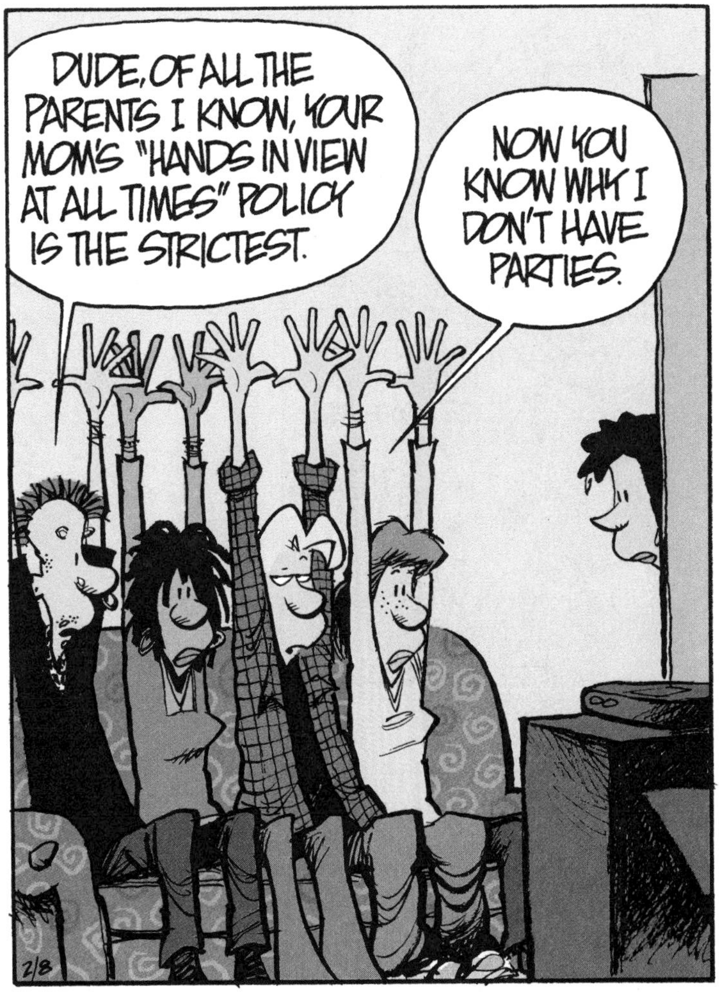
DUDE, OF ALL THE PARENTS I KNOW, YOUR MOM'S "HANDS IN VIEW AT ALL TIMES" POLICY IS THE STRICTEST.
NOW YOU KNOW WHY I DON'T HAVE PARTIES.
2/8

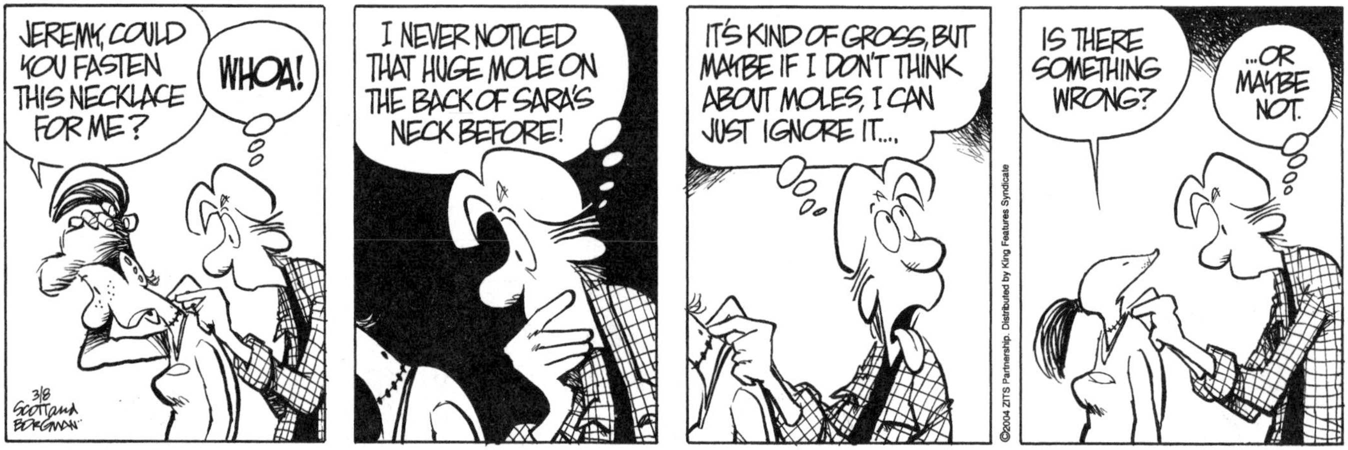
JEREMY, COULD YOU FASTEN THIS NECKLACE FOR ME?
WHOA!
3/8 SCOTT and BORGMAN
I NEVER NOTICED THAT HUGE MOLE ON THE BACK OF SARA'S NECK BEFORE!
IT'S KIND OF GROSS, BUT MAYBE IF I DON'T THINK ABOUT MOLES, I CAN JUST IGNORE IT...,
©2004 ZITS Partnership. Distributed by King Features Syndicate
IS THERE SOMETHING WRONG?
...OR MAYBE NOT.

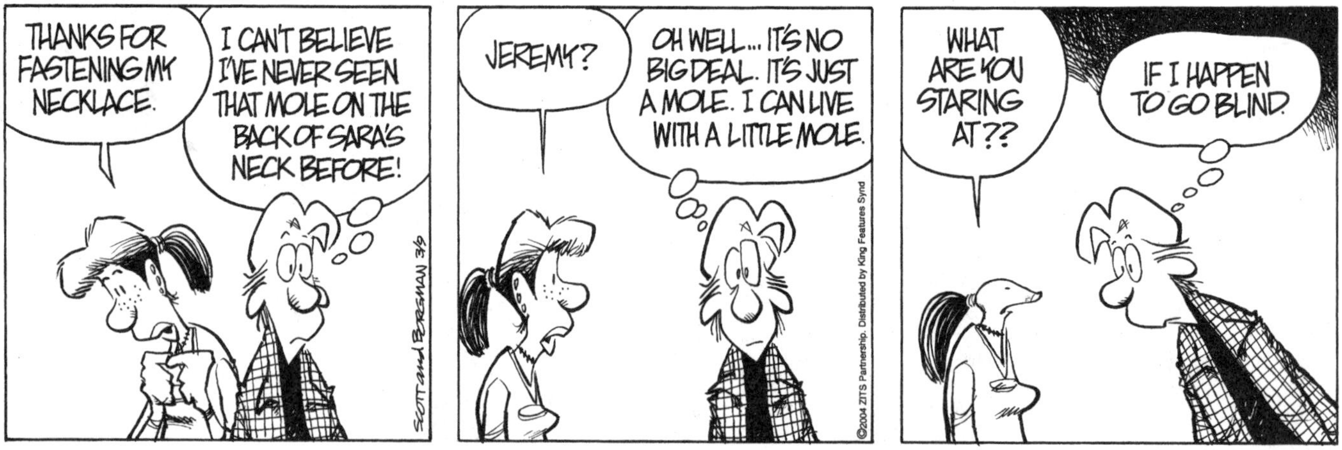
THANKS FOR FASTENING MY NECKLACE.
I CAN'T BELIEVE I'VE NEVER SEEN THAT MOLE ON THE BACK OF SARA'S NECK BEFORE!
SCOTT and BORGMAN 3/9
JEREMY?
OH WELL... IT'S NO BIG DEAL. IT'S JUST A MOLE. I CAN LIVE WITH A LITTLE MOLE.
©2004 ZITS Partnership. Distributed by King Features Synd
WHAT ARE YOU STARING AT??
IF I HAPPEN TO GO BLIND.

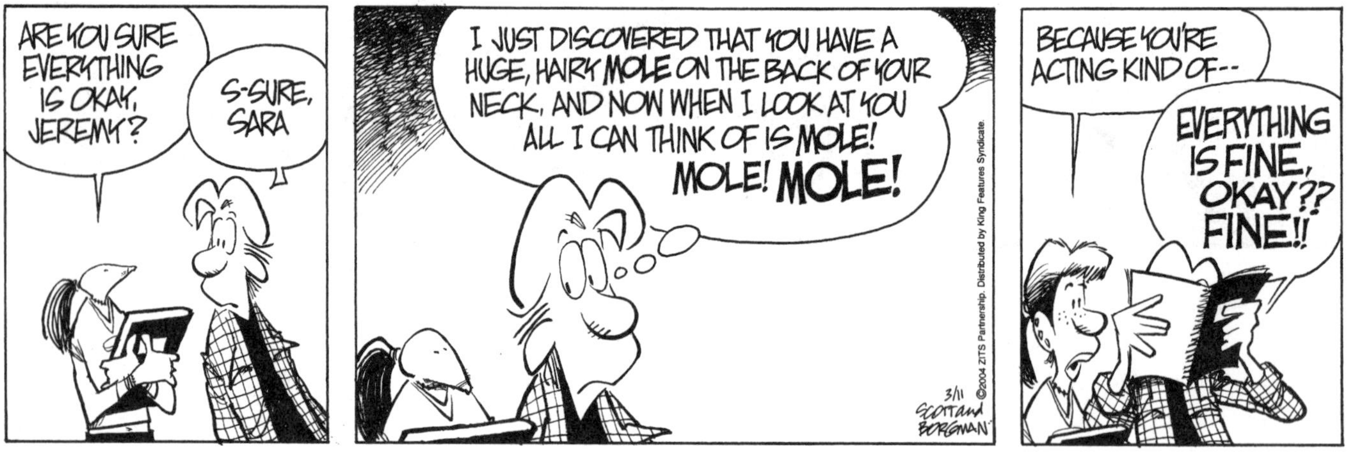
ARE YOU SURE EVERYTHING IS OKAY, JEREMY?
S-SURE, SARA
I JUST DISCOVERED THAT YOU HAVE A HUGE, HAIRY MOLE ON THE BACK OF YOUR NECK, AND NOW WHEN I LOOK AT YOU ALL I CAN THINK OF IS MOLE!
MOLE! MOLE!
©2004 ZITS Partnership. Distributed by King Features Syndicate.
3/11 SCOTT and BORGMAN
BECAUSE YOU'RE ACTING KIND OF--
EVERYTHING IS FINE, OKAY?? FINE!!

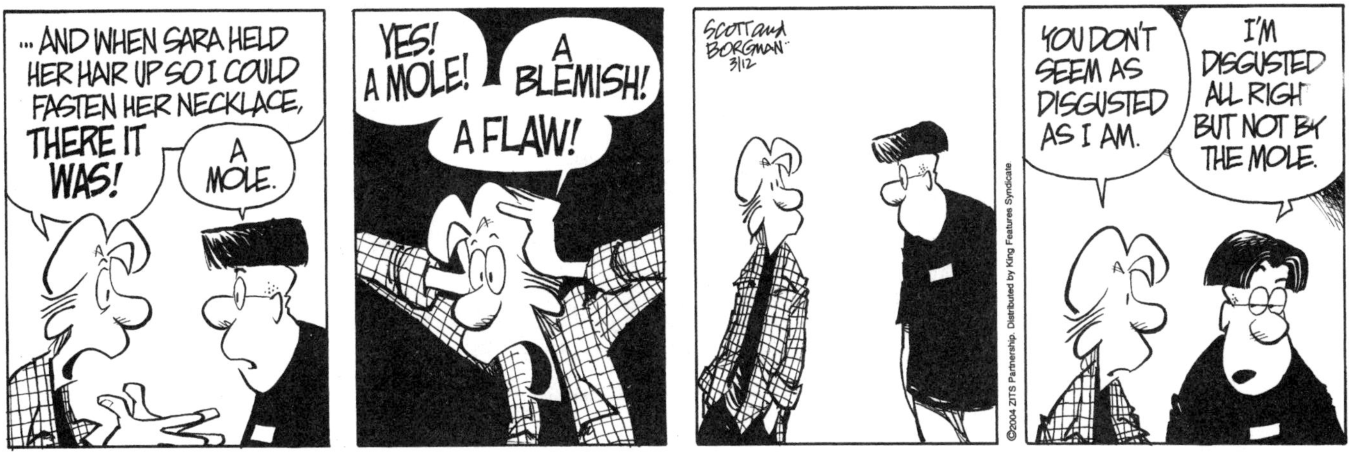
...AND WHEN SARA HELD HER HAIR UP SO I COULD FASTEN HER NECKLACE, THERE IT WAS!
A MOLE.
YES! A MOLE!
A BLEMISH!
A FLAW!
SCOTT and BORGMAN 3/12
YOU DON'T SEEM AS DISGUSTED AS I AM.
I'M DISGUSTED ALL RIGHT BUT NOT BY THE MOLE.
©2004 ZITS Partnership. Distributed by King Features Syndicate

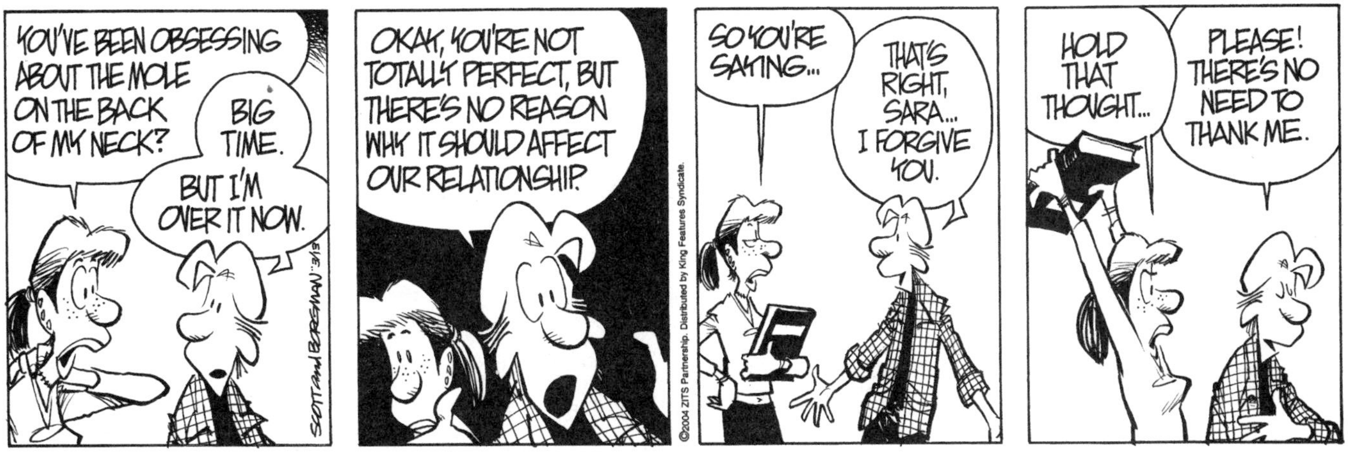
YOU'VE BEEN OBSESSING ABOUT THE MOLE ON THE BACK OF MY NECK?
BIG TIME.
BUT I'M OVER IT NOW.
SCOTT and BORGMAN 3/13
OKAY, YOU'RE NOT TOTALLY PERFECT, BUT THERE'S NO REASON WHY IT SHOULD AFFECT OUR RELATIONSHIP.
©2004 ZITS Partnership. Distributed by King Features Syndicate.
SO YOU'RE SAYING...
THAT'S RIGHT, SARA... I FORGIVE YOU.
HOLD THAT THOUGHT...
PLEASE! THERE'S NO NEED TO THANK ME.

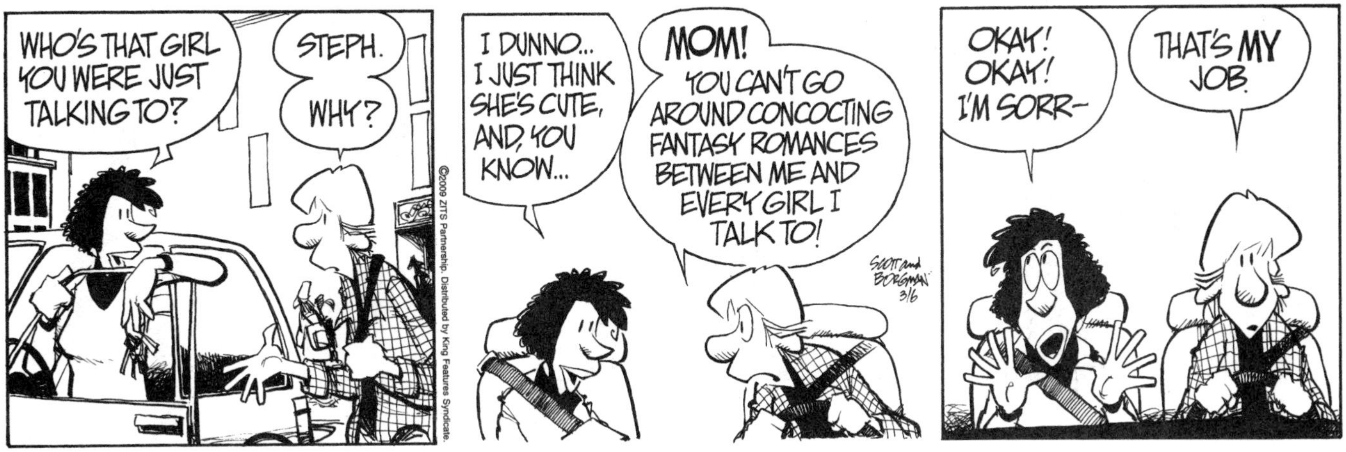
WHO'S THAT GIRL YOU WERE JUST TALKING TO?
STEPH.
WHY?
©2009 ZITS Partnership. Distributed by King Features Syndicate.
I DUNNO... I JUST THINK SHE'S CUTE, AND, YOU KNOW...
MOM! YOU CAN'T GO AROUND CONCOCTING FANTASY ROMANCES BETWEEN ME AND EVERY GIRL I TALK TO!
SCOTT and BORGMAN 3/6
OKAY! OKAY! I'M SORR–
THAT'S MY JOB.

JERRY SCOTT and JIM BORGMAN
Zits

I NEED MY OWN SPACE, JEREMY!
THERE'S NO WAY I'M MOVING MY STUFF INTO YOUR LOCKER!
WHY DO YOU ALWAYS HAVE TO BE CLOSED-MINDED TO MY IDEAS?
I'M ONLY CLOSED-MINDED TO THE STUPID ONES.
LOCKER CO-HABITATION IS SIMPLY OUT OF THE QUESTION!
IS THAT SO?
WELL, YOU MIGHT WANT TO RECONSIDER, BECAUSE I AM THIS CLOSE TO NO LONGER WORSHIPING THE GROUND YOU WALK ON, SARA!
SCOTT and BORGMAN
OKAY,... NOT REALLY!
WAY TO STRENGTHEN YOUR BARGAINING POSITION, ROMEO.
©2004 ZITS Partnership. Distributed by King Features Syndicate.

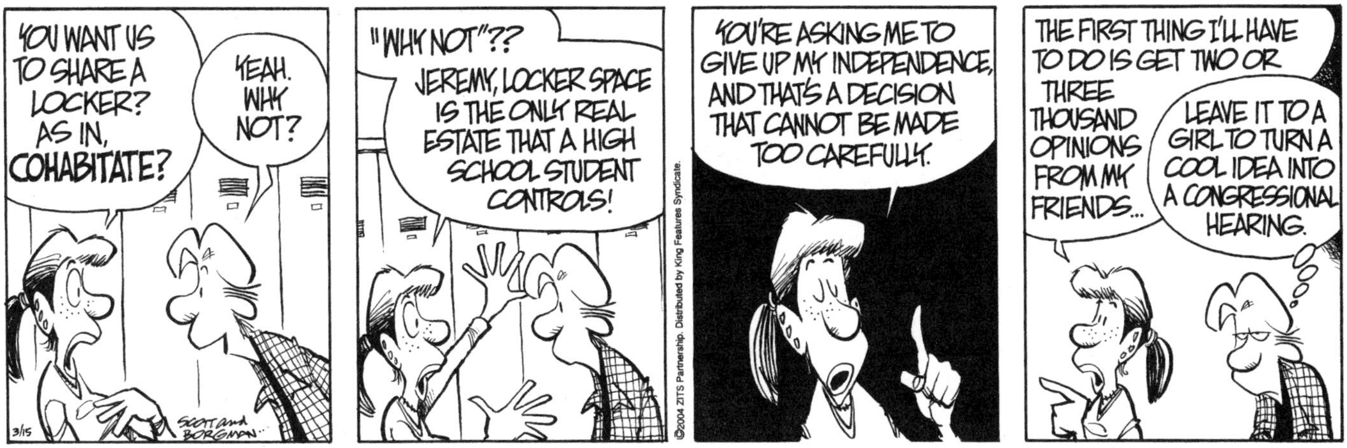
YOU WANT US TO SHARE A LOCKER? AS IN, COHABITATE?
YEAH. WHY NOT?
"WHY NOT"??
JEREMY, LOCKER SPACE IS THE ONLY REAL ESTATE THAT A HIGH SCHOOL STUDENT CONTROLS!
YOU'RE ASKING ME TO GIVE UP MY INDEPENDENCE, AND THAT'S A DECISION THAT CANNOT BE MADE TOO CAREFULLY.
THE FIRST THING I'LL HAVE TO DO IS GET TWO OR THREE THOUSAND OPINIONS FROM MY FRIENDS...
LEAVE IT TO A GIRL TO TURN A COOL IDEA INTO A CONGRESSIONAL HEARING.
3/15
SCOTT and BORGMAN
©2004 ZITS Partnership. Distributed by King Features Syndicate.

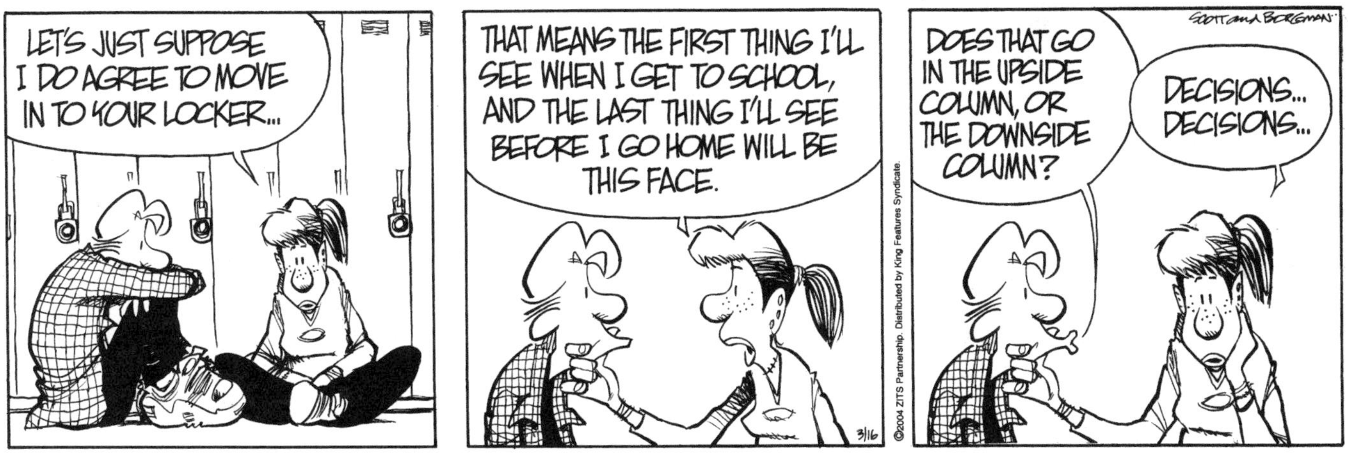
LET'S JUST SUPPOSE I DO AGREE TO MOVE IN TO YOUR LOCKER...
THAT MEANS THE FIRST THING I'LL SEE WHEN I GET TO SCHOOL, AND THE LAST THING I'LL SEE BEFORE I GO HOME WILL BE THIS FACE.
DOES THAT GO IN THE UPSIDE COLUMN, OR THE DOWNSIDE COLUMN?
DECISIONS... DECISIONS...
3/16
SCOTT and BORGMAN
©2004 ZITS Partnership. Distributed by King Features Syndicate.

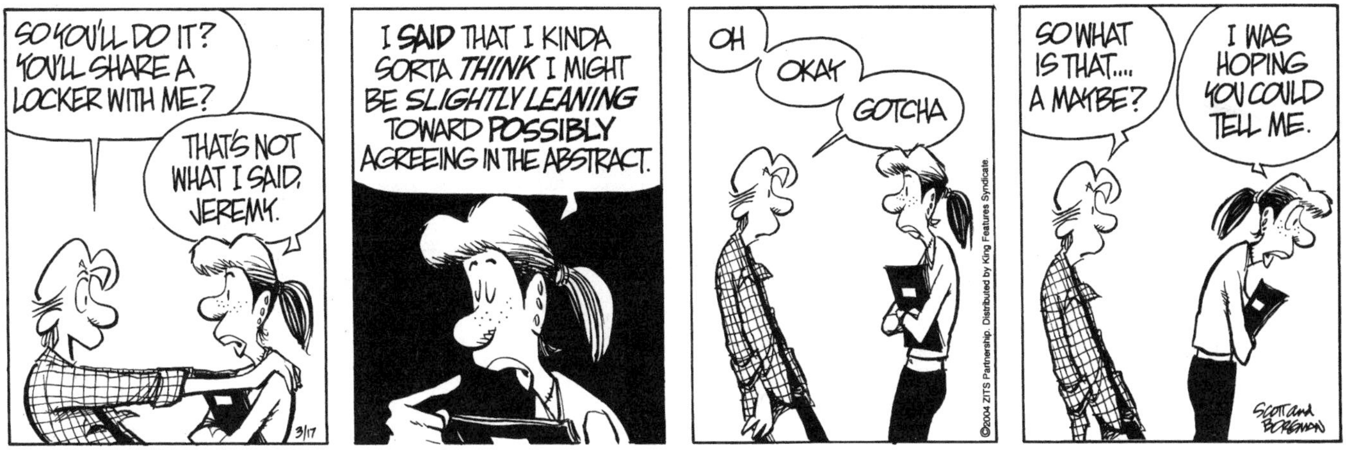
SO YOU'LL DO IT? YOU'LL SHARE A LOCKER WITH ME?
THAT'S NOT WHAT I SAID, JEREMY.
I SAID THAT I KINDA SORTA THINK I MIGHT BE SLIGHTLY LEANING TOWARD POSSIBLY AGREEING IN THE ABSTRACT.
OH
OKAY
GOTCHA
SO WHAT IS THAT.... A MAYBE?
I WAS HOPING YOU COULD TELL ME.
3/17
SCOTT and BORGMAN
©2004 ZITS Partnership. Distributed by King Features Syndicate.

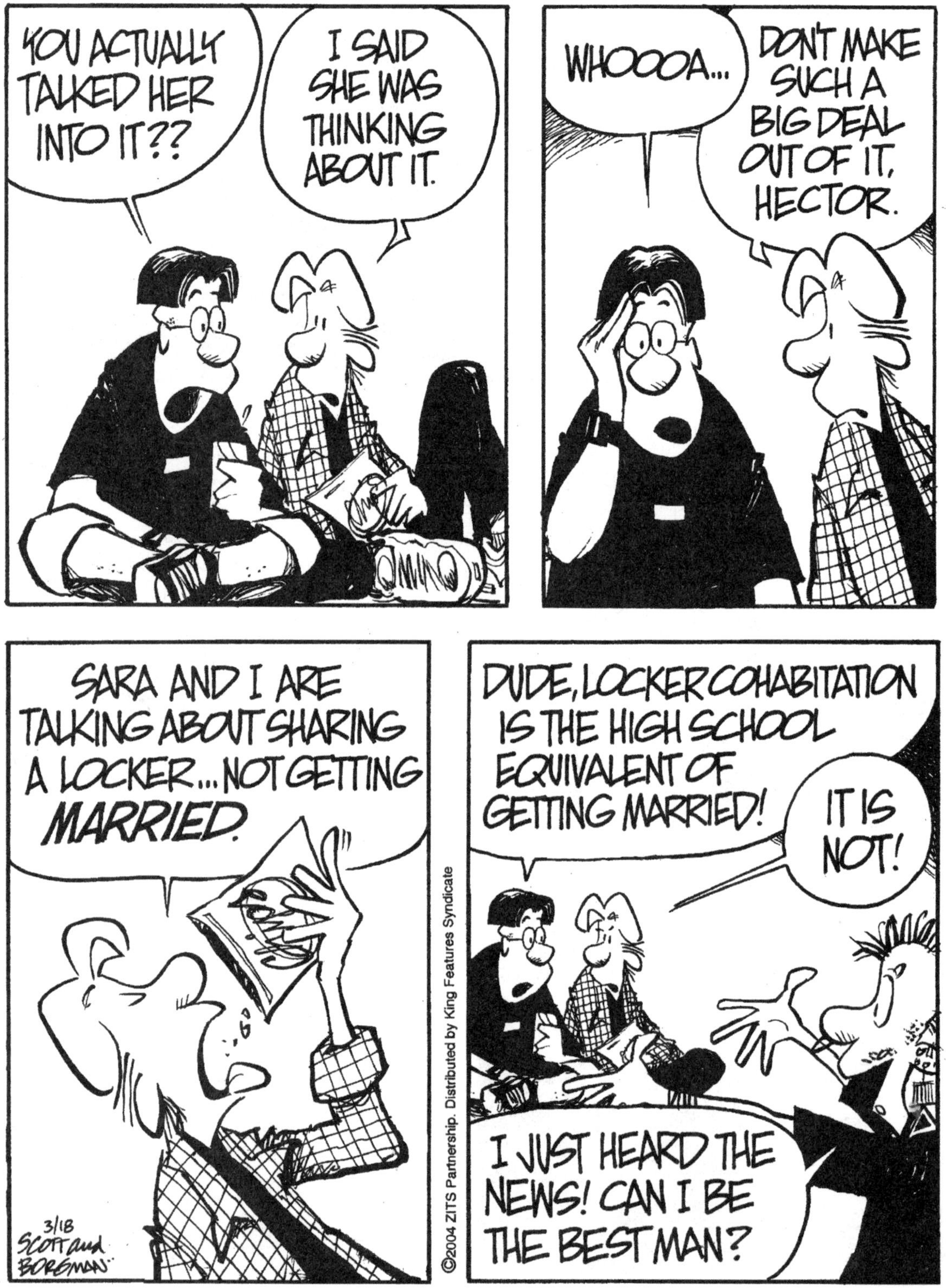
YOU ACTUALLY TALKED HER INTO IT??
I SAID SHE WAS THINKING ABOUT IT.
WHOOOOA...
DON'T MAKE SUCH A BIG DEAL OUT OF IT, HECTOR.
SARA AND I ARE TALKING ABOUT SHARING A LOCKER... NOT GETTING *MARRIED*.
3/18 SCOTT and BORGMAN
©2004 ZITS Partnership. Distributed by King Features Syndicate
DUDE, LOCKER COHABITATION IS THE HIGH SCHOOL EQUIVALENT OF GETTING MARRIED!
IT IS NOT!
I JUST HEARD THE NEWS! CAN I BE THE BEST MAN?

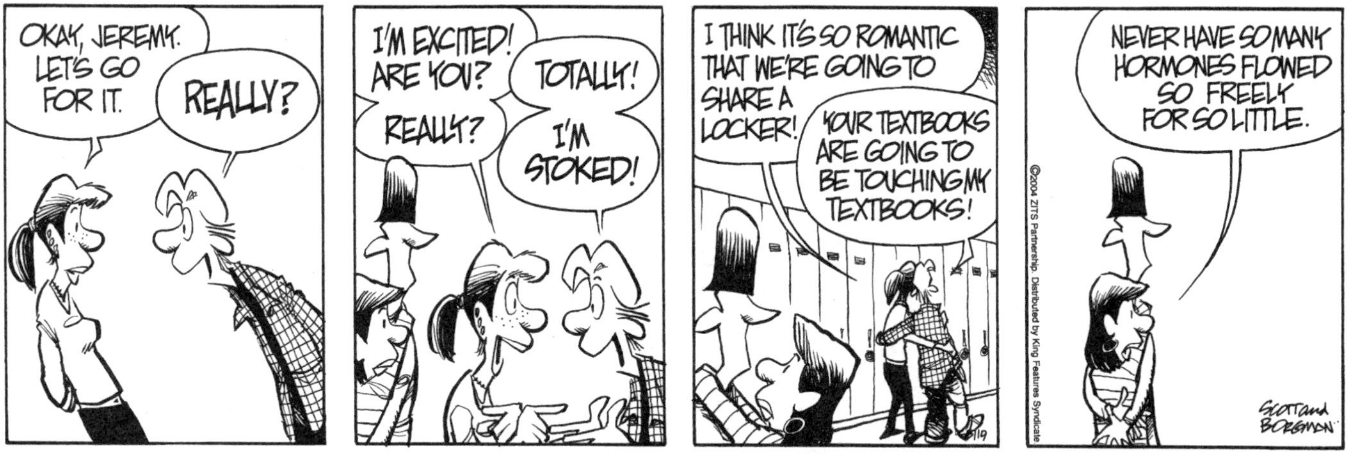
OKAY, JEREMY. LET'S GO FOR IT.
REALLY?
I'M EXCITED! ARE YOU?
TOTALLY!
REALLY?
I'M STOKED!
I THINK IT'S SO ROMANTIC THAT WE'RE GOING TO SHARE A LOCKER!
YOUR TEXTBOOKS ARE GOING TO BE TOUCHING MY TEXTBOOKS!
NEVER HAVE SO MANY HORMONES FLOWED SO FREELY FOR SO LITTLE.
©2004 ZITS Partnership. Distributed by King Features Syndicate.
SCOTT and BORGMAN

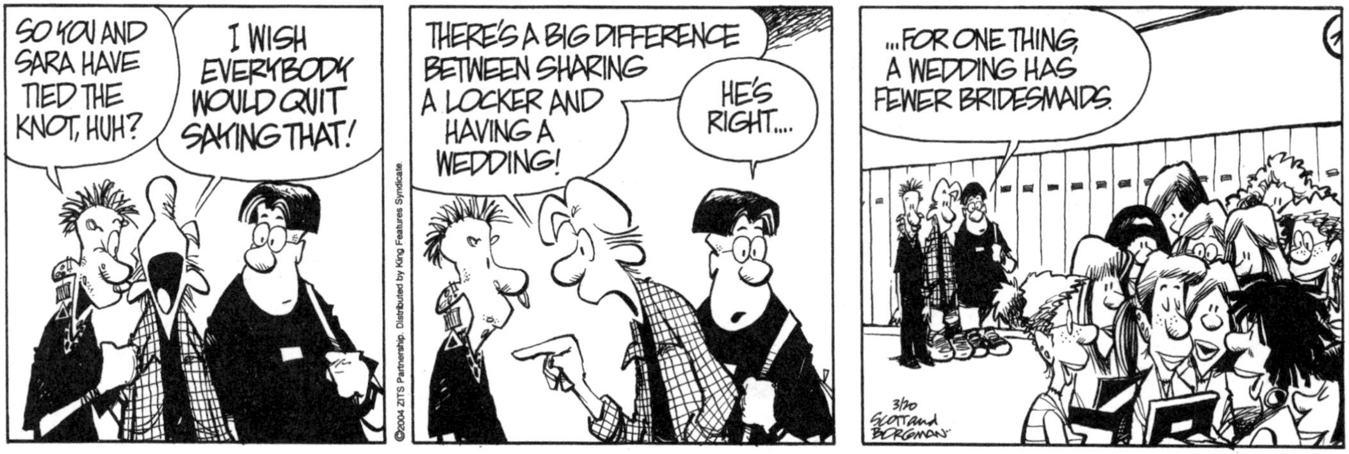
SO YOU AND SARA HAVE TIED THE KNOT, HUH?
I WISH EVERYBODY WOULD QUIT SAYING THAT!
©2004 ZITS Partnership. Distributed by King Features Syndicate.
THERE'S A BIG DIFFERENCE BETWEEN SHARING A LOCKER AND HAVING A WEDDING!
HE'S RIGHT....
...FOR ONE THING, A WEDDING HAS FEWER BRIDESMAIDS.
3/20
SCOTT and BORGMAN

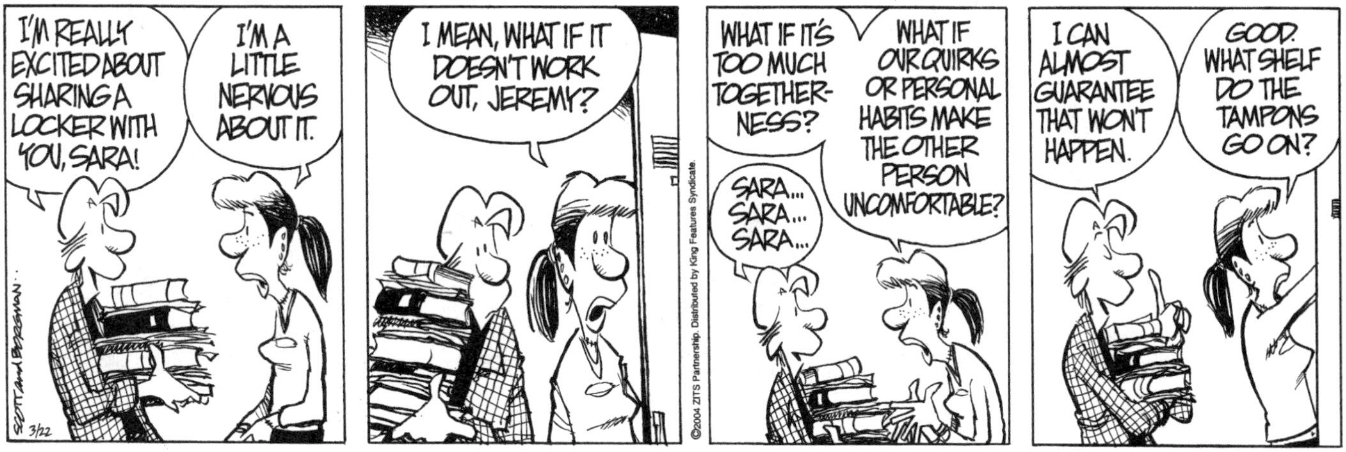
I'M REALLY EXCITED ABOUT SHARING A LOCKER WITH YOU, SARA!
I'M A LITTLE NERVOUS ABOUT IT.
SCOTT and BORGMAN
3/22
I MEAN, WHAT IF IT DOESN'T WORK OUT, JEREMY?
©2004 ZITS Partnership. Distributed by King Features Syndicate.
WHAT IF IT'S TOO MUCH TOGETHERNESS?
WHAT IF OUR QUIRKS OR PERSONAL HABITS MAKE THE OTHER PERSON UNCOMFORTABLE?
SARA... SARA... SARA...
I CAN ALMOST GUARANTEE THAT WON'T HAPPEN.
GOOD. WHAT SHELF DO THE TAMPONS GO ON?

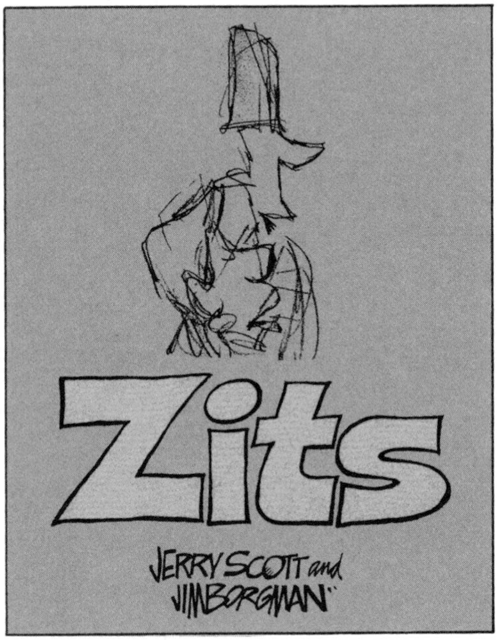
Zits
JERRY SCOTT and JIM BORGMAN

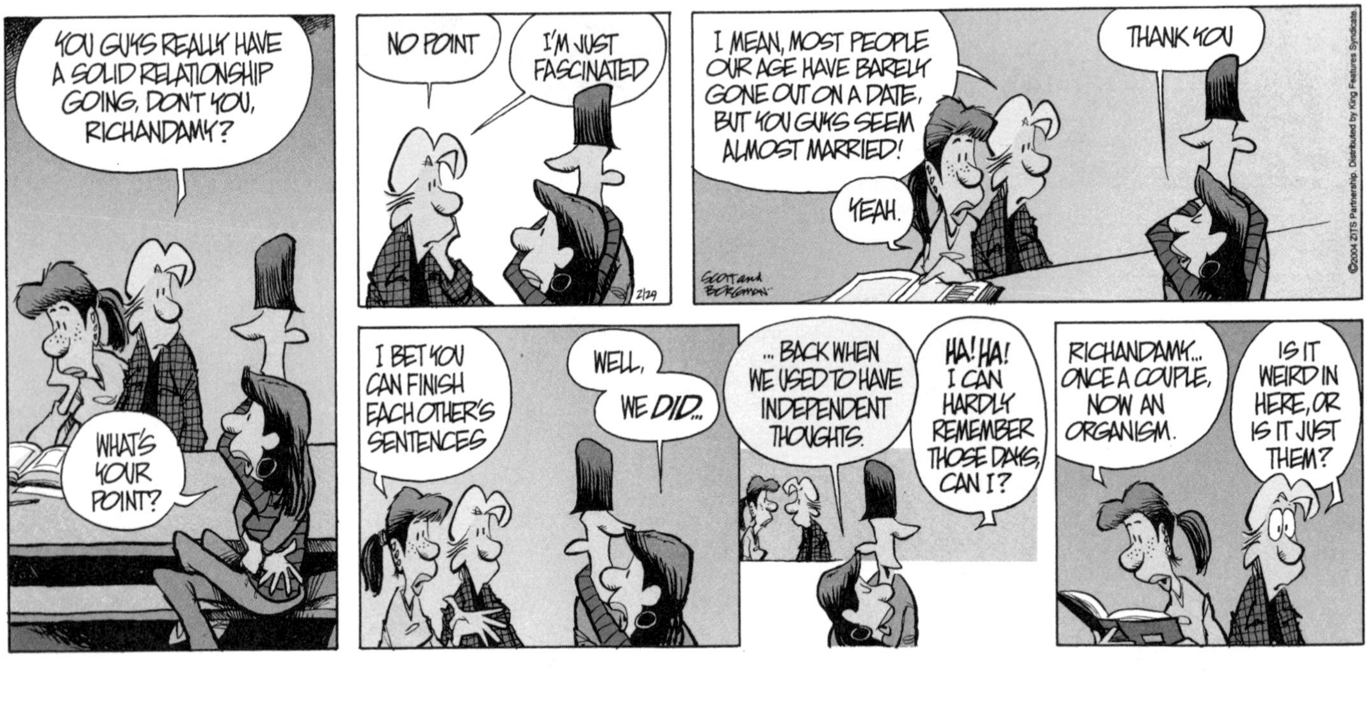
YOU GUYS REALLY HAVE A SOLID RELATIONSHIP GOING, DON'T YOU, RICHANDAMY?
WHAT'S YOUR POINT?
NO POINT
I'M JUST FASCINATED
2/29
I MEAN, MOST PEOPLE OUR AGE HAVE BARELY GONE OUT ON A DATE, BUT YOU GUYS SEEM ALMOST MARRIED!
YEAH.
THANK YOU
SCOTT and BORGMAN
©2004 ZITS Partnership. Distributed by King Features Syndicate
I BET YOU CAN FINISH EACH OTHER'S SENTENCES
WELL, WE *DID*...
... BACK WHEN WE USED TO HAVE INDEPENDENT THOUGHTS.
HA! HA! I CAN HARDLY REMEMBER THOSE DAYS, CAN I?
RICHANDAMY... ONCE A COUPLE, NOW AN ORGANISM.
IS IT WEIRD IN HERE, OR IS IT JUST THEM?

WHY DO YOU KEEP THIS IN HERE WHEN YOU DON'T EVEN PLAY BASE-BALL?
I DUNNO... IT'S ALWAYS BEEN THERE.
LOOK AT ALL THE SPACE IT WAS TAKING UP!
NOW THERE'S ROOM FOR AN EXTRA PAIR OF SHOES!
SCOTT and BORGMAN
©2004 ZITS Partnership. Distributed by King Features Syndicate.
3/23
YOU KNOW... IN CASE YOU STOP LIKING THE ONES YOU HAPPEN TO BE WEARING..?
PEOPLE OWN MORE THAN ONE PAIR OF SHOES?

WHERE'S YOUR LOCKER'S WASTEBASKET?
MY WHAT?
©2004 ZITS Partnership. Distributed by King Features Syndicate.
YOUR WASTEBASKET. DON'T YOU HAVE SOMEPLACE TO THROW AWAY GUMWRAPPERS AND JUNK?
OH, THAT— SURE...
RIGHT OVER THERE.
YO!
3/24
SCOTT and BORGMAN

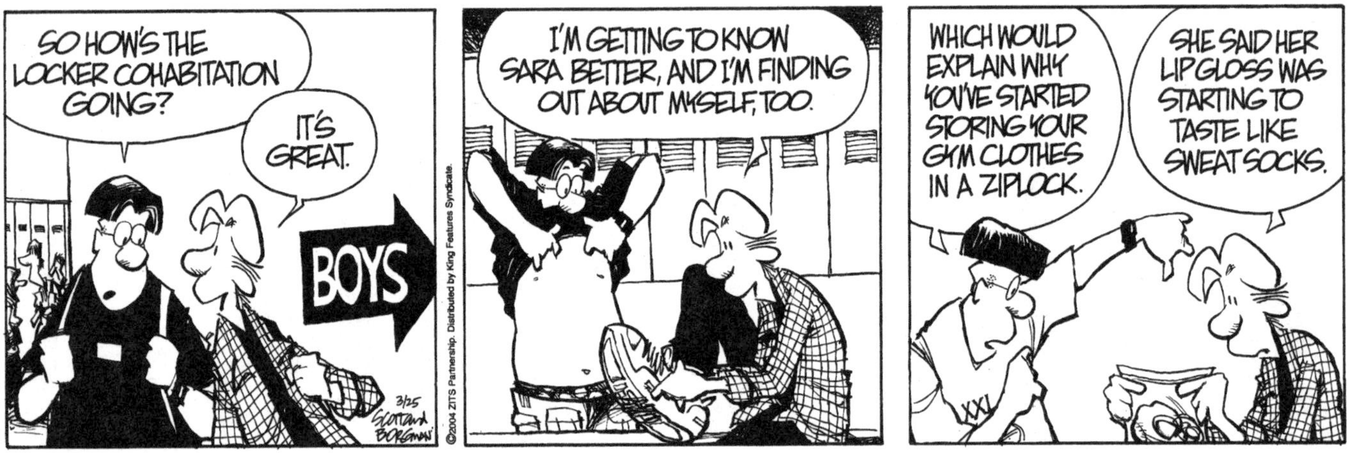
SO HOW'S THE LOCKER COHABITATION GOING?
IT'S GREAT.
BOYS
3/25 SCOTT and BORGMAN
©2004 ZITS Partnership. Distributed by King Features Syndicate.
I'M GETTING TO KNOW SARA BETTER, AND I'M FINDING OUT ABOUT MYSELF, TOO.
WHICH WOULD EXPLAIN WHY YOU'VE STARTED STORING YOUR GYM CLOTHES IN A ZIPLOCK.
SHE SAID HER LIP GLOSS WAS STARTING TO TASTE LIKE SWEAT SOCKS.
XXL

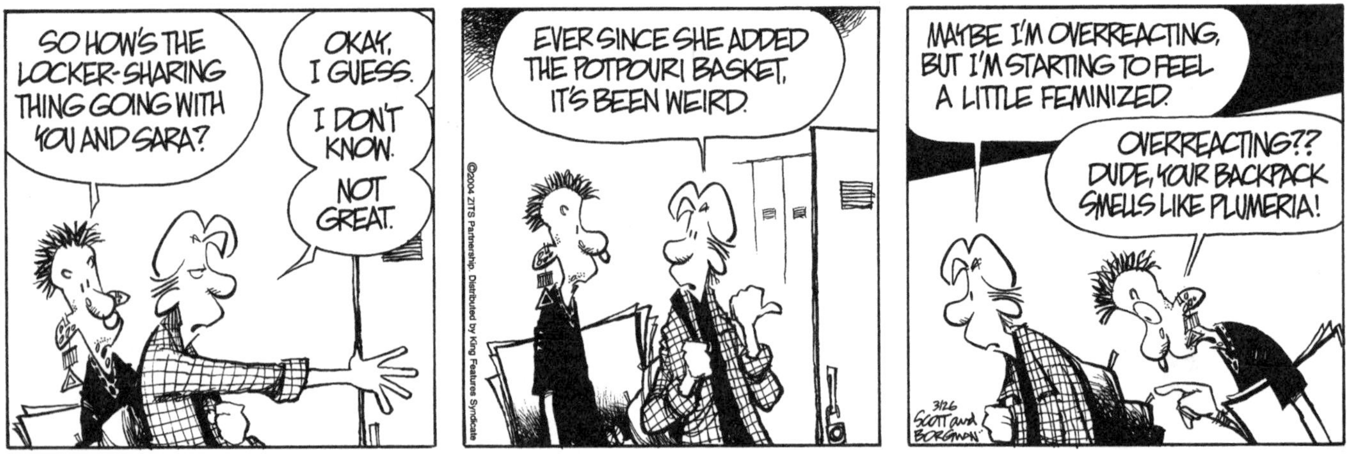
SO HOW'S THE LOCKER-SHARING THING GOING WITH YOU AND SARA?
OKAY, I GUESS.
I DON'T KNOW.
NOT GREAT.
©2004 ZITS Partnership. Distributed by King Features Syndicate
EVER SINCE SHE ADDED THE POTPOURRI BASKET, IT'S BEEN WEIRD.
MAYBE I'M OVERREACTING, BUT I'M STARTING TO FEEL A LITTLE FEMINIZED.
OVERREACTING?? DUDE, YOUR BACKPACK SMELLS LIKE PLUMERIA!
3/26 SCOTT and BORGMAN

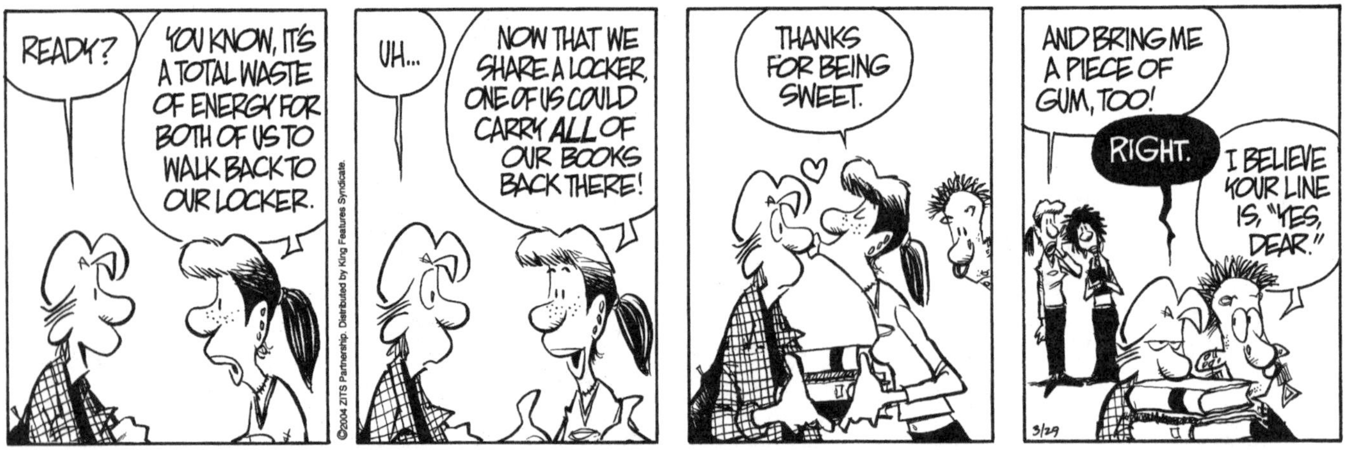
READY?
YOU KNOW, IT'S A TOTAL WASTE OF ENERGY FOR BOTH OF US TO WALK BACK TO OUR LOCKER.
©2004 ZITS Partnership. Distributed by King Features Syndicate.
UH...
NOW THAT WE SHARE A LOCKER, ONE OF US COULD CARRY ALL OF OUR BOOKS BACK THERE!
THANKS FOR BEING SWEET.
AND BRING ME A PIECE OF GUM, TOO!
RIGHT.
I BELIEVE YOUR LINE IS, "YES, DEAR."
3/29

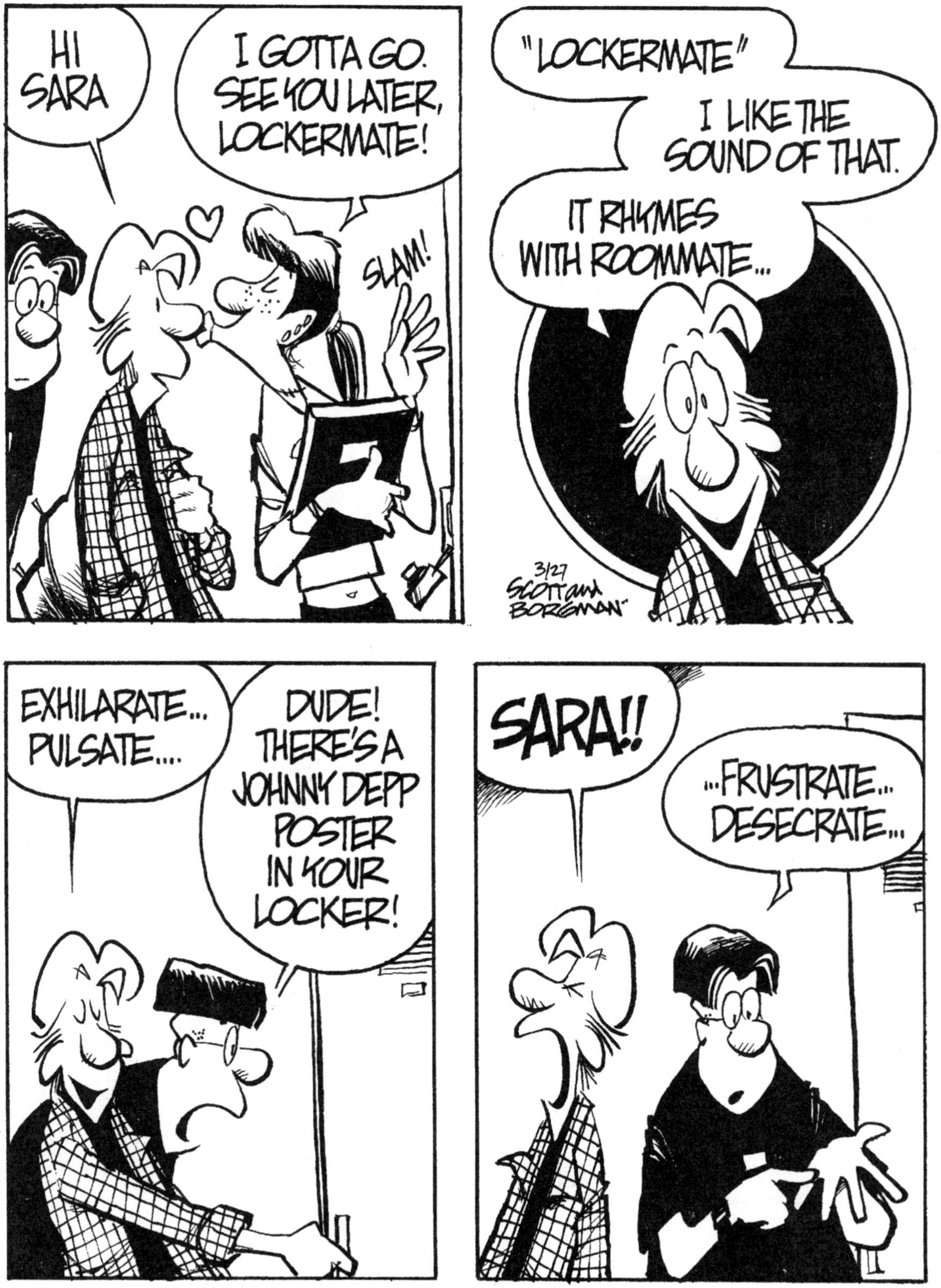
HI SARA
I GOTTA GO. SEE YOU LATER, LOCKERMATE!
SLAM!
"LOCKERMATE"
I LIKE THE SOUND OF THAT.
IT RHYMES WITH ROOMMATE...
3/27 SCOTT and BORGMAN
EXHILARATE... PULSATE....
DUDE! THERE'S A JOHNNY DEPP POSTER IN YOUR LOCKER!
SARA!!
...FRUSTRATE... DESECRATE...

Zits
by JERRY SCOTT and JIM BORGMAN

SPRING BREAK
©2004 ZITS Partnership. Distributed by King Features Syndicate
Chips
4/18 SCOTT and BORGMAN
WHY DO I KEEP FEELING A WARM, MOIST BREEZE THAT SMELLS LIKE TORTILLA CHIPS?
IT'S NOT A BREEZE... IT'S A SIGH.

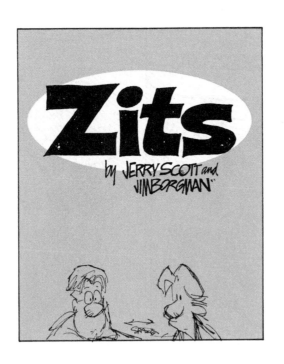

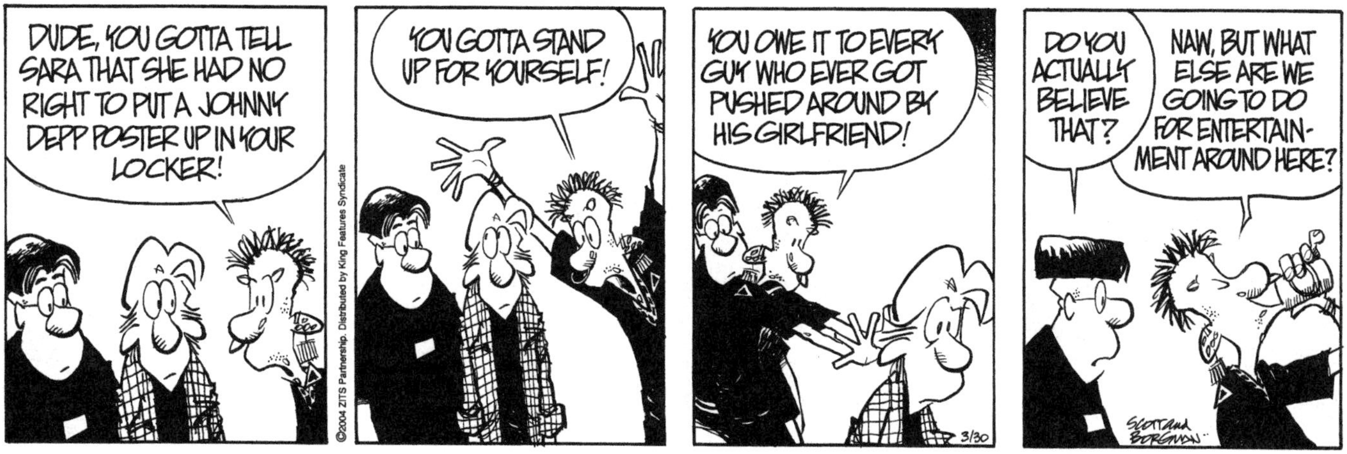
DUDE, YOU GOTTA TELL SARA THAT SHE HAD NO RIGHT TO PUT A JOHNNY DEPP POSTER UP IN YOUR LOCKER!
©2004 ZITS Partnership. Distributed by King Features Syndicate
YOU GOTTA STAND UP FOR YOURSELF!
YOU OWE IT TO EVERY GUY WHO EVER GOT PUSHED AROUND BY HIS GIRLFRIEND!
3/30
DO YOU ACTUALLY BELIEVE THAT?
NAW, BUT WHAT ELSE ARE WE GOING TO DO FOR ENTERTAIN-MENT AROUND HERE?
SCOTT AND BORGMAN

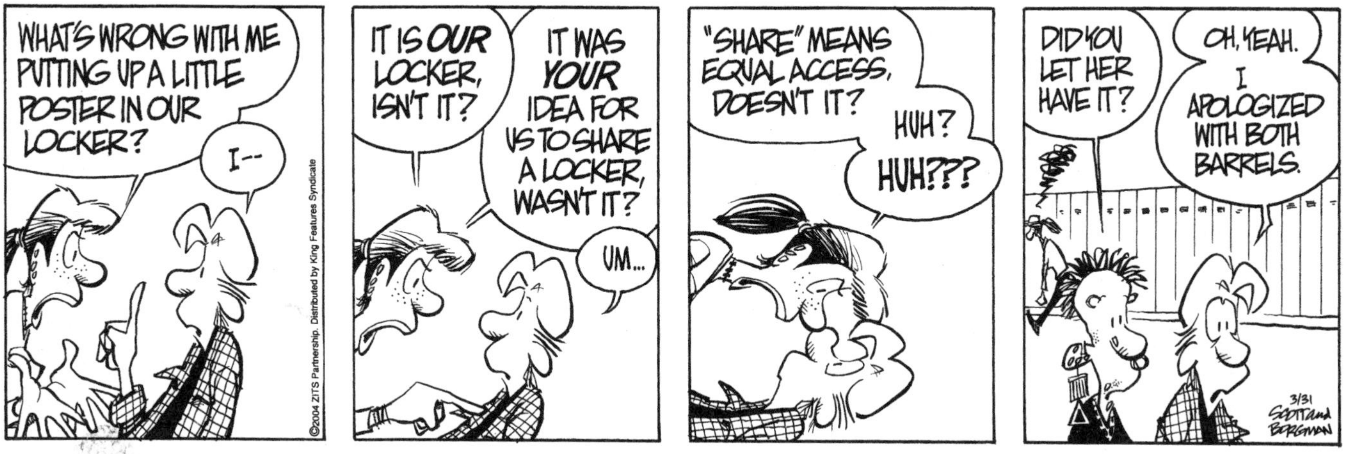
WHAT'S WRONG WITH ME PUTTING UP A LITTLE POSTER IN OUR LOCKER?
I--
©2004 ZITS Partnership. Distributed by King Features Syndicate
IT IS **OUR** LOCKER, ISN'T IT?
IT WAS **YOUR** IDEA FOR US TO SHARE A LOCKER, WASN'T IT?
UM...
"SHARE" MEANS EQUAL ACCESS, DOESN'T IT?
HUH?
HUH???
DID YOU LET HER HAVE IT?
OH, YEAH.
I APOLOGIZED WITH BOTH BARRELS.
3/31
SCOTT AND BORGMAN

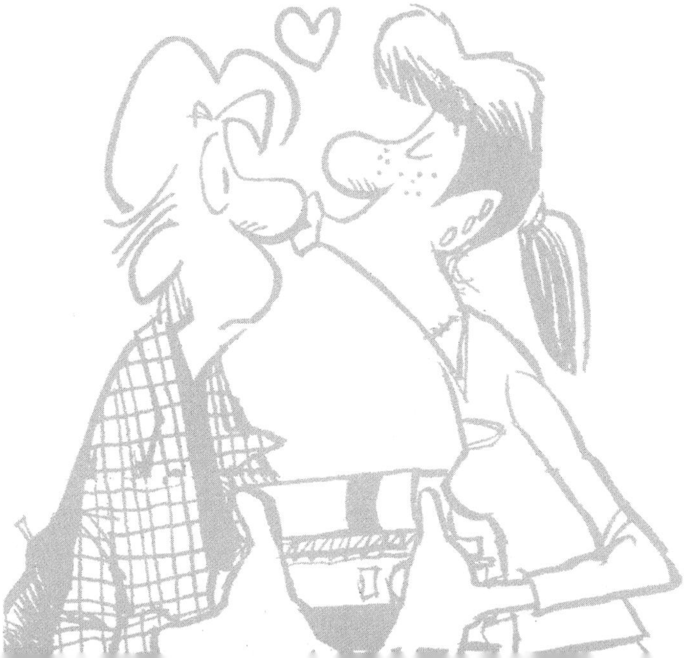

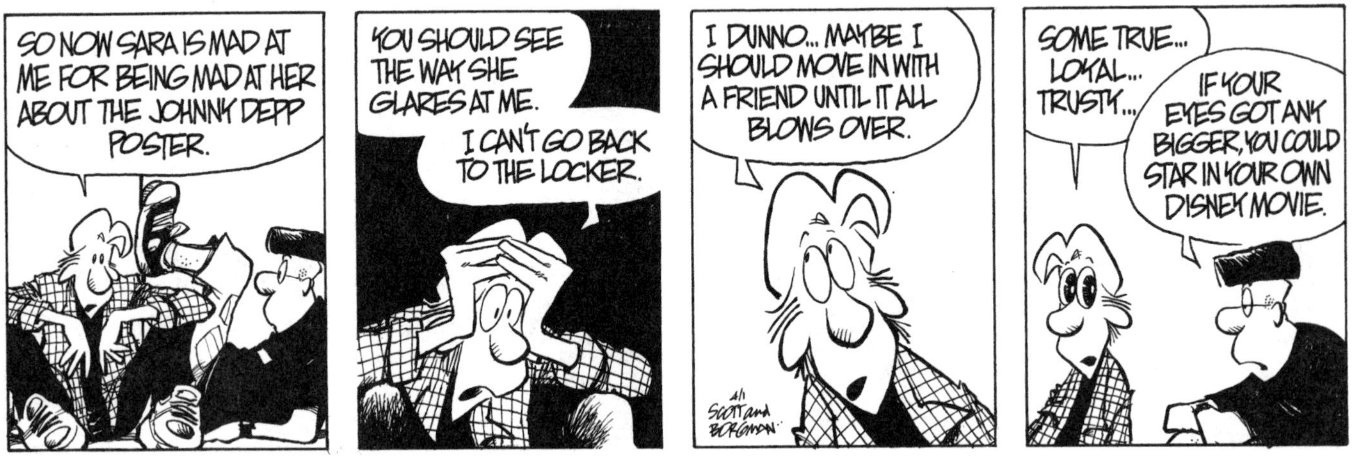
SO NOW SARA IS MAD AT ME FOR BEING MAD AT HER ABOUT THE JOHNNY DEPP POSTER.
YOU SHOULD SEE THE WAY SHE GLARES AT ME.
I CAN'T GO BACK TO THE LOCKER.
I DUNNO... MAYBE I SHOULD MOVE IN WITH A FRIEND UNTIL IT ALL BLOWS OVER.
4/1 SCOTT and BORGMAN
SOME TRUE... LOYAL... TRUSTY...
IF YOUR EYES GOT ANY BIGGER, YOU COULD STAR IN YOUR OWN DISNEY MOVIE.

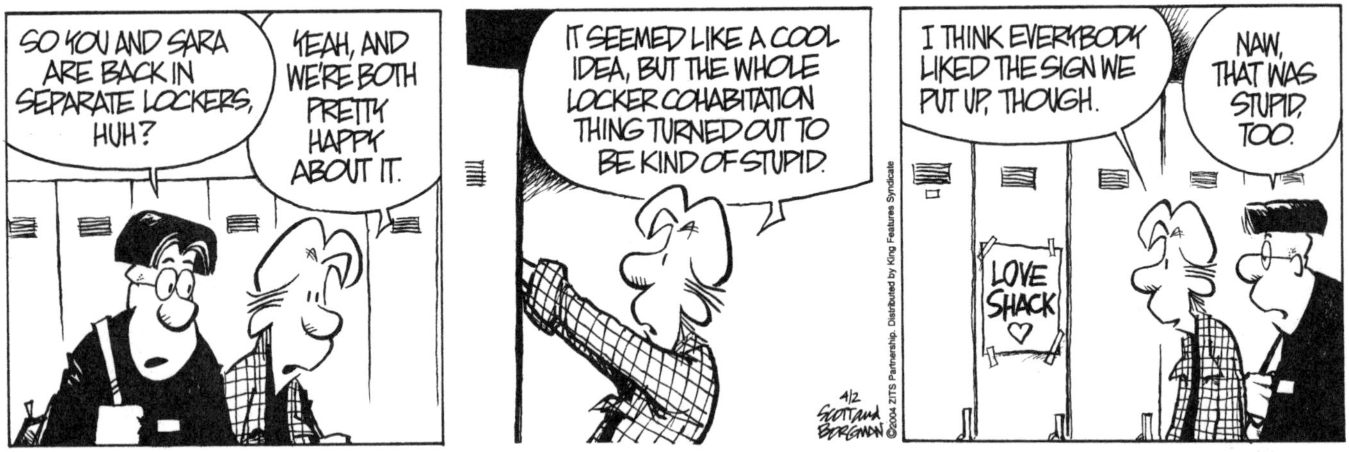
SO YOU AND SARA ARE BACK IN SEPARATE LOCKERS, HUH?
YEAH, AND WE'RE BOTH PRETTY HAPPY ABOUT IT.
IT SEEMED LIKE A COOL IDEA, BUT THE WHOLE LOCKER COHABITATION THING TURNED OUT TO BE KIND OF STUPID.
4/2 SCOTT and BORGMAN
©2004 ZITS Partnership. Distributed by King Features Syndicate
I THINK EVERYBODY LIKED THE SIGN WE PUT UP, THOUGH.
NAW, THAT WAS STUPID, TOO.
LOVE SHACK

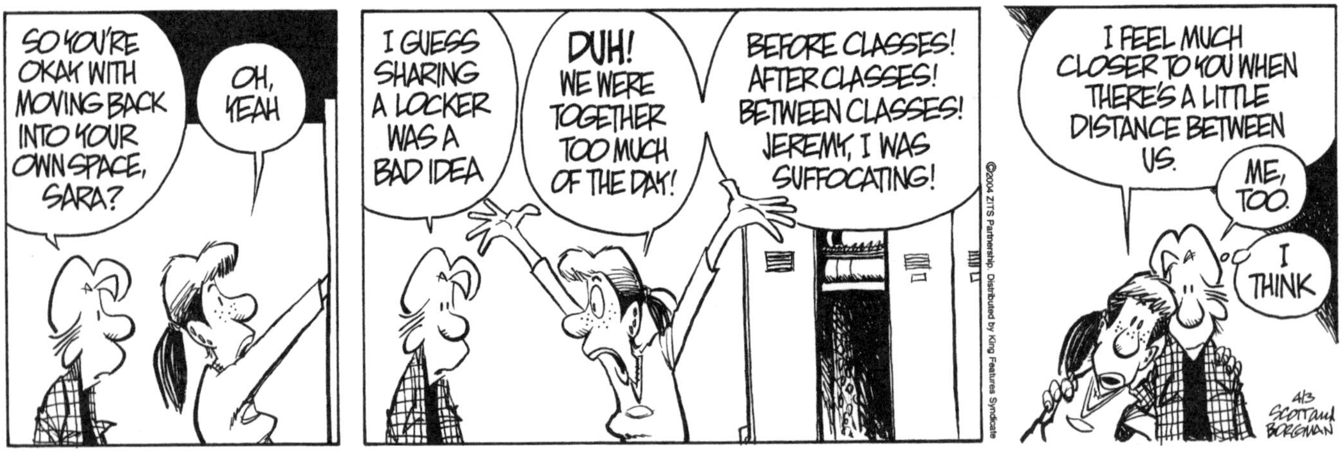
SO YOU'RE OKAY WITH MOVING BACK INTO YOUR OWN SPACE, SARA?
OH, YEAH
I GUESS SHARING A LOCKER WAS A BAD IDEA
DUH! WE WERE TOGETHER TOO MUCH OF THE DAY!
BEFORE CLASSES! AFTER CLASSES! BETWEEN CLASSES! JEREMY, I WAS SUFFOCATING!
©2004 ZITS Partnership. Distributed by King Features Syndicate
I FEEL MUCH CLOSER TO YOU WHEN THERE'S A LITTLE DISTANCE BETWEEN US.
ME, TOO.
I THINK
4/3 SCOTT and BORGMAN

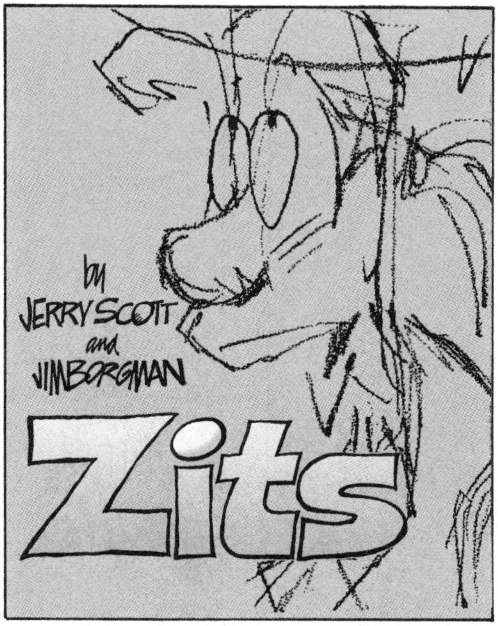
by
JERRY SCOTT
and
JIM BORGMAN
Zits

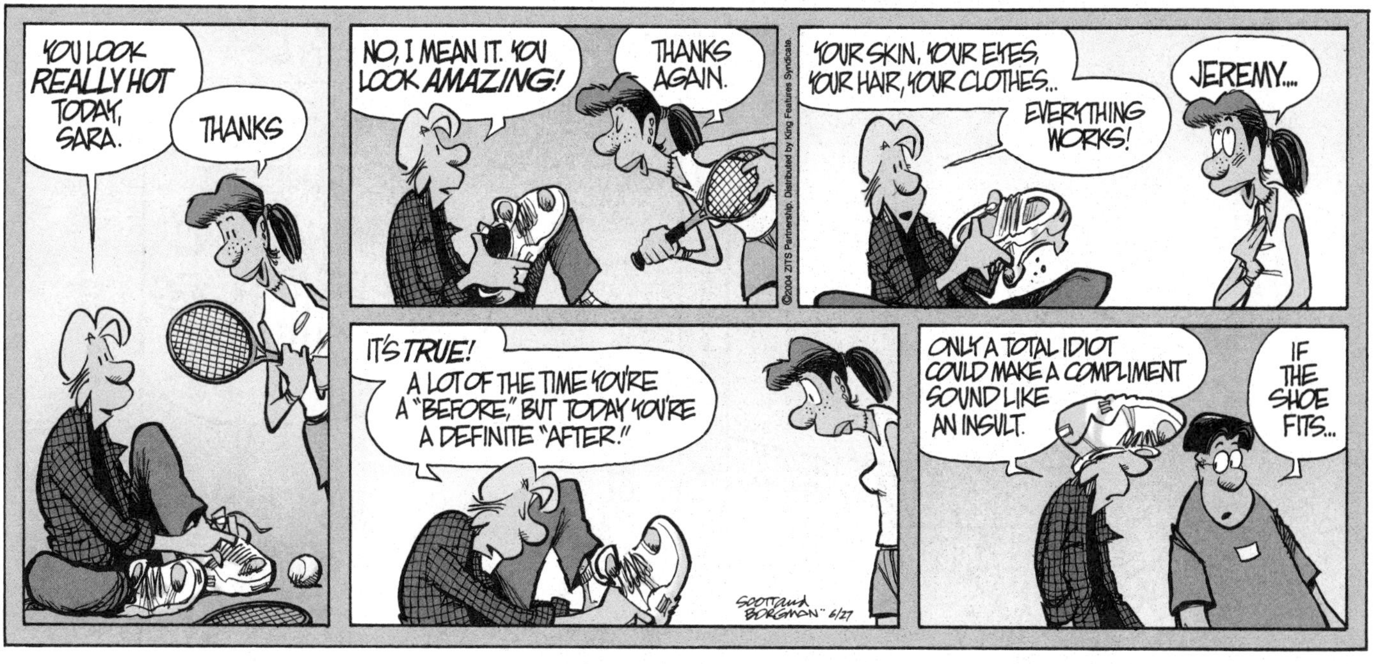
YOU LOOK REALLY HOT TODAY, SARA.
THANKS
NO, I MEAN IT. YOU LOOK AMAZING!
THANKS AGAIN.
©2004 ZITS Partnership. Distributed by King Features Syndicate.
YOUR SKIN, YOUR EYES, YOUR HAIR, YOUR CLOTHES...
EVERYTHING WORKS!
JEREMY....
IT'S TRUE!
A LOT OF THE TIME YOU'RE A "BEFORE," BUT TODAY YOU'RE A DEFINITE "AFTER."
SCOTT and BORGMAN 6/27
ONLY A TOTAL IDIOT COULD MAKE A COMPLIMENT SOUND LIKE AN INSULT.
IF THE SHOE FITS...

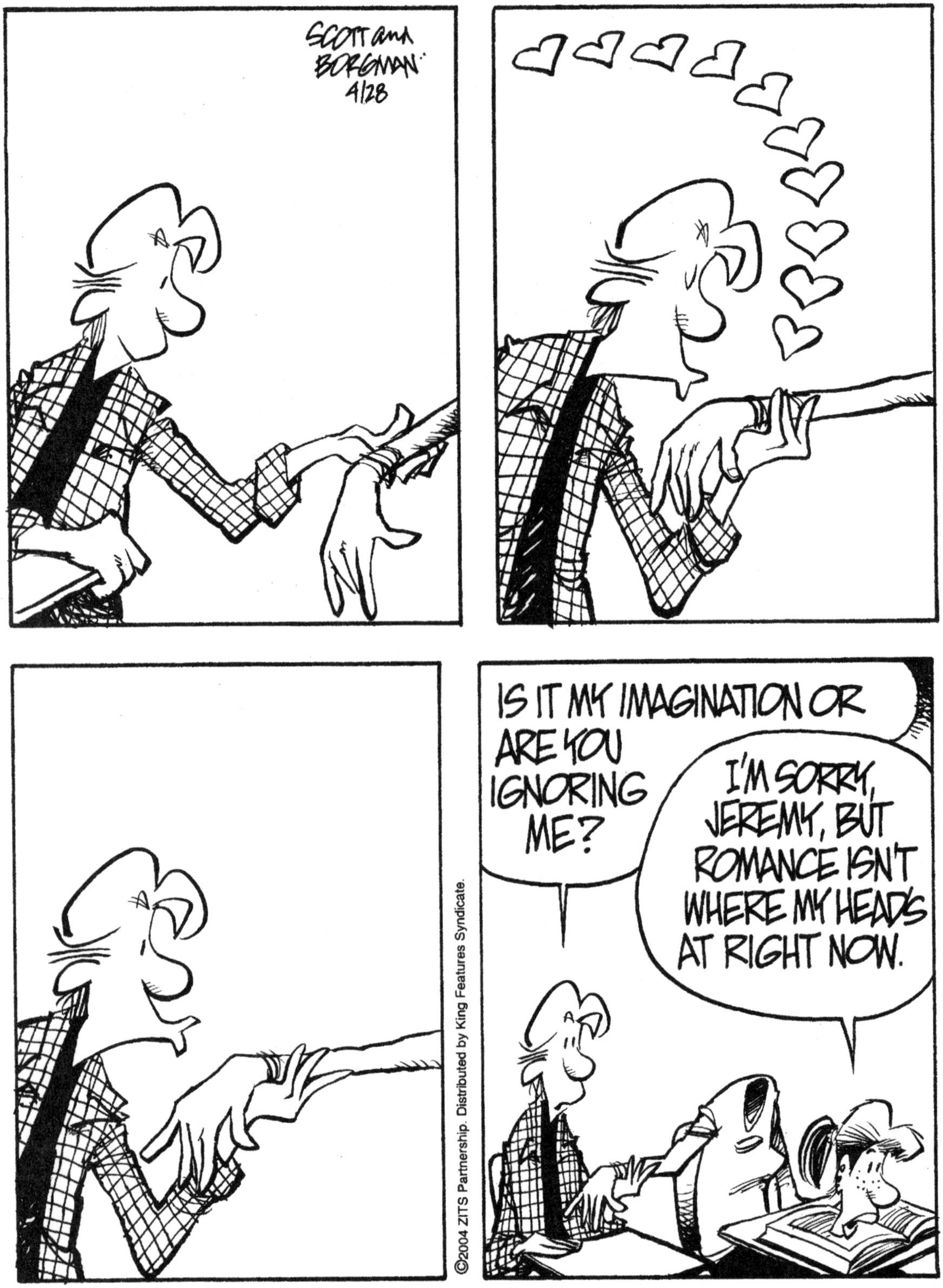
SCOTT and BORGMAN 4/28
IS IT MY IMAGINATION OR ARE YOU IGNORING ME?
I'M SORRY, JEREMY, BUT ROMANCE ISN'T WHERE MY HEAD'S AT RIGHT NOW.
©2004 ZITS Partnership. Distributed by King Features Syndicate.

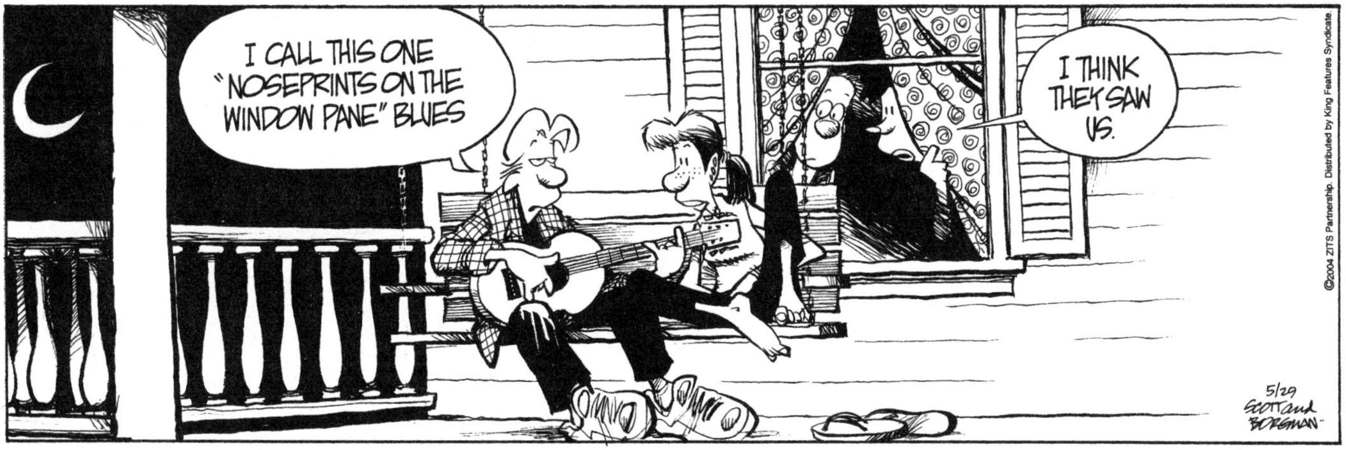
I CALL THIS ONE "NOSEPRINTS ON THE WINDOW PANE" BLUES
I THINK THEY SAW US.
5/29 SCOTT and BORGMAN
©2004 ZITS Partnership. Distributed by King Features Syndicate.

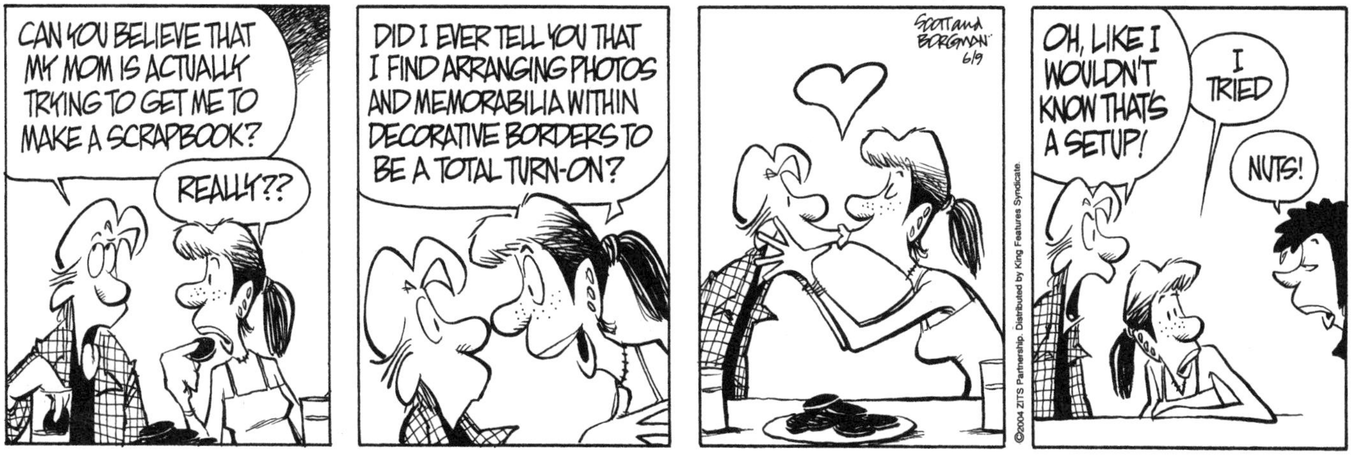
CAN YOU BELIEVE THAT MY MOM IS ACTUALLY TRYING TO GET ME TO MAKE A SCRAPBOOK?
REALLY??
DID I EVER TELL YOU THAT I FIND ARRANGING PHOTOS AND MEMORABILIA WITHIN DECORATIVE BORDERS TO BE A TOTAL TURN-ON?
SCOTT and BORGMAN 6/9
©2004 ZITS Partnership. Distributed by King Features Syndicate.
OH, LIKE I WOULDN'T KNOW THAT'S A SETUP!
I TRIED
NUTS!

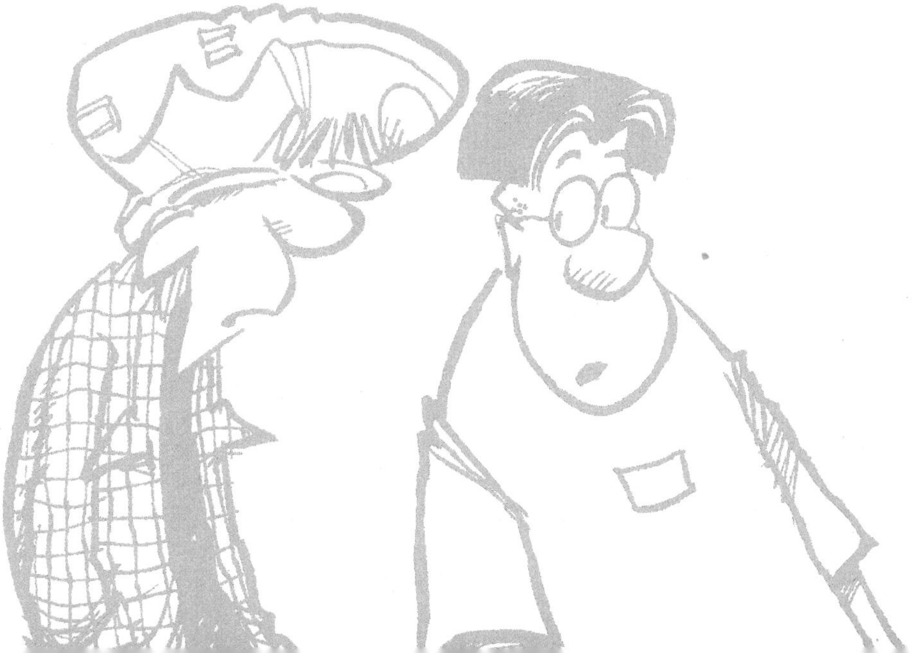

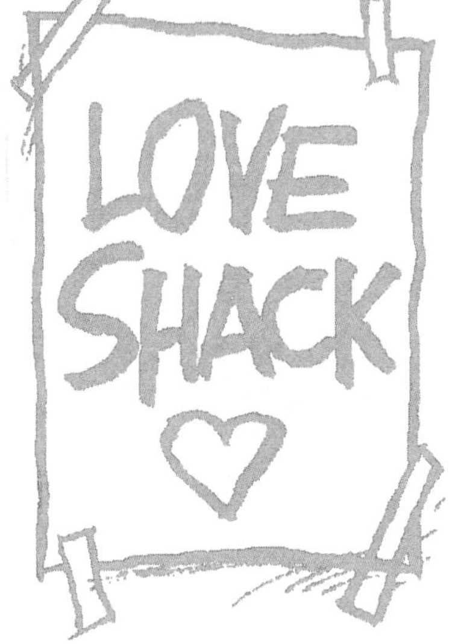
LOVE SHACK

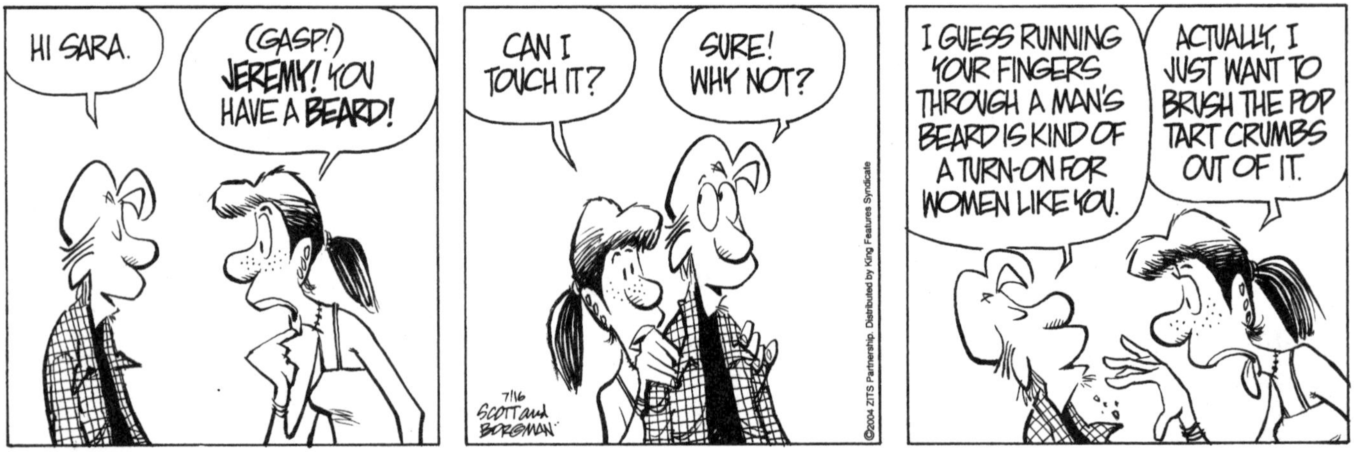
HI SARA.
(GASP!) JEREMY! YOU HAVE A BEARD!
CAN I TOUCH IT?
SURE! WHY NOT?
7/16 SCOTT and BORGMAN
©2004 ZITS Partnership. Distributed by King Features Syndicate
I GUESS RUNNING YOUR FINGERS THROUGH A MAN'S BEARD IS KIND OF A TURN-ON FOR WOMEN LIKE YOU.
ACTUALLY, I JUST WANT TO BRUSH THE POP TART CRUMBS OUT OF IT.

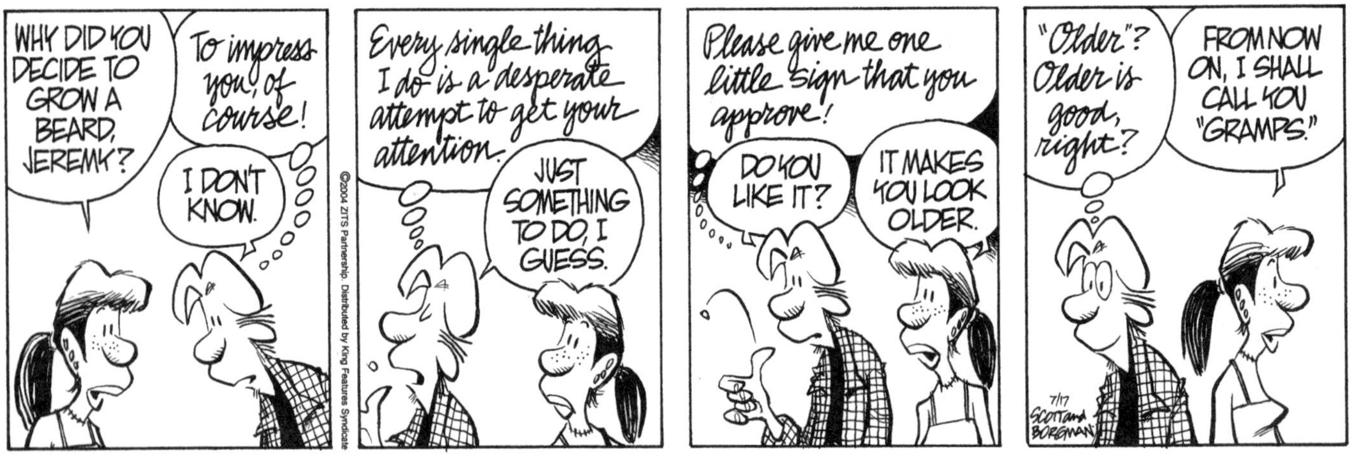
WHY DID YOU DECIDE TO GROW A BEARD, JEREMY?
To impress you, of course!
I DON'T KNOW.
©2004 ZITS Partnership. Distributed by King Features Syndicate
Every single thing I do is a desperate attempt to get your attention.
JUST SOMETHING TO DO, I GUESS.
Please give me one little sign that you approve!
DO YOU LIKE IT?
IT MAKES YOU LOOK OLDER.
"Older"? Older is good, right?
FROM NOW ON, I SHALL CALL YOU "GRAMPS."
7/17 SCOTT and BORGMAN

Zits
by JERRY SCOTT and JIM BORGMAN

GUY HAIR
BARB SHO
GUY HAIR
SNIP! SNIP! SNIP! SNIP! SNIP! SNIP! SNIP!
BRUSH! BRUSH! BRUSH! BRUSH!
SCOTT and BORGMAN
WHAT?
©2004 ZITS Partnership. Distributed by King Features Syndicate

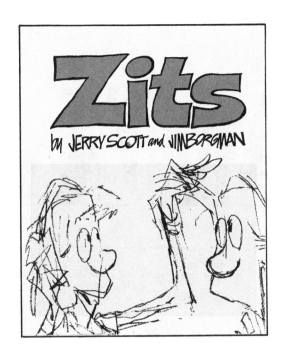

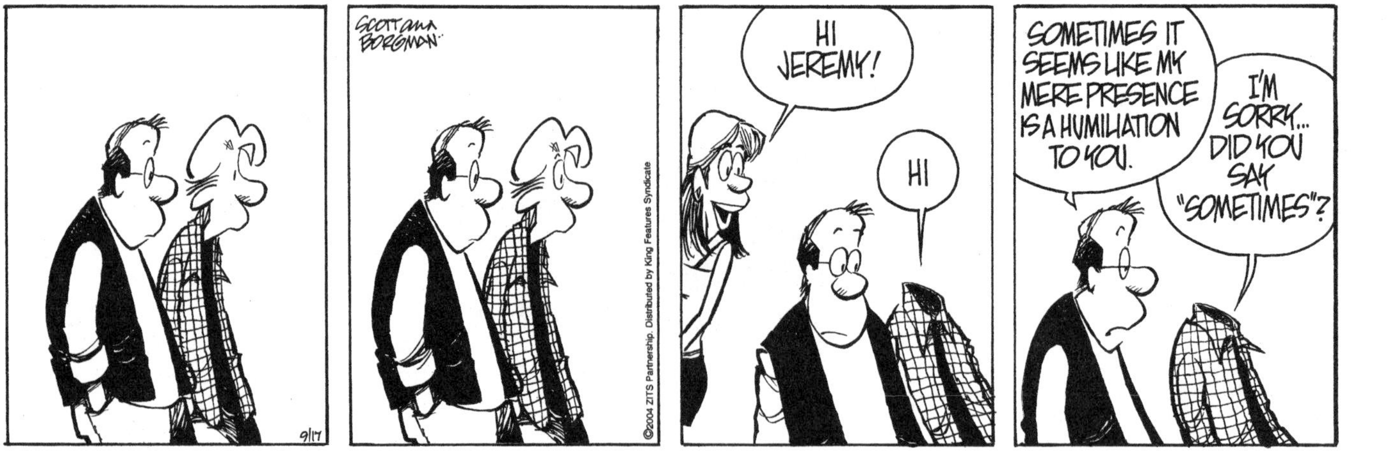
©2004 ZITS Partnership. Distributed by King Features Syndicate
HI JEREMY!
HI
SOMETIMES IT SEEMS LIKE MY MERE PRESENCE IS A HUMILIATION TO YOU.
I'M SORRY... DID YOU SAY "SOMETIMES"?

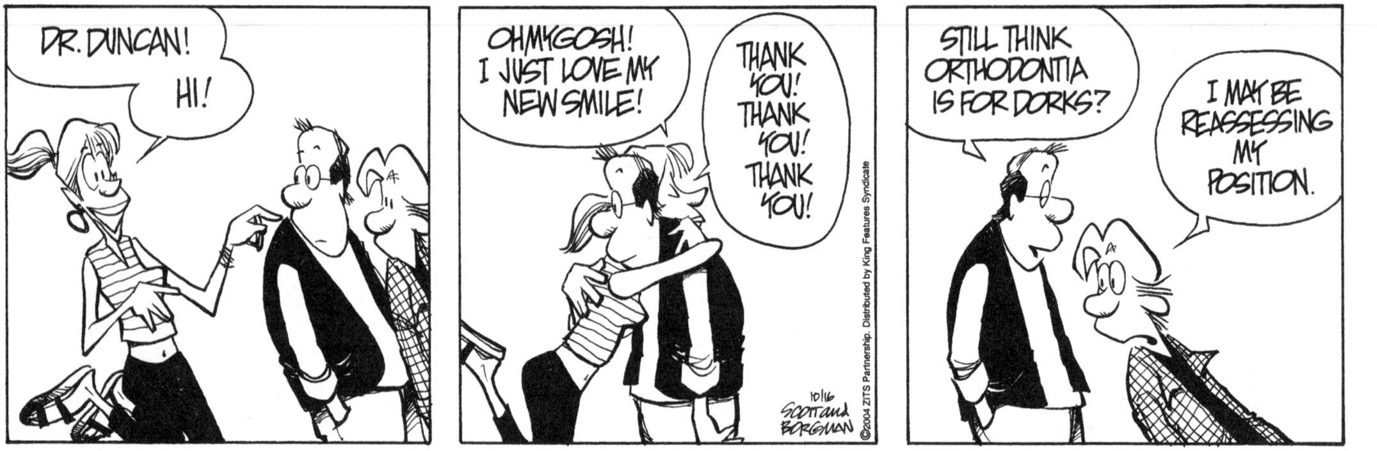
DR. DUNCAN!
HI!
OHMYGOSH! I JUST LOVE MY NEW SMILE!
THANK YOU! THANK YOU! THANK YOU!
©2004 ZITS Partnership. Distributed by King Features Syndicate
STILL THINK ORTHODONTIA IS FOR DORKS?
I MAY BE REASSESSING MY POSITION.

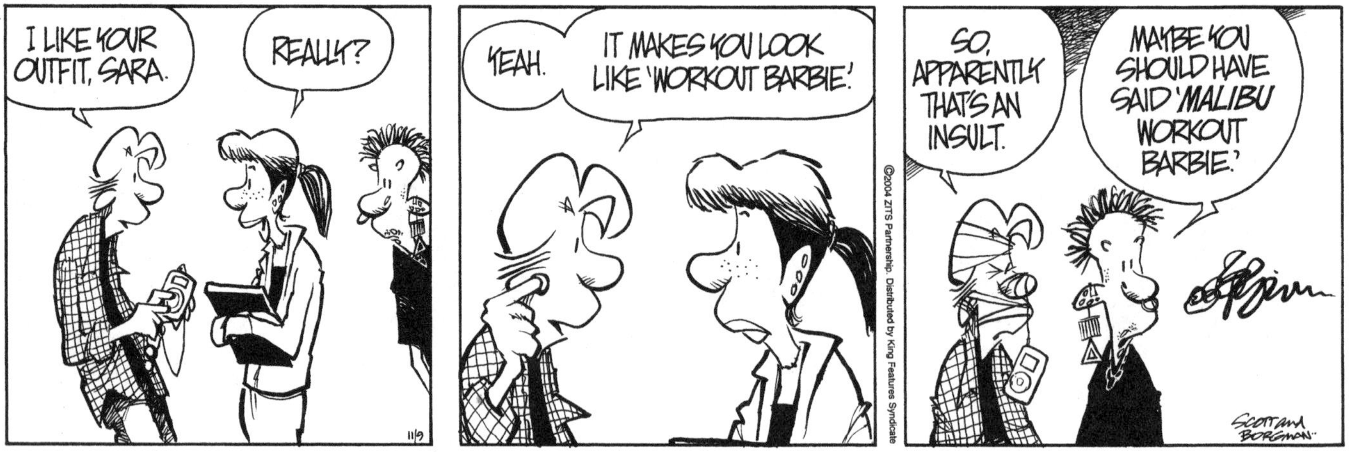
I LIKE YOUR OUTFIT, SARA.
REALLY?
YEAH.
IT MAKES YOU LOOK LIKE 'WORKOUT BARBIE.'
©2004 ZITS Partnership. Distributed by King Features Syndicate
SO, APPARENTLY THAT'S AN INSULT.
MAYBE YOU SHOULD HAVE SAID '*MALIBU* WORKOUT BARBIE.'

Zits
by JERRY SCOTT and JIM BORGMAN

WOW... SO YOU AND SARA HAD A FIGHT, HUH?
JUST NOW. HOW DID YOU--?
OOH. YOU SHOULDN'T HAVE CALLED HER "IRRATIONAL," JEREMY.
I DIDN'T CALL HER IRRATIONAL!
SCOTT and BORGMAN
ACCORDING TO THE TRANSCRIPT YOU DID... AND YOU DO LOOK PRETTY MAD IN THE PICTURES.
OKAY, BUT SHE -- WHAT PICTURES??
12/19
HOWEVER, THE GOOD NEWS IS THAT POPULAR OPINION SEEMS TO INDICATE THAT YOU TWO SHOULD STAY TOGETHER.
©2004 ZITS Partnership. Distributed by King Features Syndicate
CONGRATULATIONS!
HOLD ON... MORE POLL RESULTS ARE COMING IN FROM NEW ZEALAND.....
SCROLL SCROLL SCROLL
SOMETIMES I REALLY HATE THE INTERNET.

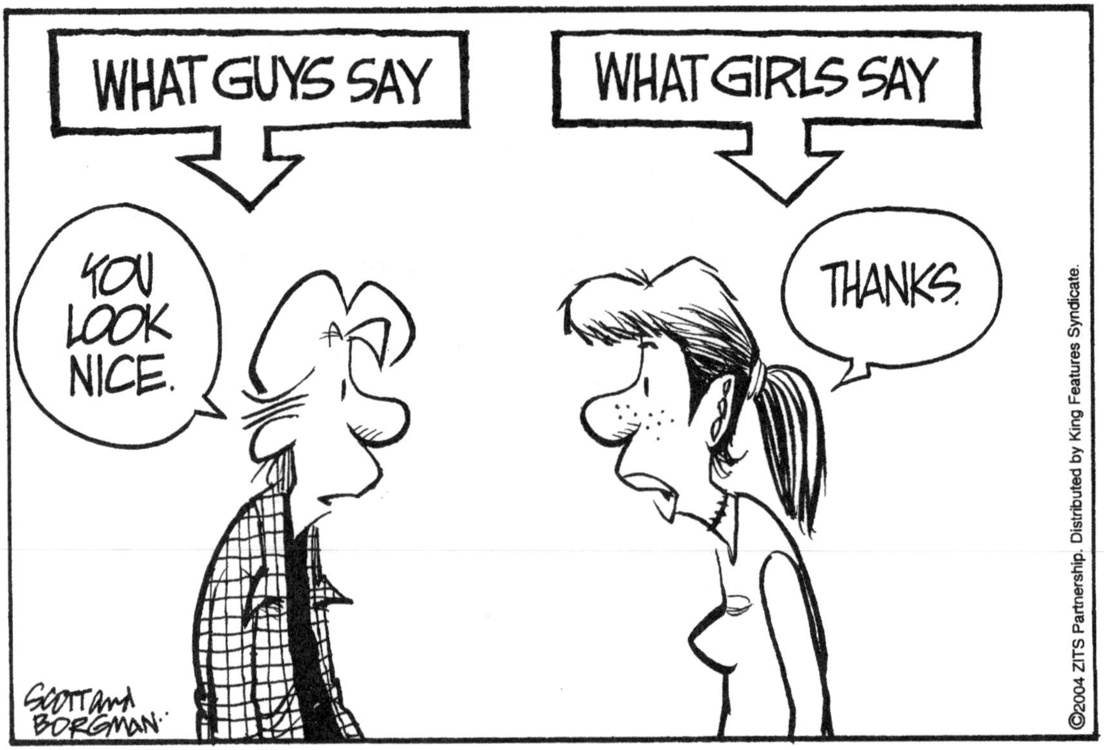
WHAT GUYS SAY
WHAT GIRLS SAY
YOU LOOK NICE.
THANKS.
SCOTT AND BORGMAN
©2004 ZITS Partnership. Distributed by King Features Syndicate.

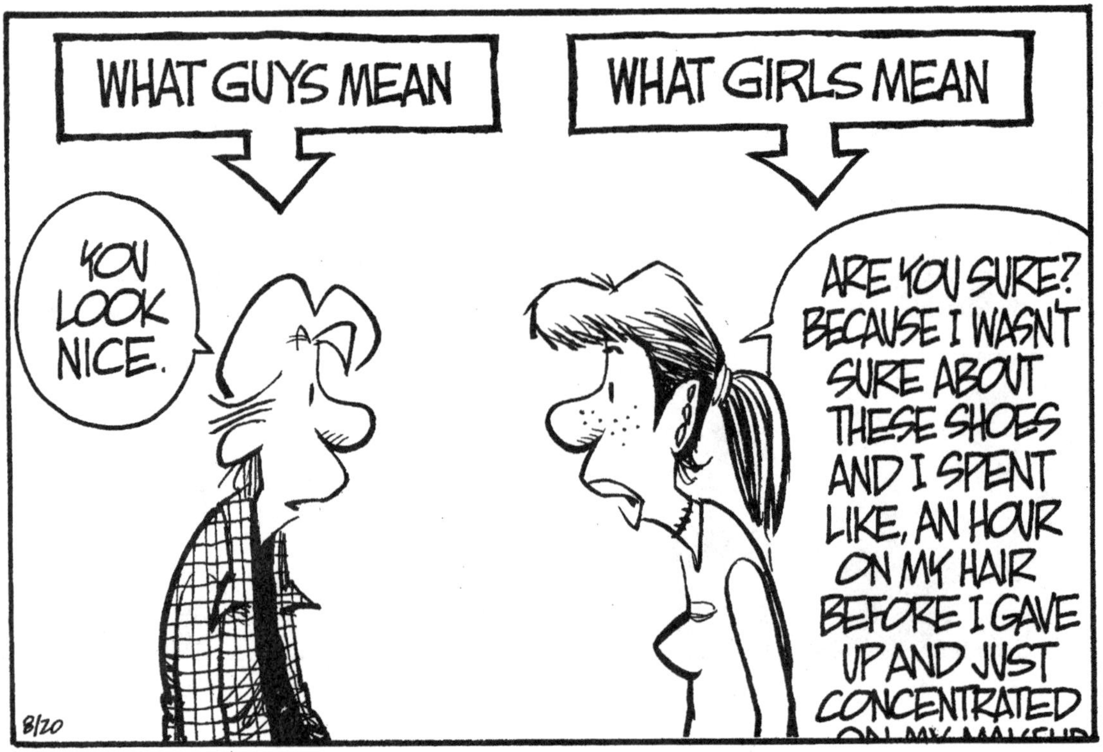
WHAT GUYS MEAN
WHAT GIRLS MEAN
YOU LOOK NICE.
ARE YOU SURE? BECAUSE I WASN'T SURE ABOUT THESE SHOES AND I SPENT LIKE, AN HOUR ON MY HAIR BEFORE I GAVE UP AND JUST CONCENTRATED
8/20

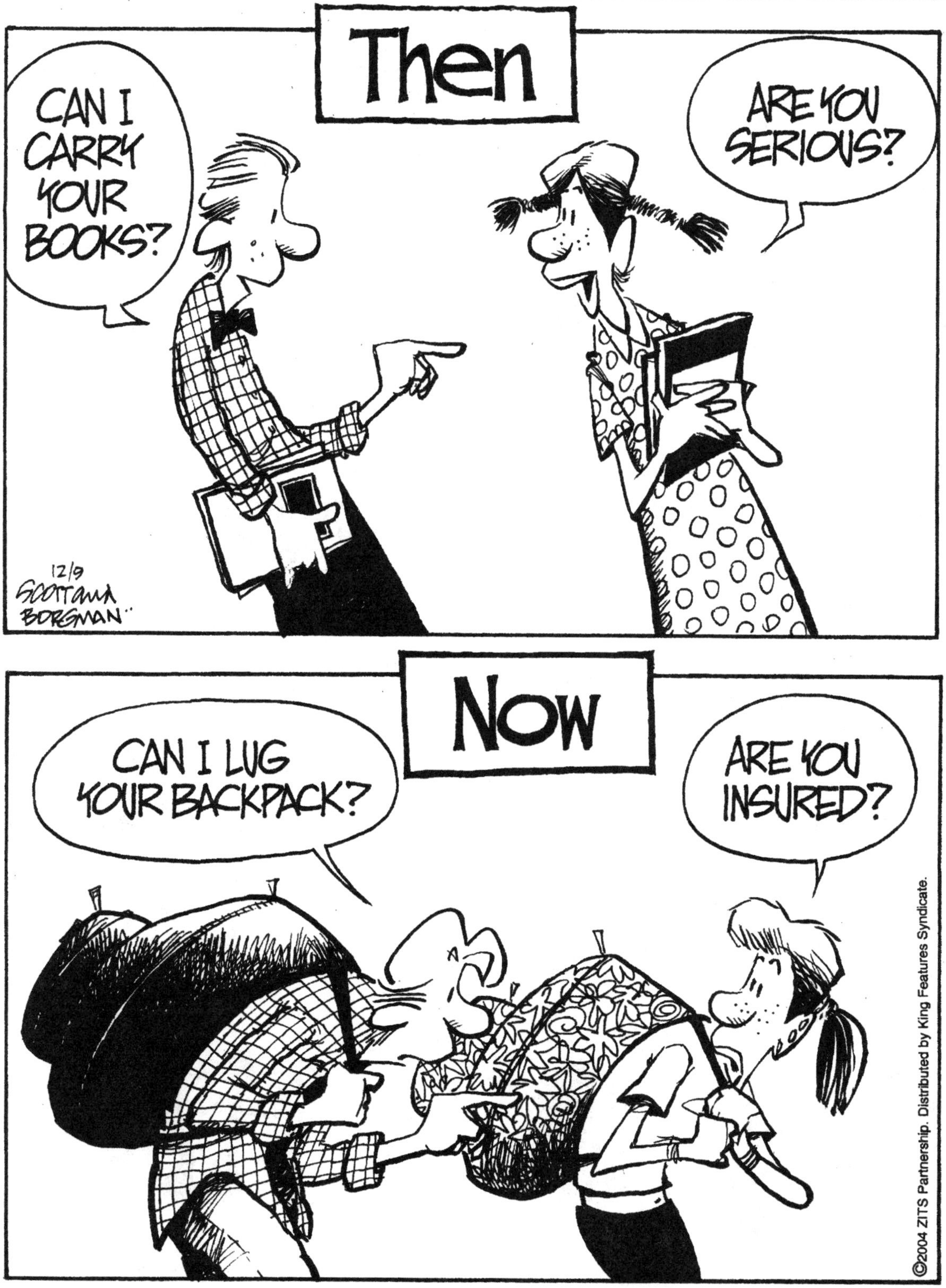
Then
CAN I CARRY YOUR BOOKS?
ARE YOU SERIOUS?
12/9
SCOTT AND BORGMAN
Now
CAN I LUG YOUR BACKPACK?
ARE YOU INSURED?
©2004 ZITS Partnership. Distributed by King Features Syndicate.

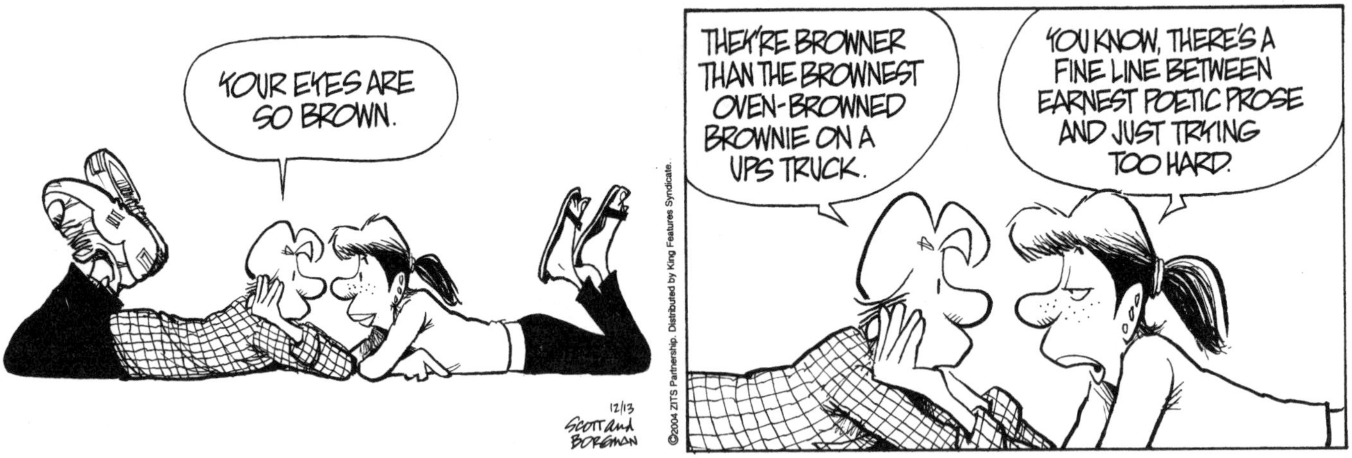
YOUR EYES ARE SO BROWN.
THEY'RE BROWNER THAN THE BROWNEST OVEN-BROWNED BROWNIE ON A UPS TRUCK.
YOU KNOW, THERE'S A FINE LINE BETWEEN EARNEST POETIC PROSE AND JUST TRYING TOO HARD.
12/13 SCOTT and BORGMAN
©2004 ZITS Partnership. Distributed by King Features Syndicate.

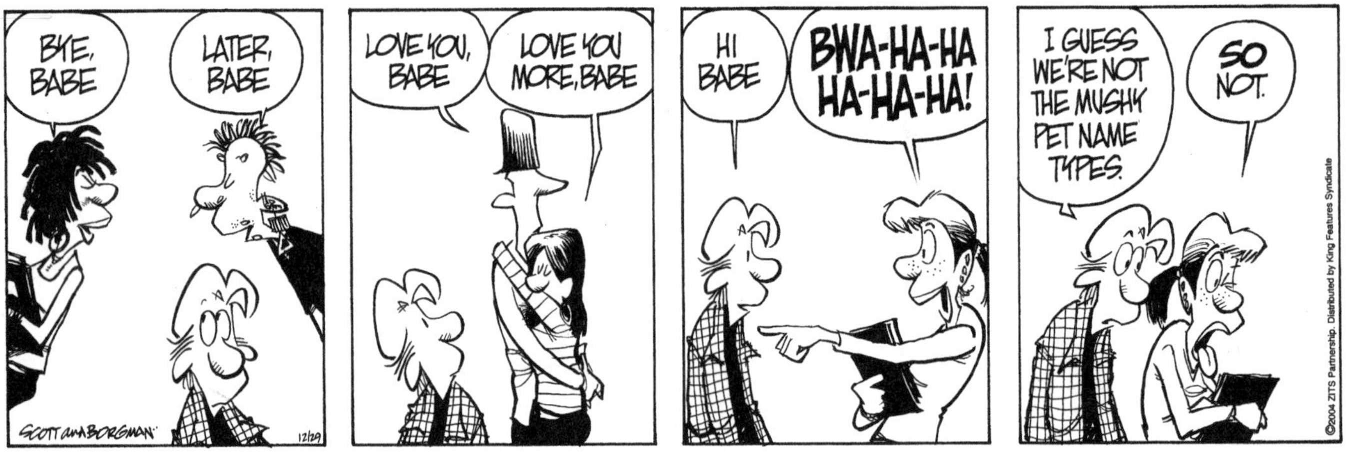
BYE, BABE
LATER, BABE
SCOTT and BORGMAN 12/29
LOVE YOU, BABE
LOVE YOU MORE, BABE
HI BABE
BWA-HA-HA HA-HA-HA!
I GUESS WE'RE NOT THE MUSHY PET NAME TYPES.
SO NOT.
©2004 ZITS Partnership. Distributed by King Features Syndicate

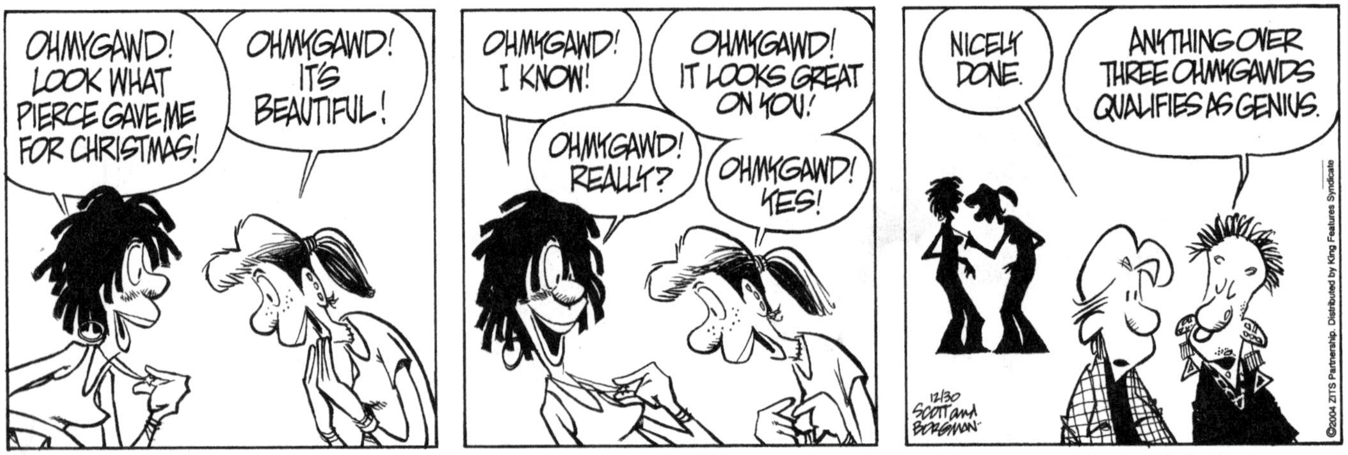
OHMYGAWD! LOOK WHAT PIERCE GAVE ME FOR CHRISTMAS!
OHMYGAWD! IT'S BEAUTIFUL!
OHMYGAWD! I KNOW!
OHMYGAWD! IT LOOKS GREAT ON YOU!
OHMYGAWD! REALLY?
OHMYGAWD! YES!
NICELY DONE.
ANYTHING OVER THREE OHMYGAWDS QUALIFIES AS GENIUS.
12/30 SCOTT and BORGMAN
©2004 ZITS Partnership. Distributed by King Features Syndicate

Zits
by JERRY SCOTT and JIM BORGMAN

SOMETHING WEIRD IS GOING ON WITH JEREMY, BUT I DON'T KNOW WHAT IT IS.
HMM
DID YOU WAIT FOR HIM AT HIS LOCKER THIS MORNING?
NO
DID YOU GUYS TALK IN THE HALL?
NO
AND I DIDN'T TEXT-MESSAGE HIM IN THE LIBRARY, HAVE LUNCH WITH HIM **OR** OFFER HIM A RIDE HOME!
WOW! NO WONDER YOU'RE CONFUSED!
I KNOW!
HOW MANY TIMES DO YOU HAVE TO IGNORE A GUY TO GET HIS ATTENTION?
3/20 SCOTT and BORGMAN
©2005 ZITS Partnership. Distributed by King Features Syndicate

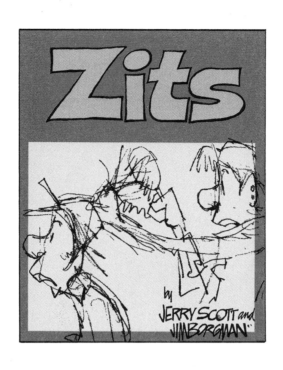

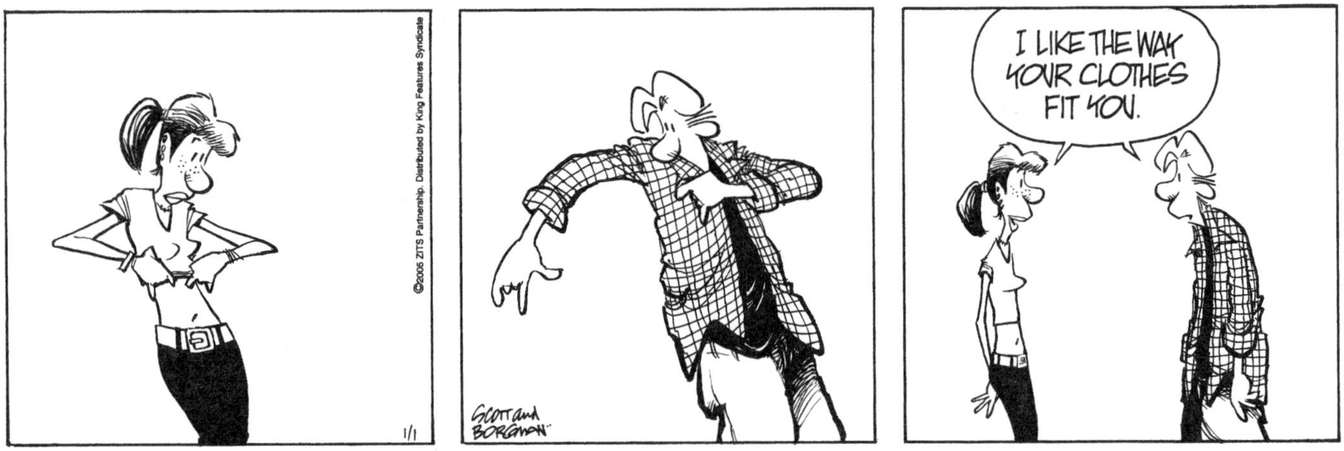
©2005 ZITS Partnership. Distributed by King Features Syndicate
1/1
SCOTT and BORGMAN
I LIKE THE WAY YOUR CLOTHES FIT YOU.

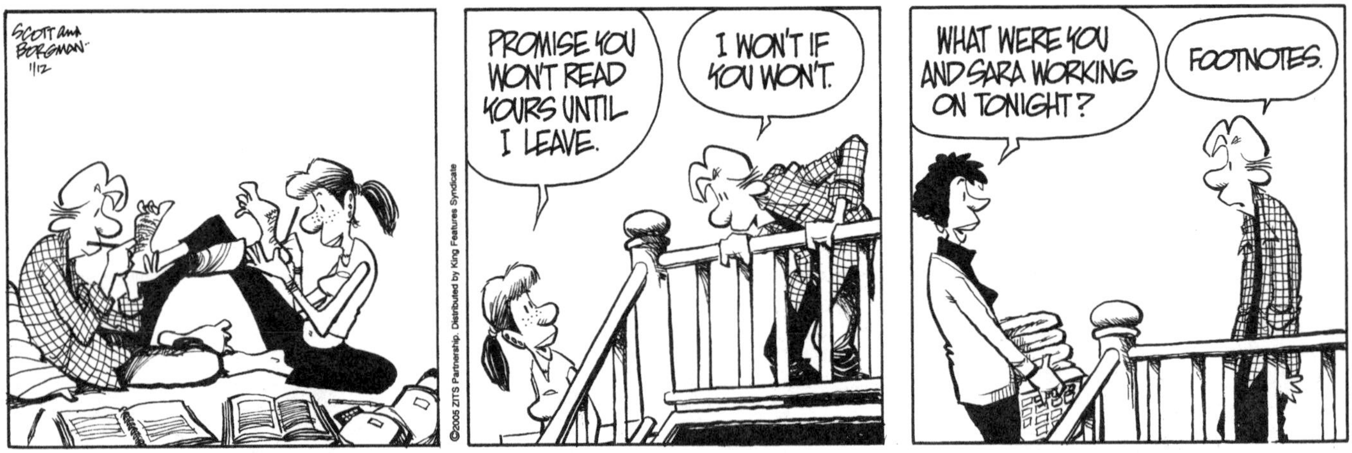
SCOTT and BORGMAN 1/12
©2005 ZITS Partnership. Distributed by King Features Syndicate
PROMISE YOU WON'T READ YOURS UNTIL I LEAVE.
I WON'T IF YOU WON'T.
WHAT WERE YOU AND SARA WORKING ON TONIGHT?
FOOTNOTES.

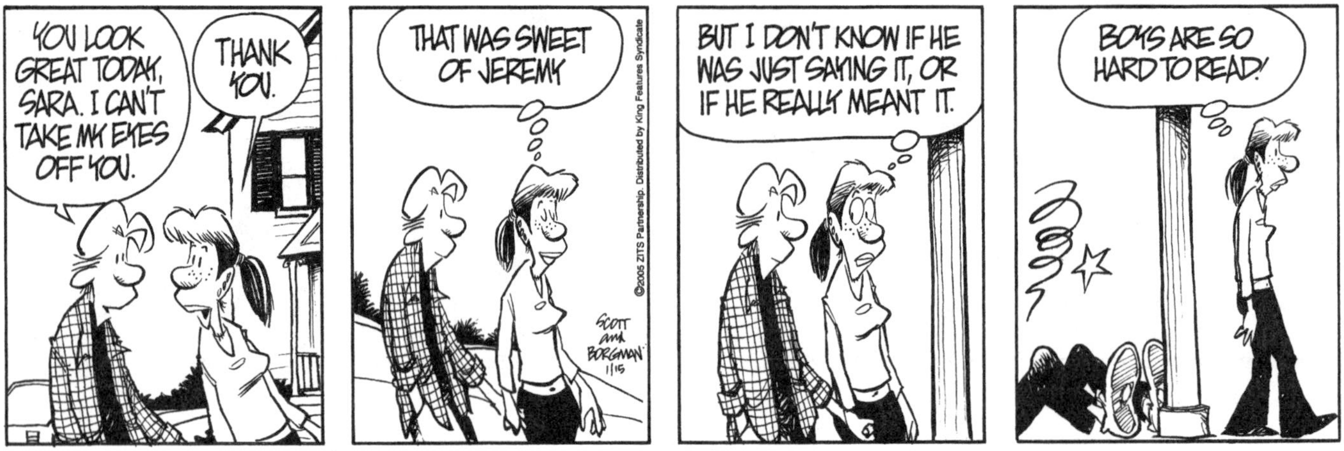
YOU LOOK GREAT TODAY, SARA. I CAN'T TAKE MY EYES OFF YOU.
THANK YOU.
THAT WAS SWEET OF JEREMY
©2005 ZITS Partnership. Distributed by King Features Syndicate
SCOTT and BORGMAN 1/15
BUT I DON'T KNOW IF HE WAS JUST SAYING IT, OR IF HE REALLY MEANT IT.
BOYS ARE SO HARD TO READ!

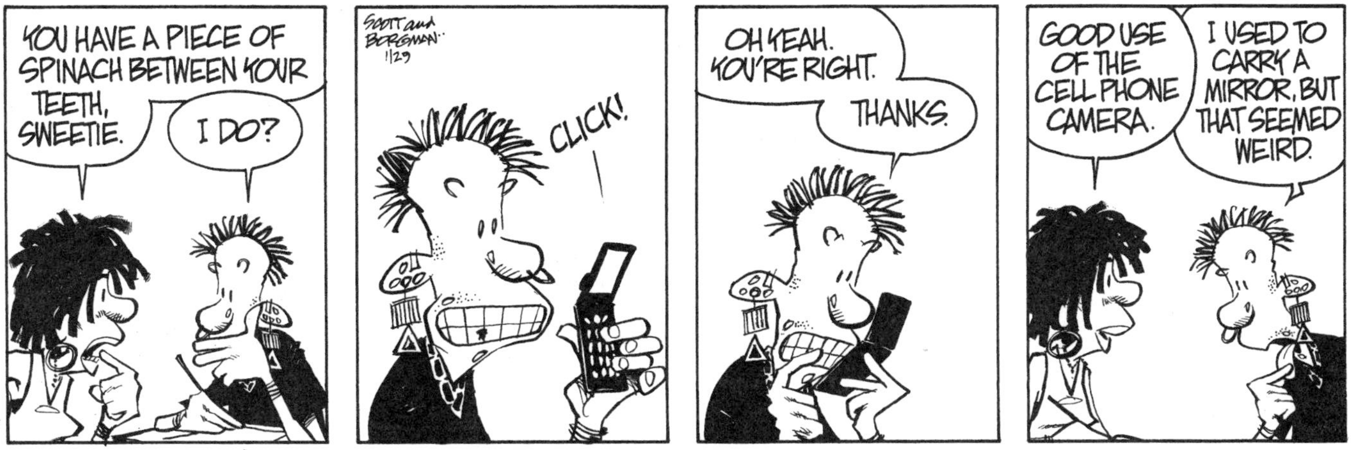
YOU HAVE A PIECE OF SPINACH BETWEEN YOUR TEETH, SWEETIE.
I DO?
SCOTT and BORGMAN 1/29
CLICK!
OH YEAH. YOU'RE RIGHT.
THANKS.
GOOD USE OF THE CELL PHONE CAMERA.
I USED TO CARRY A MIRROR, BUT THAT SEEMED WEIRD.

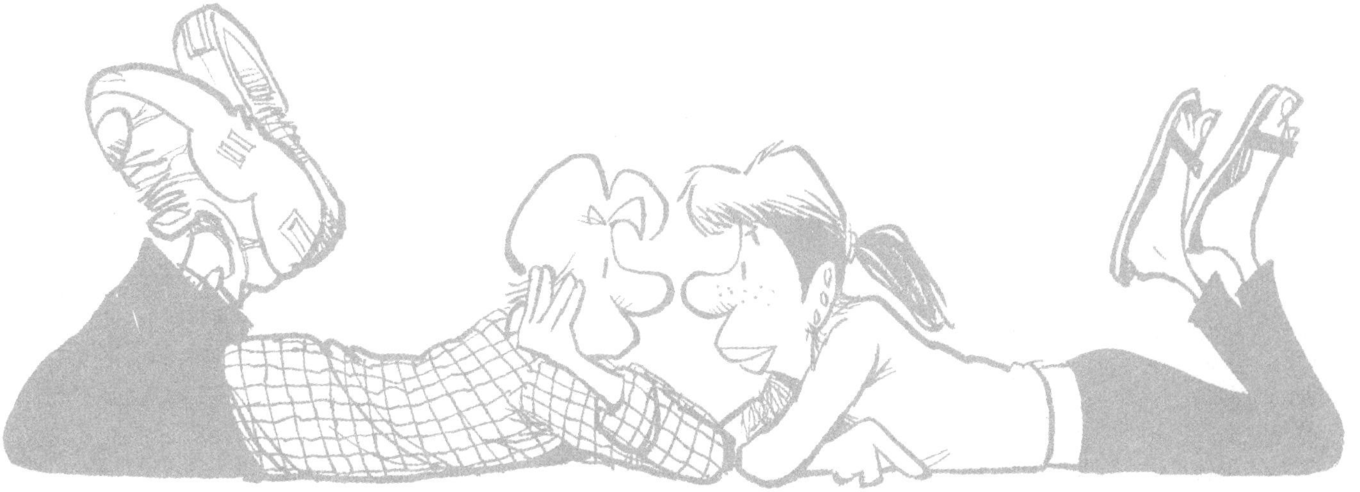

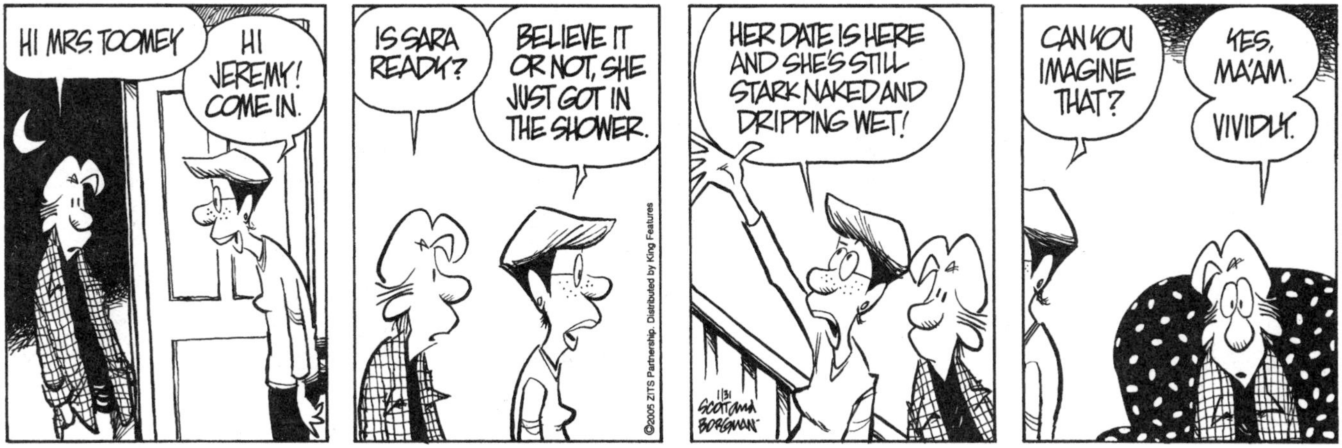
HI MRS. TOOMEY
HI JEREMY! COME IN.
IS SARA READY?
BELIEVE IT OR NOT, SHE JUST GOT IN THE SHOWER.
©2005 ZITS Partnership. Distributed by King Features
HER DATE IS HERE AND SHE'S STILL STARK NAKED AND DRIPPING WET!
1/31 SCOTT and BORGMAN
CAN YOU IMAGINE THAT?
YES, MA'AM.
VIVIDLY.

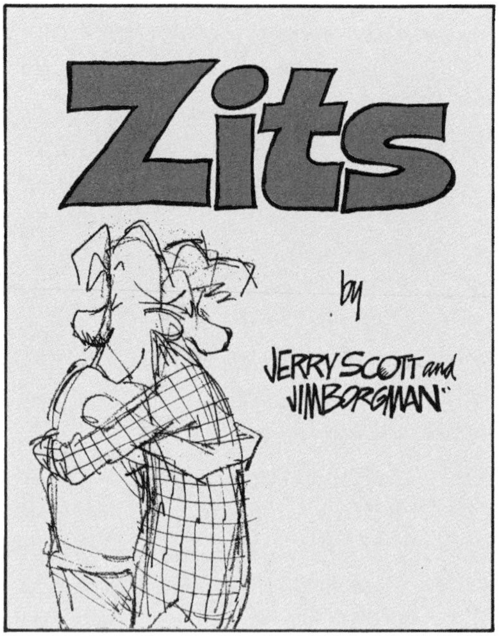
Zits
by
JERRY SCOTT and
JIM BORGMAN

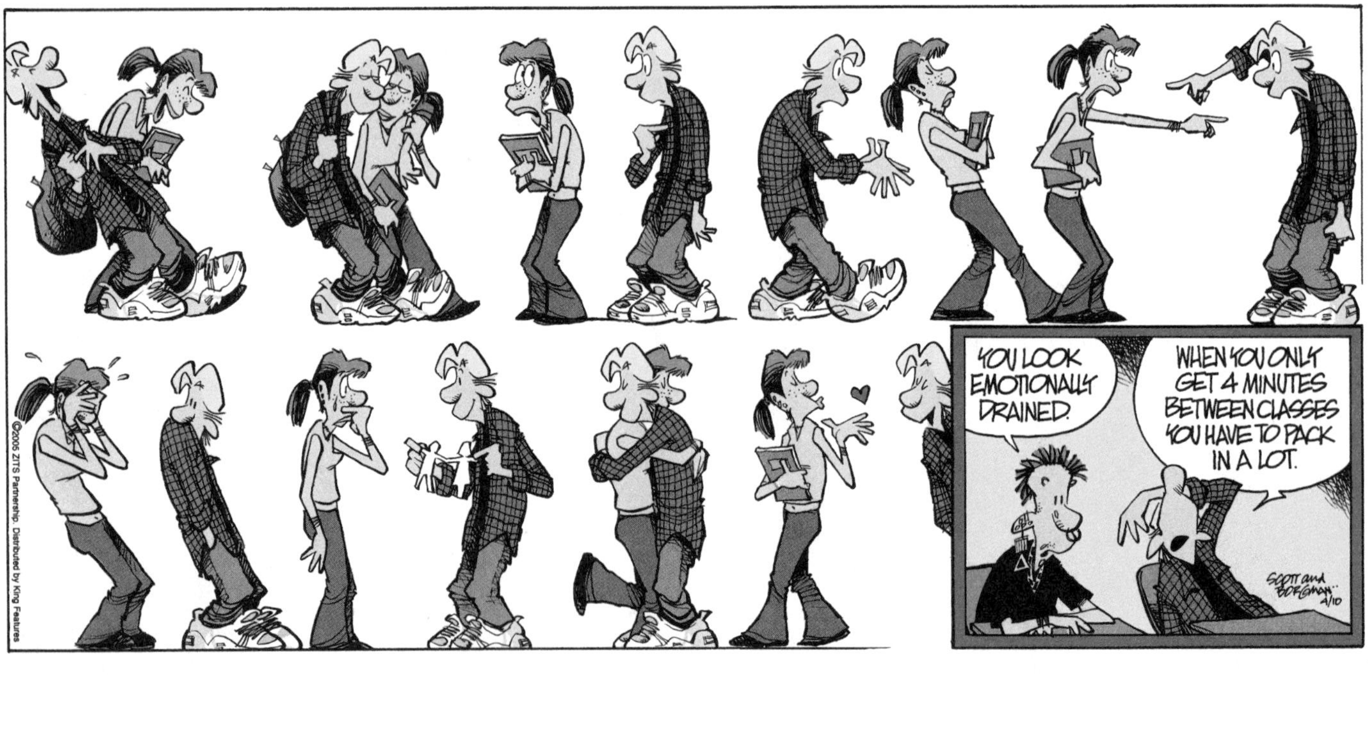
©2005 ZITS Partnership. Distributed by King Features
YOU LOOK EMOTIONALLY DRAINED.
WHEN YOU ONLY GET 4 MINUTES BETWEEN CLASSES YOU HAVE TO PACK IN A LOT.
SCOTT and BORGMAN 4/10

Zits
by
JERRY SCOTT and
JIM BORGMAN

©2005 ZITS Partnership. Distributed by King Features Syndicate
6:00
6:12
6:29
6:43
6:57
I DID MY HAIR IN UNDER AN HOUR TODAY!
SOMETIMES WE ARE SO ALIKE, IT'S ALMOST SCARY.
SCOTT and BORGMAN 4/24

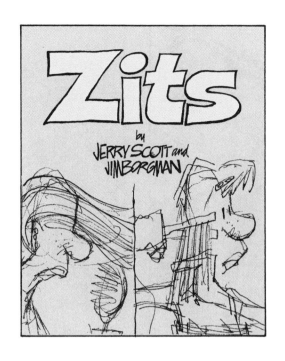

SCOTT AND BORGMAN
©2005 ZITS Partnership. Distributed by King Features Syndicate
2/14
OH, I'M SORRY. I DIDN'T NOTICE THAT I WAS TOUCHING YOUR LEG, JEREMY.
OH. UM,... YEAH. ME EITHER.

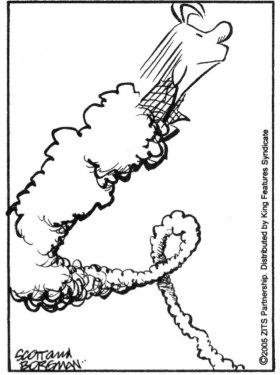

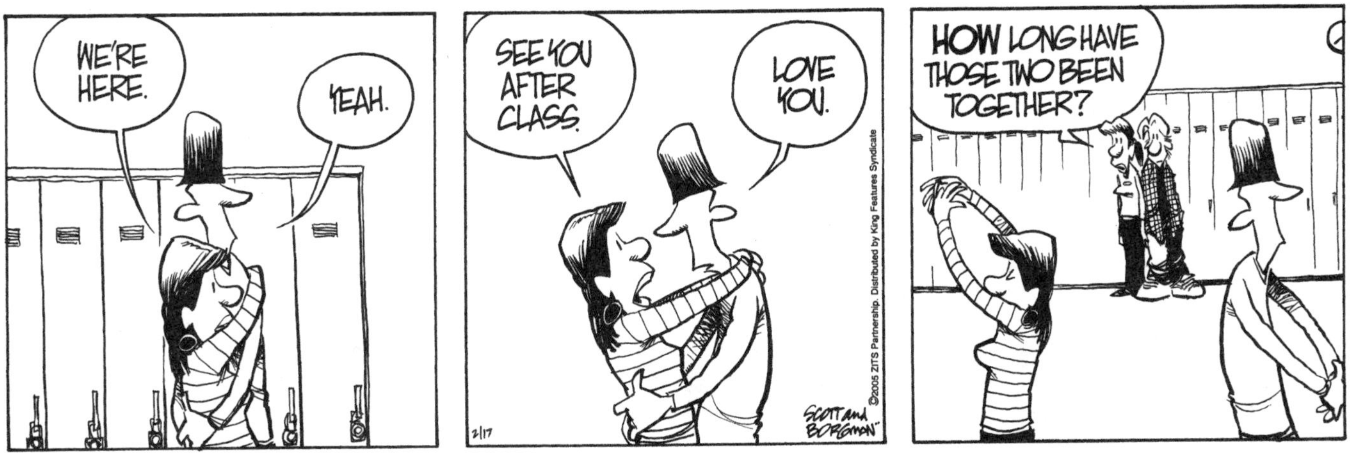
WE'RE HERE.
YEAH.
SEE YOU AFTER CLASS.
LOVE YOU.
2/17
SCOTT and BORGMAN
©2005 ZITS Partnership. Distributed by King Features Syndicate
HOW LONG HAVE THOSE TWO BEEN TOGETHER?

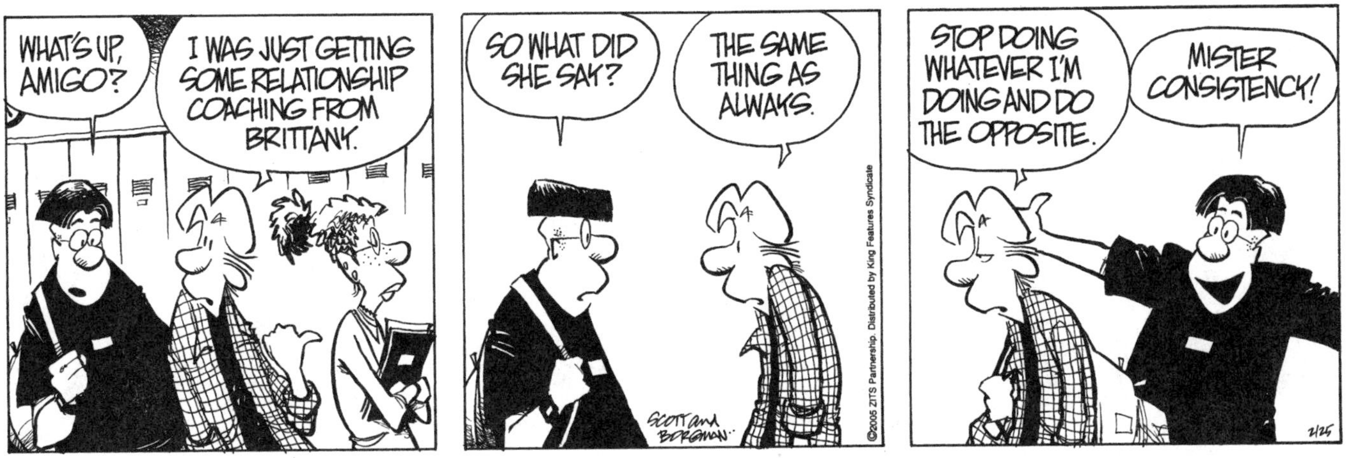
WHAT'S UP, AMIGO?
I WAS JUST GETTING SOME RELATIONSHIP COACHING FROM BRITTANY.
SO WHAT DID SHE SAY?
THE SAME THING AS ALWAYS.
SCOTT and BORGMAN
©2005 ZITS Partnership. Distributed by King Features Syndicate
STOP DOING WHATEVER I'M DOING AND DO THE OPPOSITE.
MISTER CONSISTENCY!
2/25

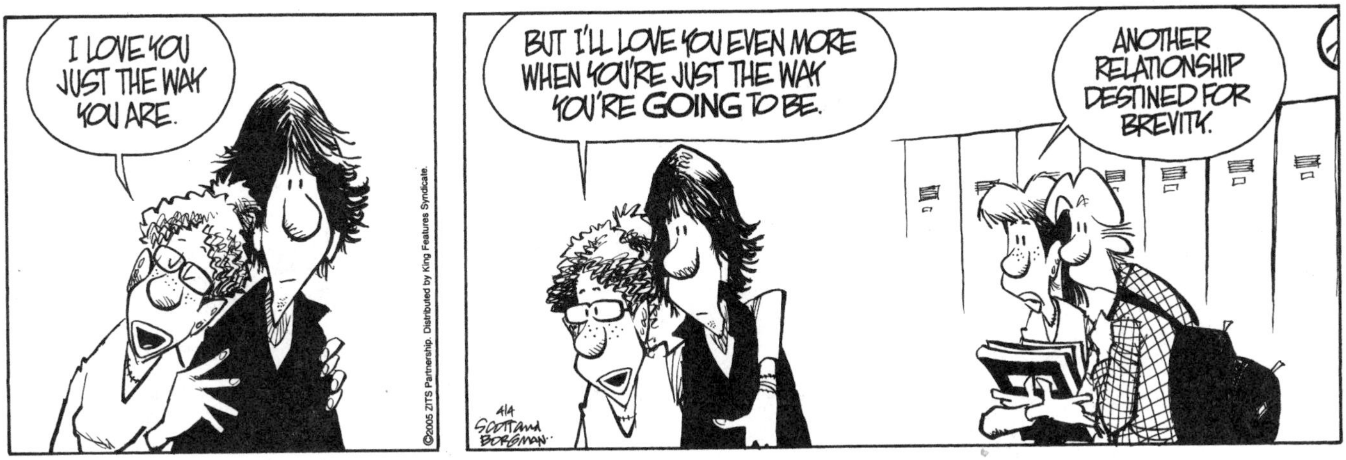
I LOVE YOU JUST THE WAY YOU ARE.
©2005 ZITS Partnership. Distributed by King Features Syndicate.
BUT I'LL LOVE YOU EVEN MORE WHEN YOU'RE JUST THE WAY YOU'RE GOING TO BE.
ANOTHER RELATIONSHIP DESTINED FOR BREVITY.
4/14
SCOTT and BORGMAN

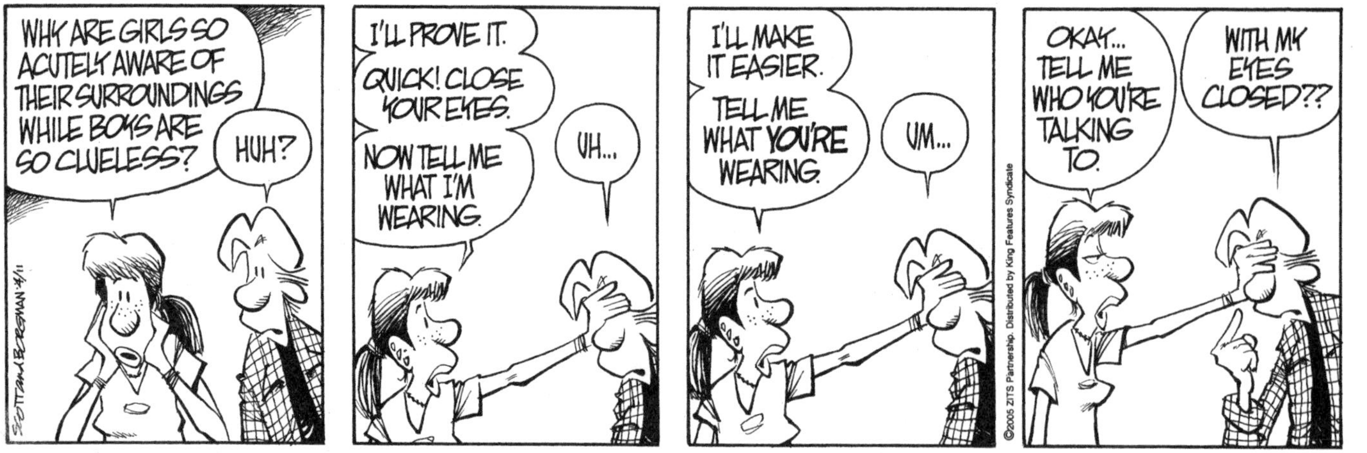
WHY ARE GIRLS SO ACUTELY AWARE OF THEIR SURROUNDINGS WHILE BOYS ARE SO CLUELESS?
HUH?
I'LL PROVE IT.
QUICK! CLOSE YOUR EYES.
NOW TELL ME WHAT I'M WEARING.
UH...
I'LL MAKE IT EASIER.
TELL ME WHAT YOU'RE WEARING.
UM...
OKAY... TELL ME WHO YOU'RE TALKING TO.
WITH MY EYES CLOSED??
©2005 ZITS Partnership. Distributed by King Features Syndicate

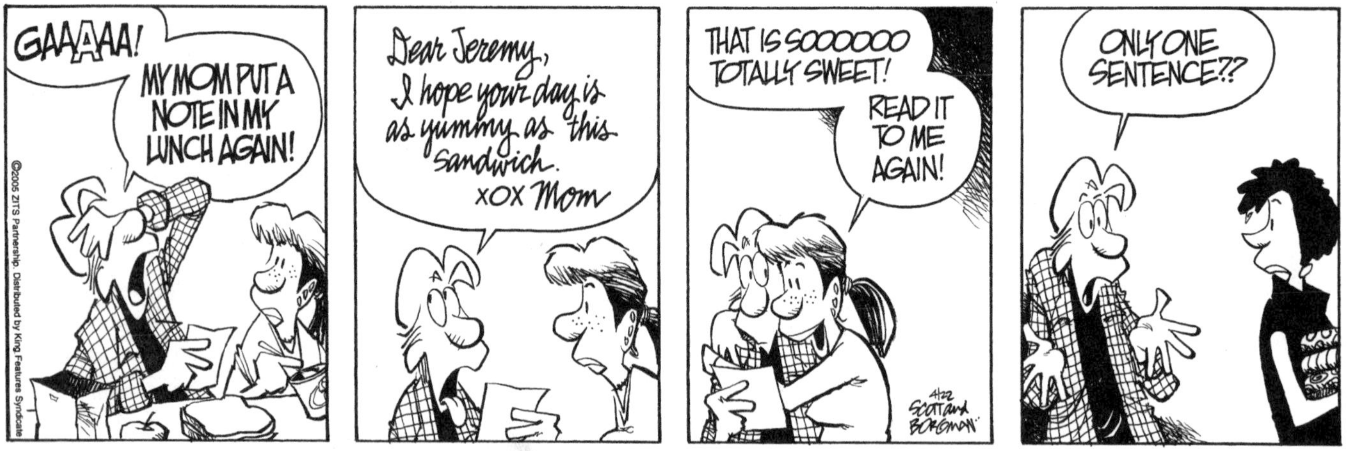
GAAAAA!
MY MOM PUT A NOTE IN MY LUNCH AGAIN!
©2005 ZITS Partnership. Distributed by King Features Syndicate
Dear Jeremy,
I hope your day is as yummy as this sandwich.
xox Mom
THAT IS SOOOOOO TOTALLY SWEET!
READ IT TO ME AGAIN!
ONLY ONE SENTENCE??

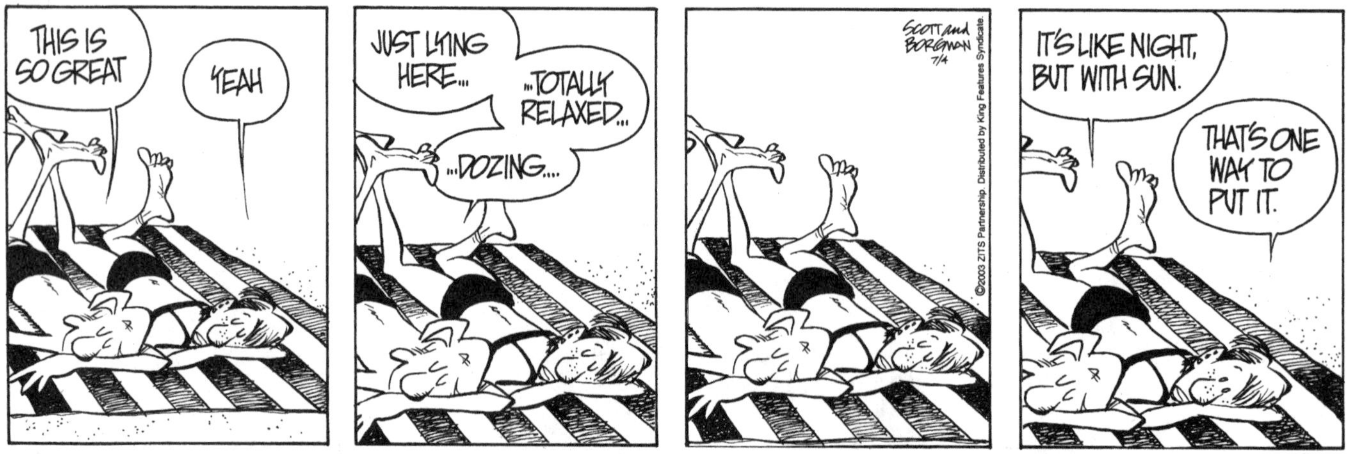
THIS IS SO GREAT
YEAH
JUST LYING HERE...
...TOTALLY RELAXED...
...DOZING....
©2003 ZITS Partnership. Distributed by King Features Syndicate.
IT'S LIKE NIGHT, BUT WITH SUN.
THAT'S ONE WAY TO PUT IT.

SCOTT and BORGMAN
2/22
PSSSHT
DUDE, THIS ISN'T DEODORANT, IT'S ROGAINE!
YOU DEAL WITH LOCKER ROOM INSECURITIES YOUR WAY, AND I'LL DEAL WITH THEM MY WAY.
©2005 ZITS Partnership. Distributed by King Features Syndicate

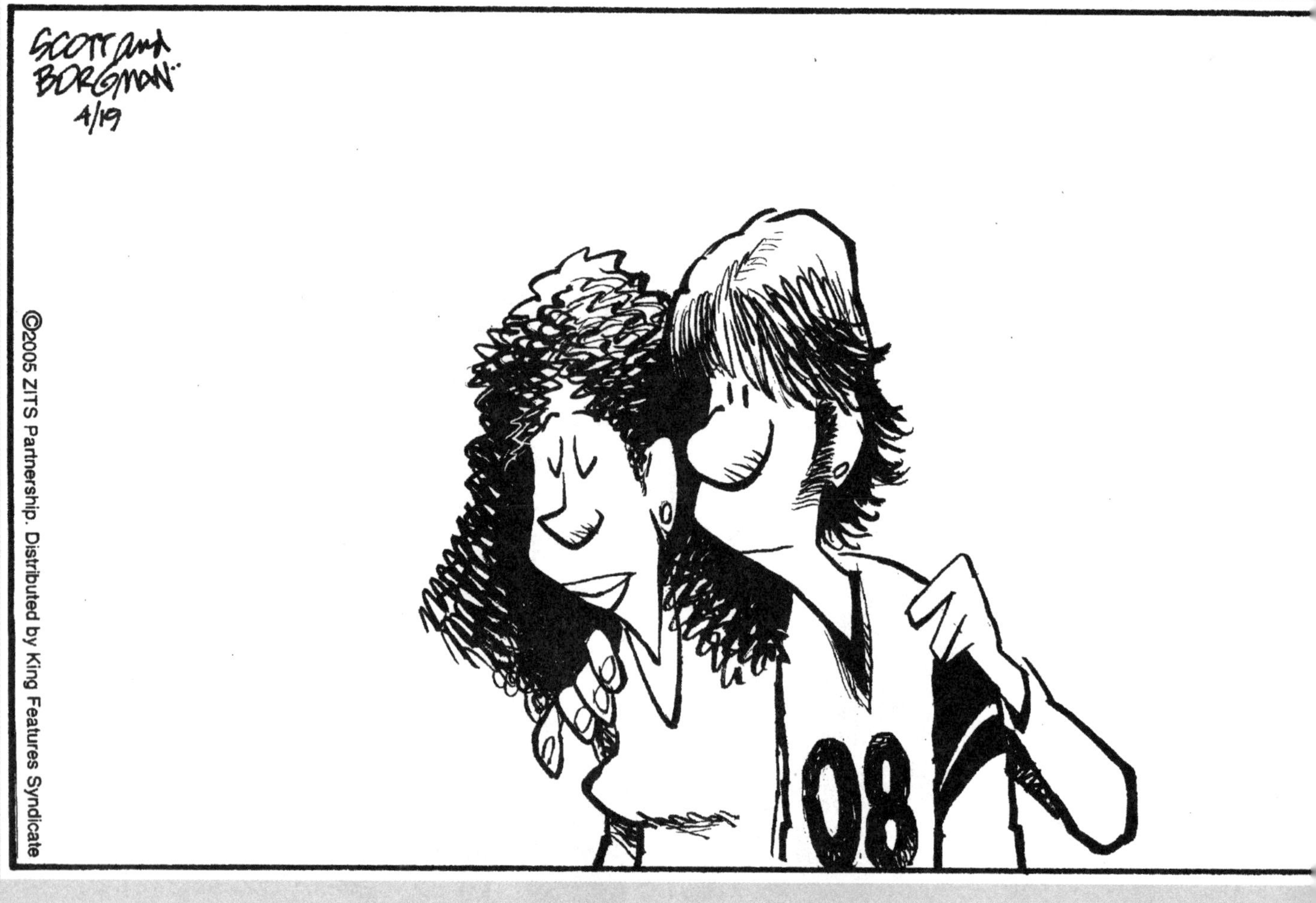
SCOTT and BORGMAN
4/19
©2005 ZITS Partnership. Distributed by King Features Syndicate
08

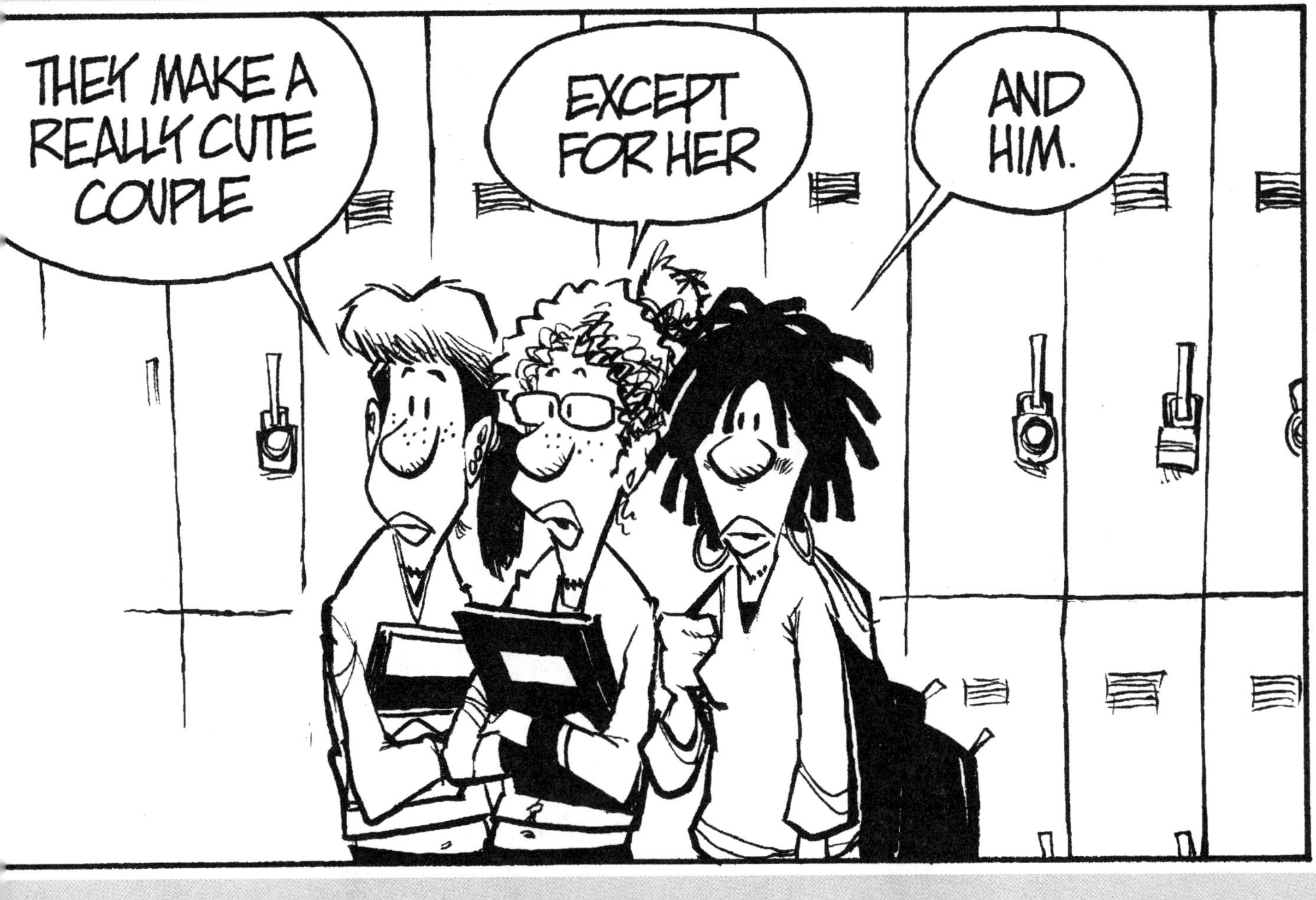
THEY MAKE A REALLY CUTE COUPLE
EXCEPT FOR HER
AND HIM.

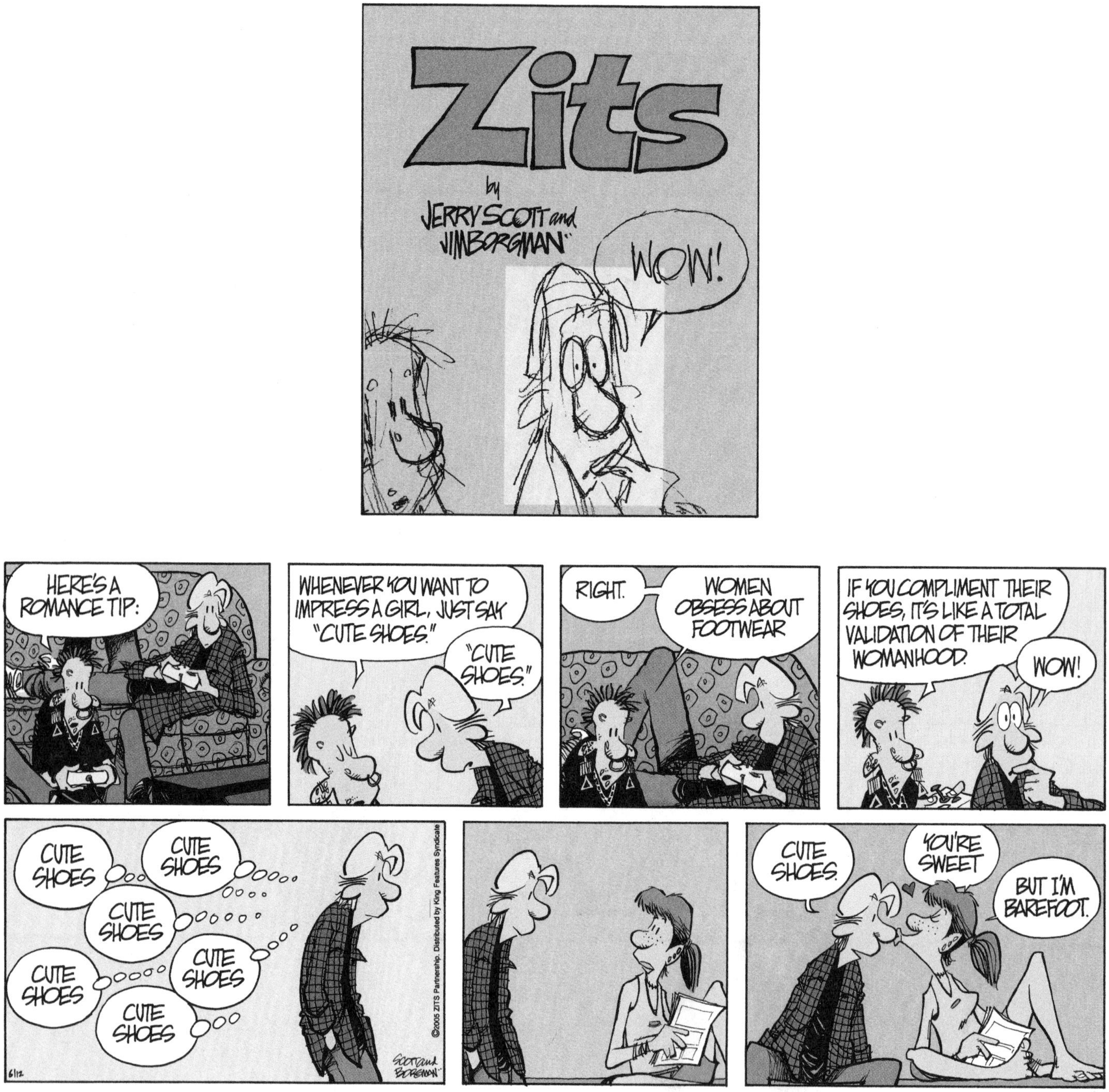
Zits
by
JERRY SCOTT and
JIM BORGMAN
WOW!
HERE'S A ROMANCE TIP:
WHENEVER YOU WANT TO IMPRESS A GIRL, JUST SAY "CUTE SHOES."
"CUTE SHOES."
RIGHT.
WOMEN OBSESS ABOUT FOOTWEAR
IF YOU COMPLIMENT THEIR SHOES, IT'S LIKE A TOTAL VALIDATION OF THEIR WOMANHOOD.
WOW!
CUTE SHOES
CUTE SHOES
CUTE SHOES
CUTE SHOES
CUTE SHOES
CUTE SHOES
©2005 ZITS Partnership. Distributed by King Features Syndicate
6/12
SCOTT and BORGMAN
CUTE SHOES.
YOU'RE SWEET
BUT I'M BAREFOOT.

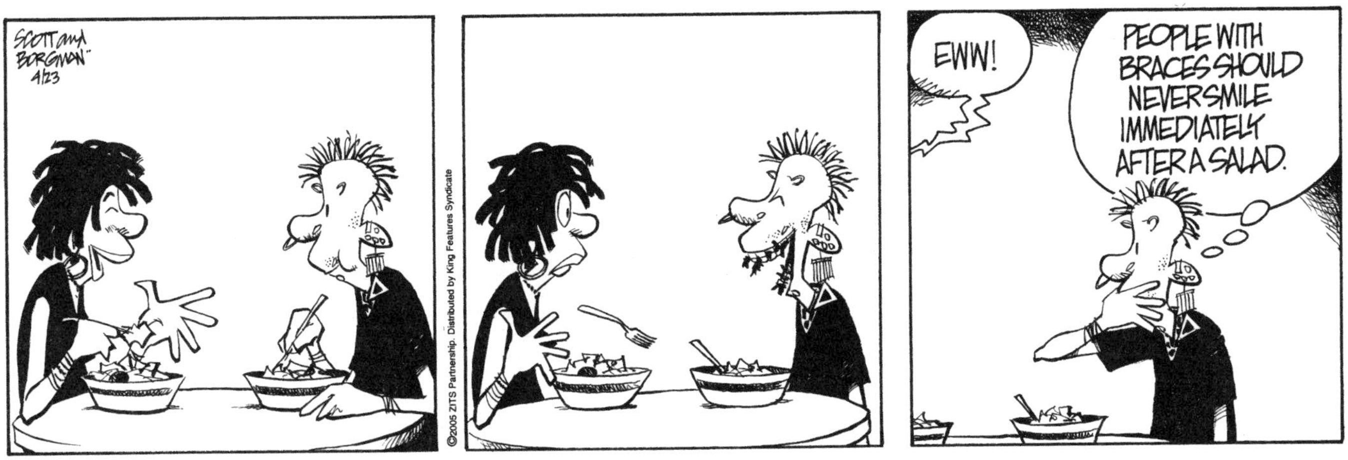
SCOTT and BORGMAN 4/23
©2005 ZITS Partnership. Distributed by King Features Syndicate
EWW!
PEOPLE WITH BRACES SHOULD NEVER SMILE IMMEDIATELY AFTER A SALAD.

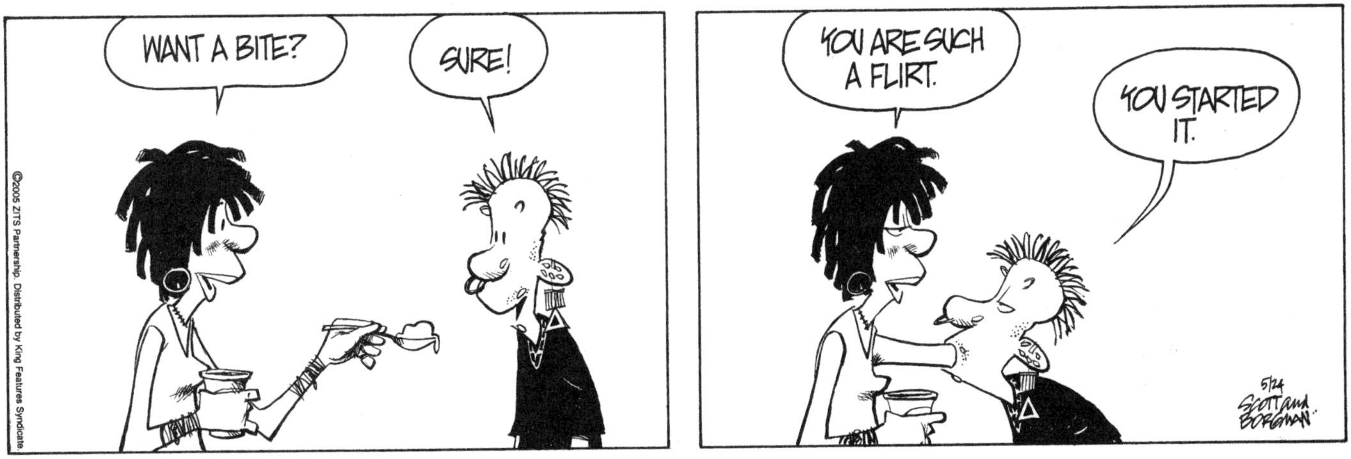
©2005 ZITS Partnership. Distributed by King Features Syndicate.
WANT A BITE?
SURE!
YOU ARE SUCH A FLIRT.
YOU STARTED IT.
5/24 SCOTT and BORGMAN

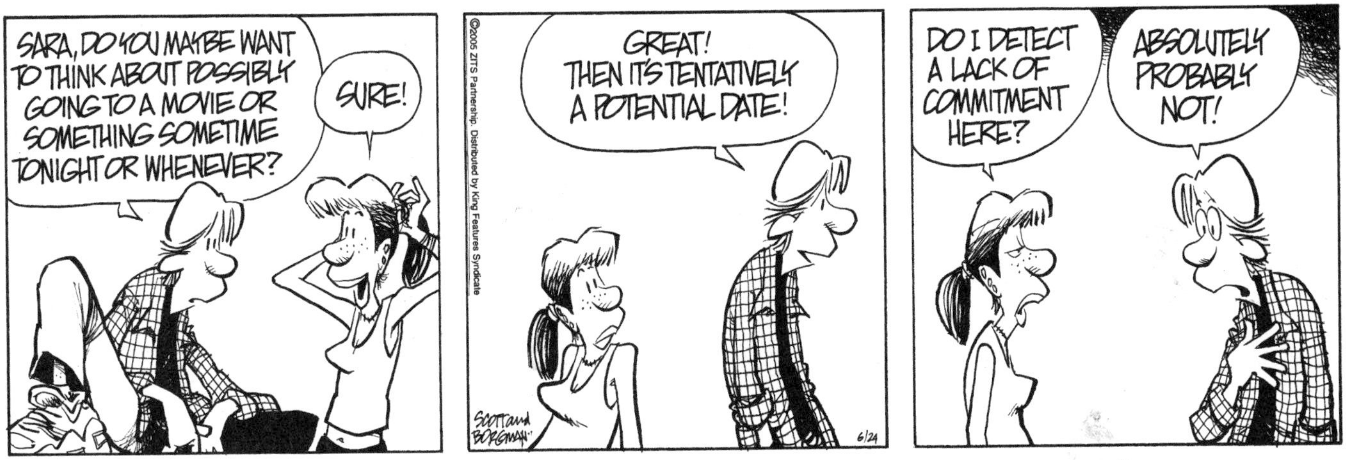
SARA, DO YOU MAYBE WANT TO THINK ABOUT POSSIBLY GOING TO A MOVIE OR SOMETHING SOMETIME TONIGHT OR WHENEVER?
SURE!
©2005 ZITS Partnership. Distributed by King Features Syndicate
GREAT! THEN IT'S TENTATIVELY A POTENTIAL DATE!
SCOTT and BORGMAN
6/24
DO I DETECT A LACK OF COMMITMENT HERE?
ABSOLUTELY PROBABLY NOT!

Zits
by
JERRY SCOTT and
JIM BORGMAN

WELL, YOU'D BETTER GET GOING.
YEAH...
WOW!
The End
WELL, YOU'D BETTER GET GOING.
YEAH
SCOTT AND BORGMAN
7/31
©2005 ZITS Partnership. Distributed by King Features Syndicate

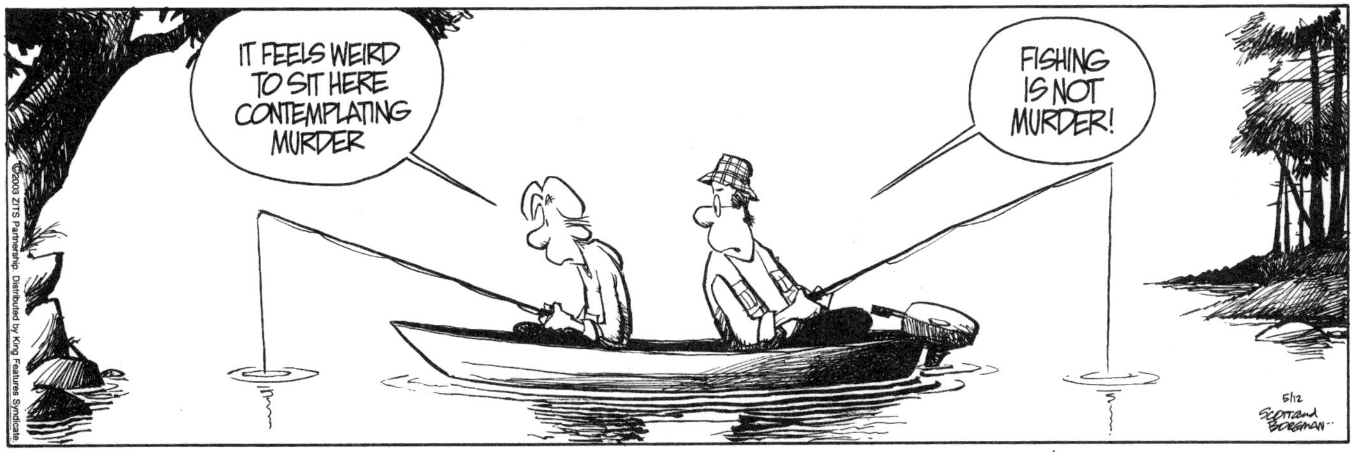
IT FEELS WEIRD TO SIT HERE CONTEMPLATING MURDER
FISHING IS NOT MURDER!
©2003 ZITS Partnership. Distributed by King Features Syndicate.
5/12
SCOTT and BORGMAN

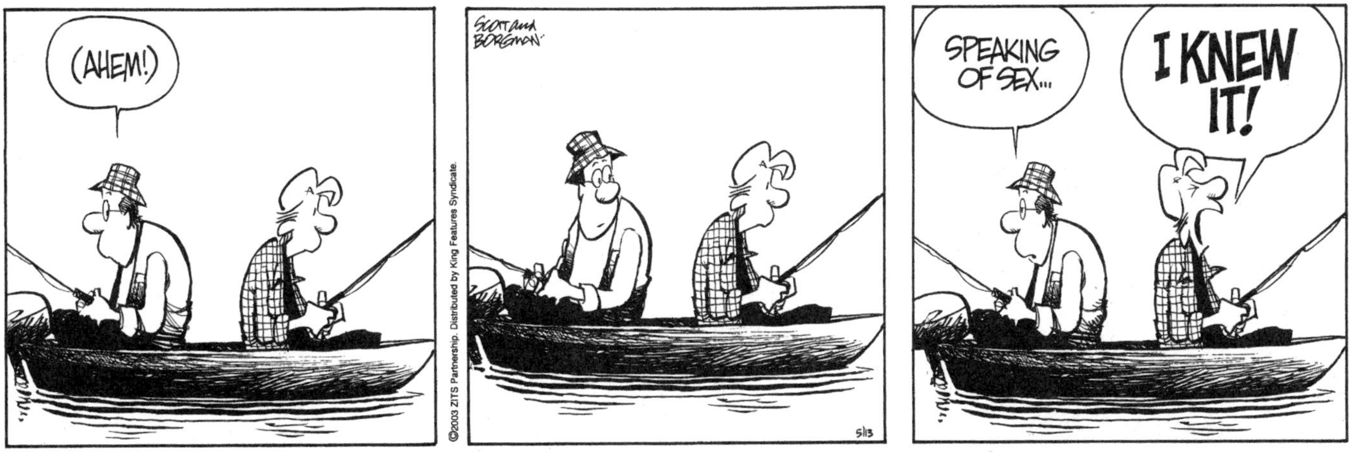
(AHEM!)
SCOTT and BORGMAN
©2003 ZITS Partnership. Distributed by King Features Syndicate.
5/13
SPEAKING OF SEX...
I KNEW IT!

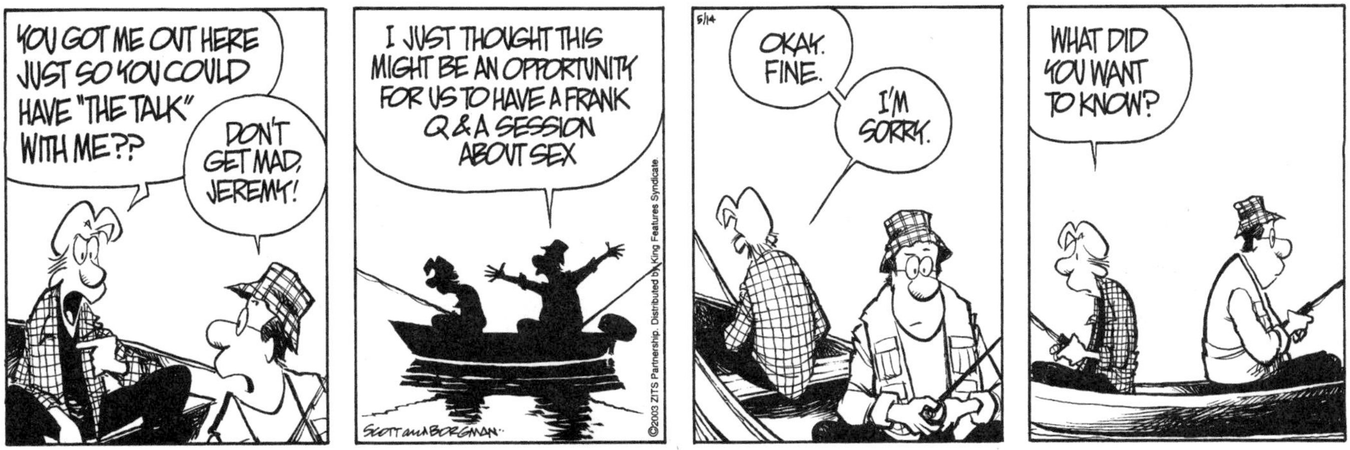
YOU GOT ME OUT HERE JUST SO YOU COULD HAVE "THE TALK" WITH ME??
DON'T GET MAD, JEREMY!
I JUST THOUGHT THIS MIGHT BE AN OPPORTUNITY FOR US TO HAVE A FRANK Q & A SESSION ABOUT SEX
SCOTT and BORGMAN
©2003 ZITS Partnership. Distributed by King Features Syndicate.
5/14
OKAY. FINE.
I'M SORRY.
WHAT DID YOU WANT TO KNOW?

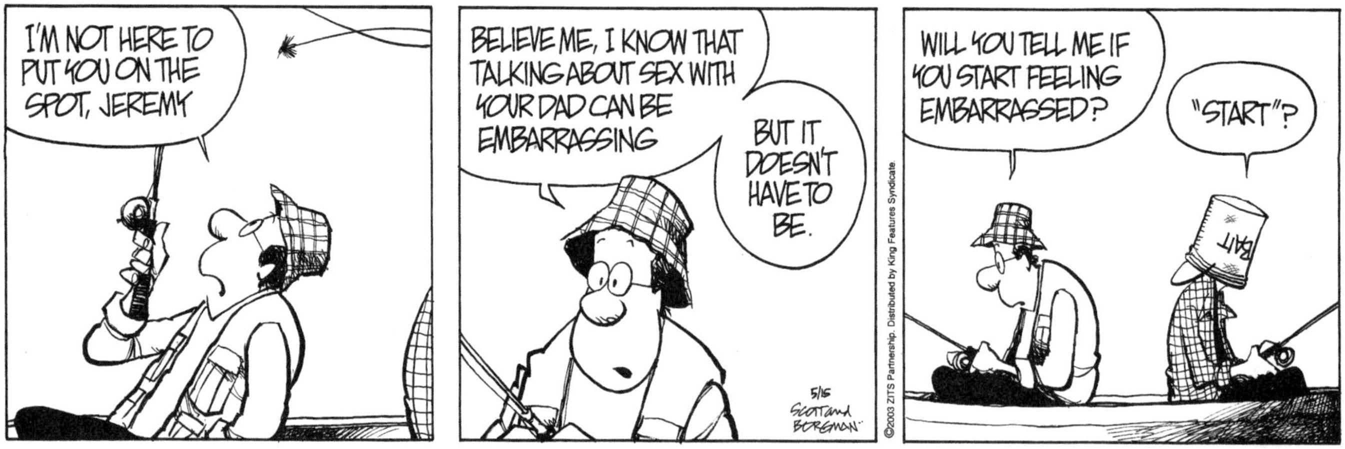
I'M NOT HERE TO PUT YOU ON THE SPOT, JEREMY.
BELIEVE ME, I KNOW THAT TALKING ABOUT SEX WITH YOUR DAD CAN BE EMBARRASSING.
BUT IT DOESN'T HAVE TO BE.
5/15 SCOTT and BORGMAN
WILL YOU TELL ME IF YOU START FEELING EMBARRASSED?
"START"?
BAIT
©2003 ZITS Partnership. Distributed by King Features Syndicate.

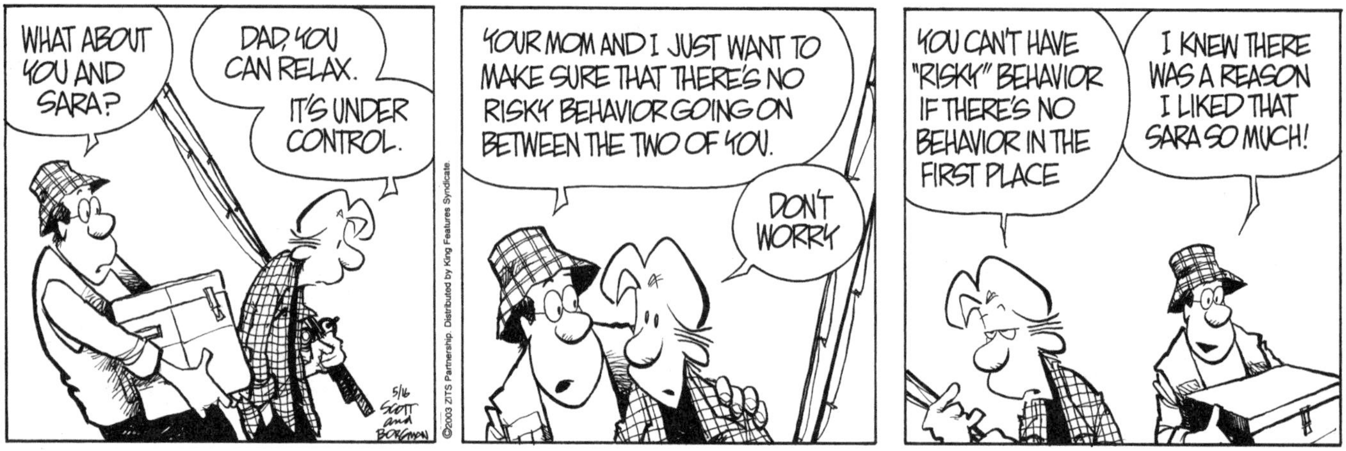
WHAT ABOUT YOU AND SARA?
DAD, YOU CAN RELAX.
IT'S UNDER CONTROL.
5/16 SCOTT and BORGMAN
©2003 ZITS Partnership. Distributed by King Features Syndicate.
YOUR MOM AND I JUST WANT TO MAKE SURE THAT THERE'S NO RISKY BEHAVIOR GOING ON BETWEEN THE TWO OF YOU.
DON'T WORRY.
YOU CAN'T HAVE "RISKY" BEHAVIOR IF THERE'S NO BEHAVIOR IN THE FIRST PLACE.
I KNEW THERE WAS A REASON I LIKED THAT SARA SO MUCH!

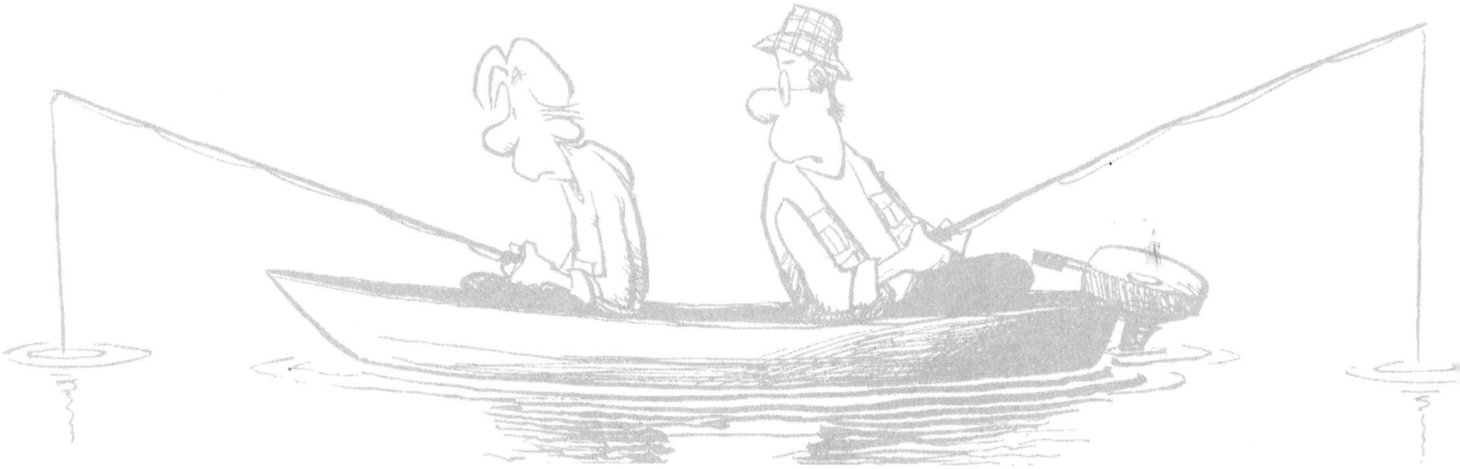

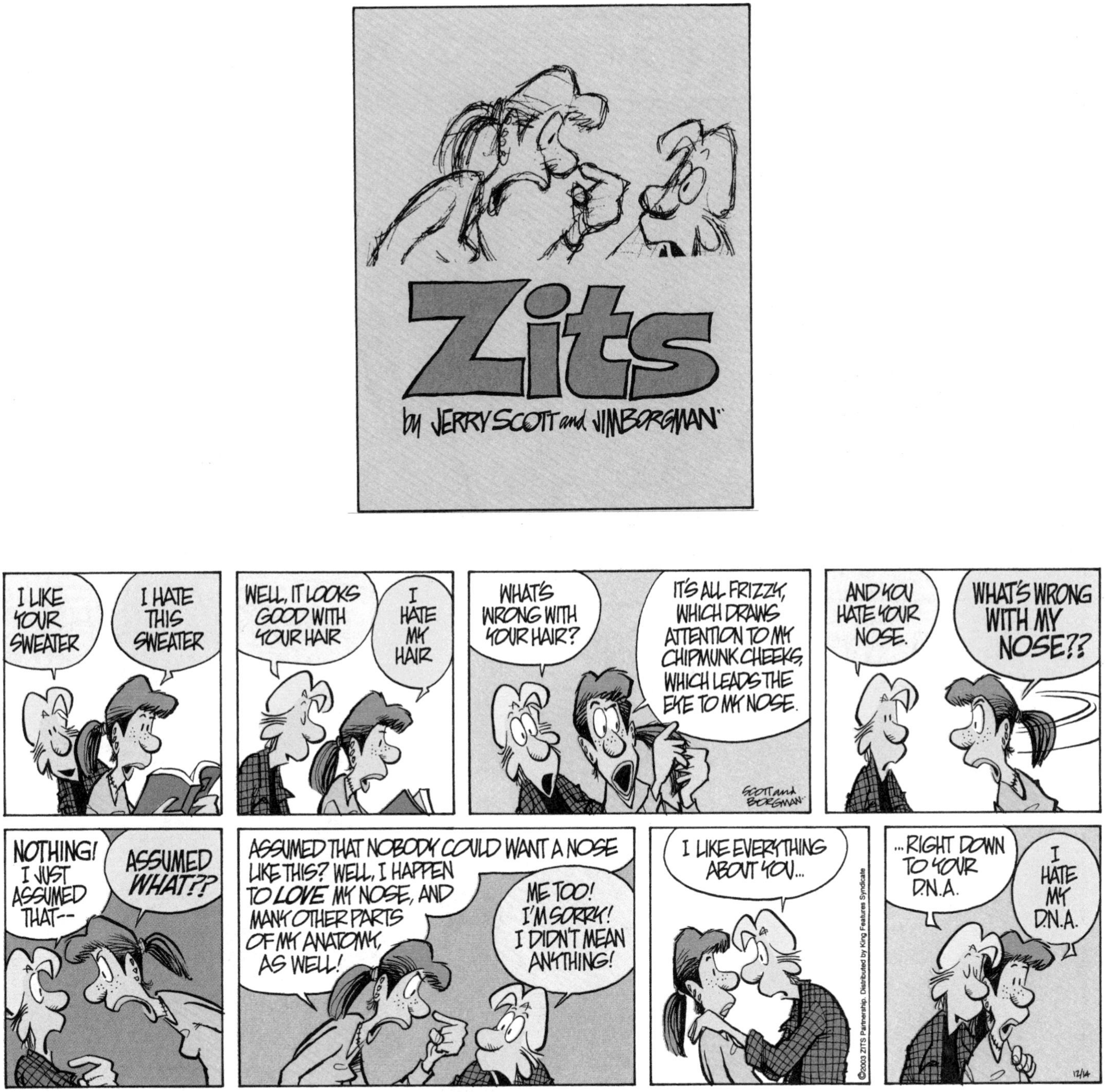
Zits
by JERRY SCOTT and JIM BORGMAN
I LIKE YOUR SWEATER
I HATE THIS SWEATER
WELL, IT LOOKS GOOD WITH YOUR HAIR
I HATE MY HAIR
WHAT'S WRONG WITH YOUR HAIR?
IT'S ALL FRIZZY, WHICH DRAWS ATTENTION TO MY CHIPMUNK CHEEKS, WHICH LEADS THE EYE TO MY NOSE.
SCOTT and BORGMAN
AND YOU HATE YOUR NOSE.
WHAT'S WRONG WITH MY NOSE??
NOTHING! I JUST ASSUMED THAT--
ASSUMED WHAT??
ASSUMED THAT NOBODY COULD WANT A NOSE LIKE THIS? WELL, I HAPPEN TO LOVE MY NOSE, AND MANY OTHER PARTS OF MY ANATOMY, AS WELL!
ME TOO! I'M SORRY! I DIDN'T MEAN ANYTHING!
I LIKE EVERYTHING ABOUT YOU...
©2003 ZITS Partnership. Distributed by King Features Syndicate
...RIGHT DOWN TO YOUR D.N.A.
I HATE MY D.N.A.
12/14

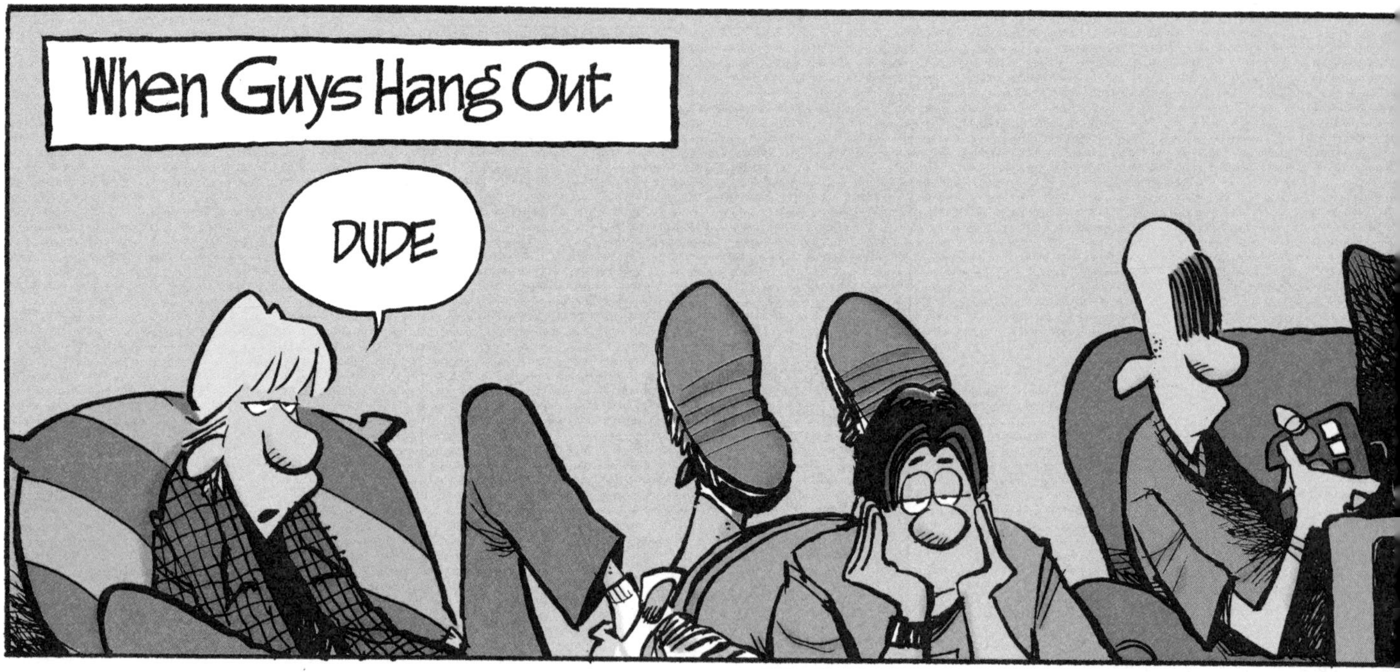
When Guys Hang Out
DUDE

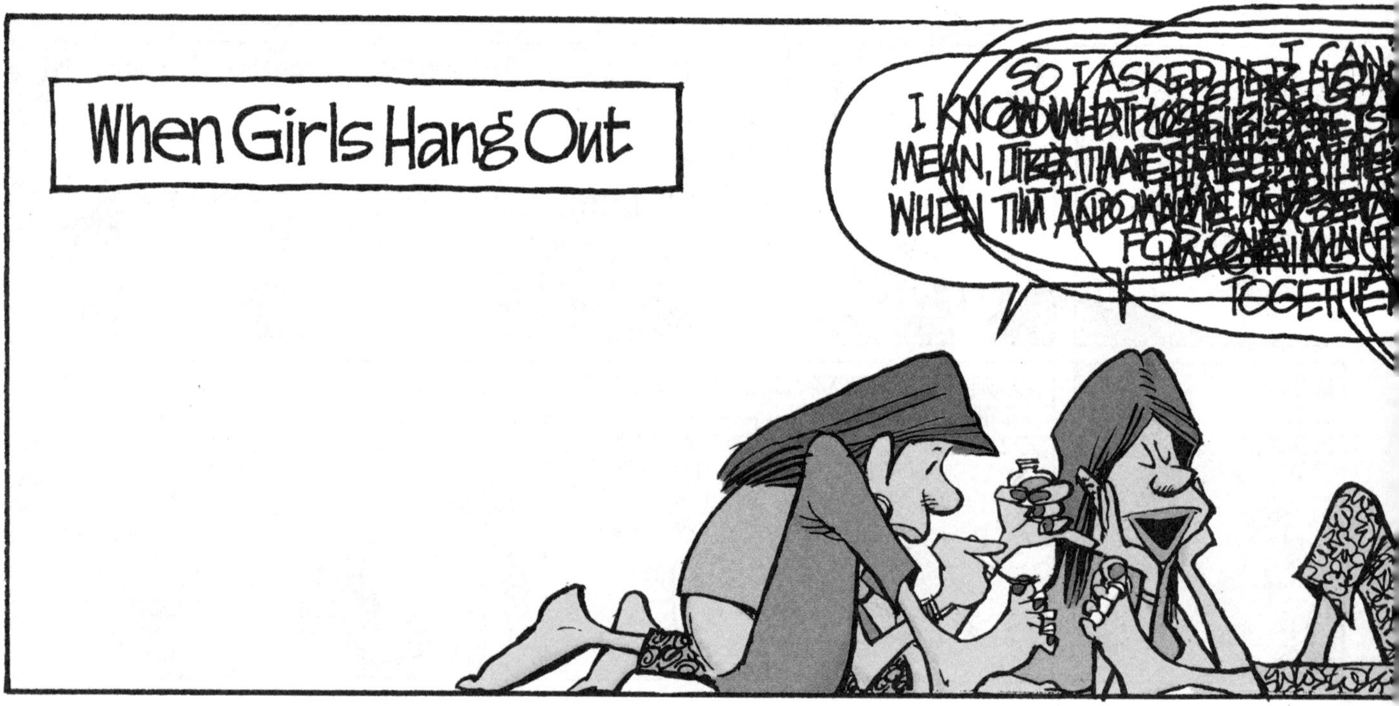
When Girls Hang Out

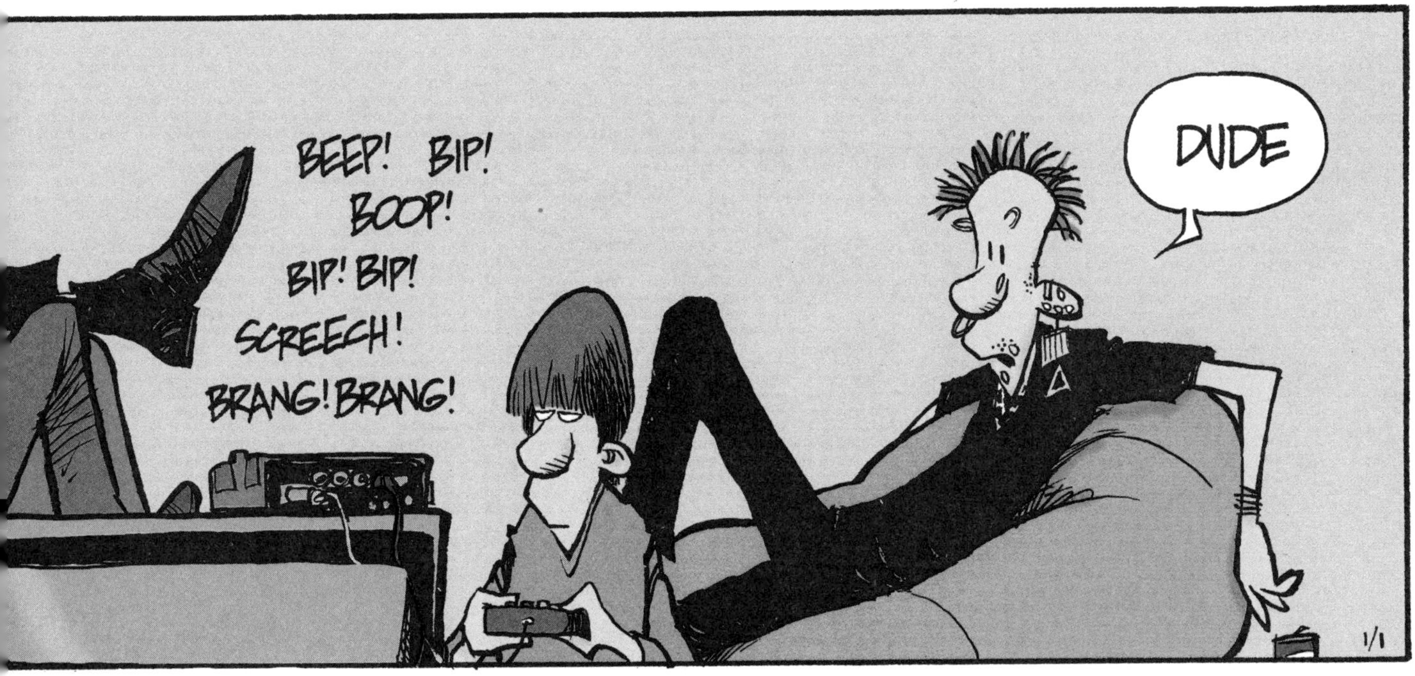
BEEP! BIP!
BOOP!
BIP! BIP!
SCREECH!
BRANG! BRANG!
DUDE
1/1

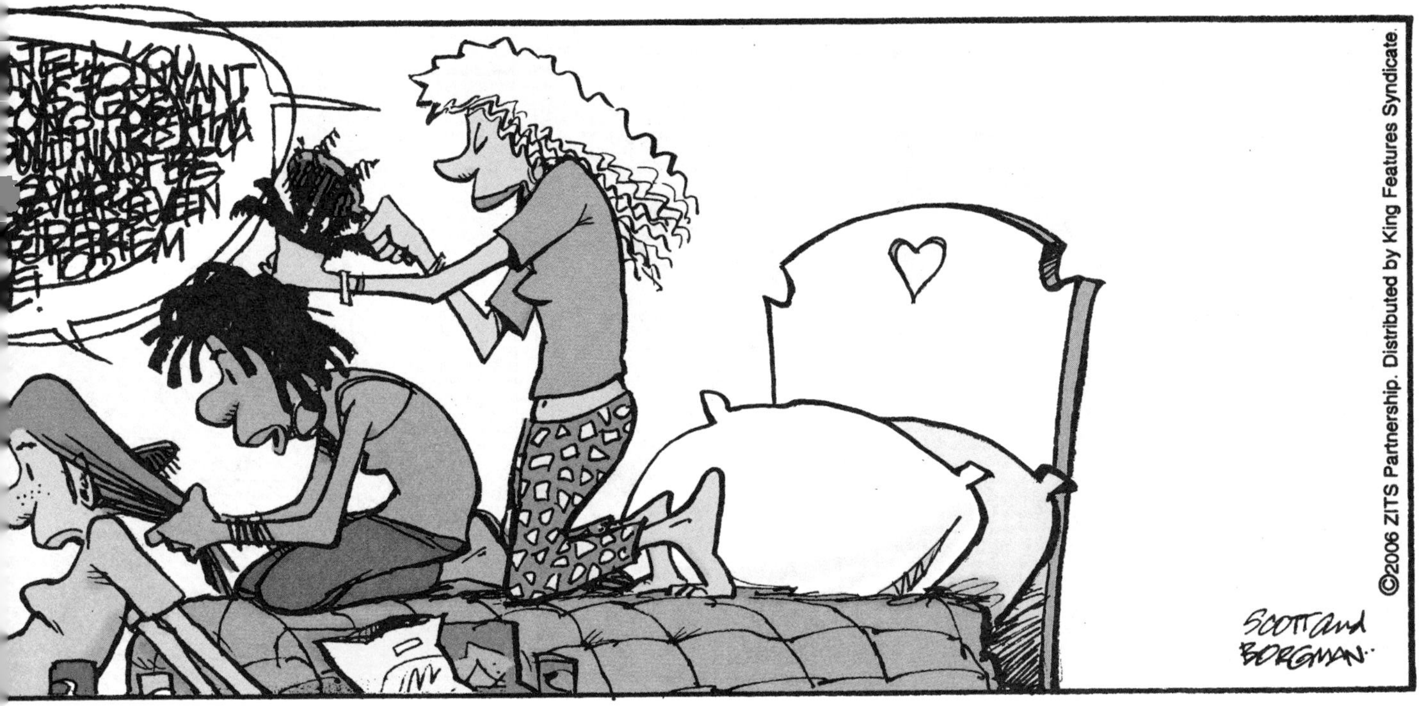
©2006 ZITS Partnership. Distributed by King Features Syndicate.
SCOTT and BORGMAN

Zits
JERRY SCOTT and JIM BORGMAN

I HAVE AN APPOINTMENT WITH THE GUIDANCE COUNSELOR TODAY.
COOL.
YEAH. MAYBE.
HECTOR, DO YOU HAVE ANY TROUBLE, UM, CONCENTRATING WHEN YOU'RE IN HER OFFICE?
NO.
1/9
REALLY? WHEN YOU'RE IN THERE YOUR MIND DOESN'T WANDER INTO WEIRD FANTASIES THAT MAKE IT IMPOSSIBLE TO FOCUS ON THE REASON YOU'RE IN THERE?
©2005 ZITS Partnership. Distributed by King Features Syndicate
I DON'T THINK SO.
SCOTT and BORGMAN
GREAT. THEN THAT MEANS IT'S JUST ME.
LET'S DISCUSS YOUR G.P.A....
COUNSELOR

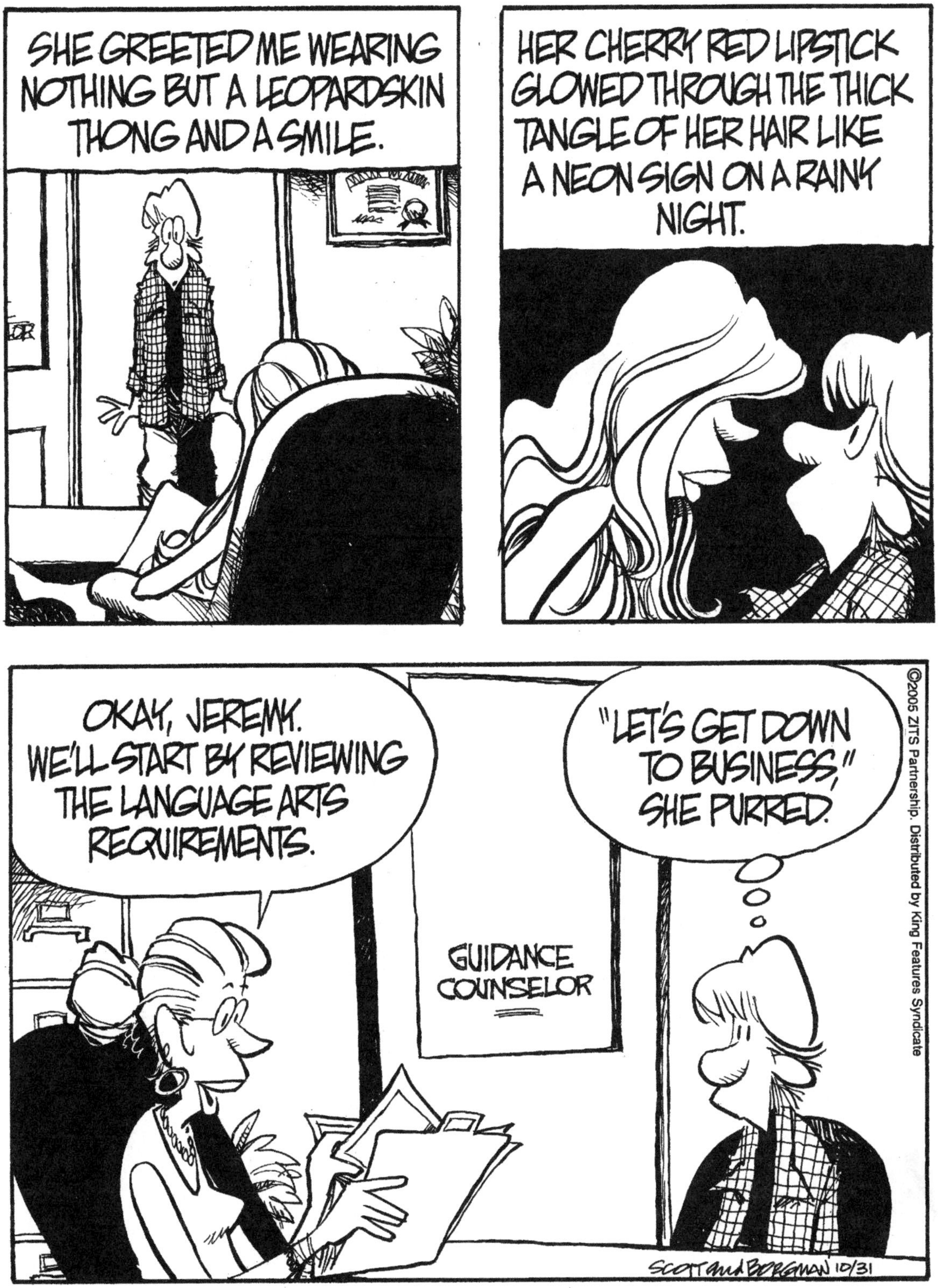
SHE GREETED ME WEARING NOTHING BUT A LEOPARDSKIN THONG AND A SMILE.
HER CHERRY RED LIPSTICK GLOWED THROUGH THE THICK TANGLE OF HER HAIR LIKE A NEON SIGN ON A RAINY NIGHT.
OKAY, JEREMY. WE'LL START BY REVIEWING THE LANGUAGE ARTS REQUIREMENTS.
"LET'S GET DOWN TO BUSINESS," SHE PURRED.
GUIDANCE COUNSELOR
©2005 ZITS Partnership. Distributed by King Features Syndicate
SCOTT and BORGMAN 10/31

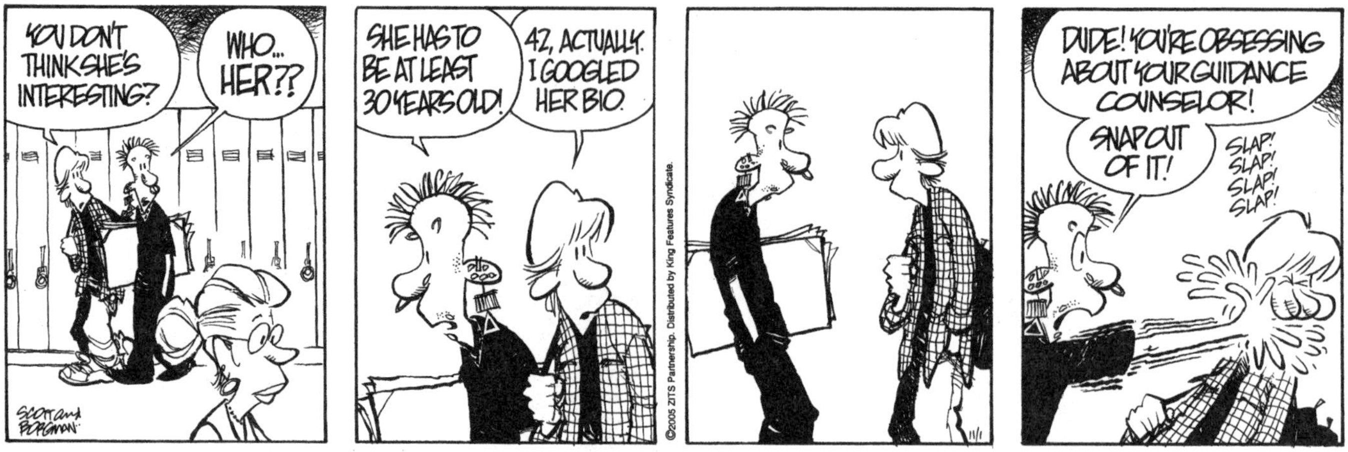
YOU DON'T THINK SHE'S INTERESTING?
WHO... HER??
SHE HAS TO BE AT LEAST 30 YEARS OLD!
42, ACTUALLY. I GOOGLED HER BIO.
©2005 ZITS Partnership. Distributed by King Features Syndicate.
DUDE! YOU'RE OBSESSING ABOUT YOUR GUIDANCE COUNSELOR!
SNAP OUT OF IT!
SLAP! SLAP! SLAP! SLAP!

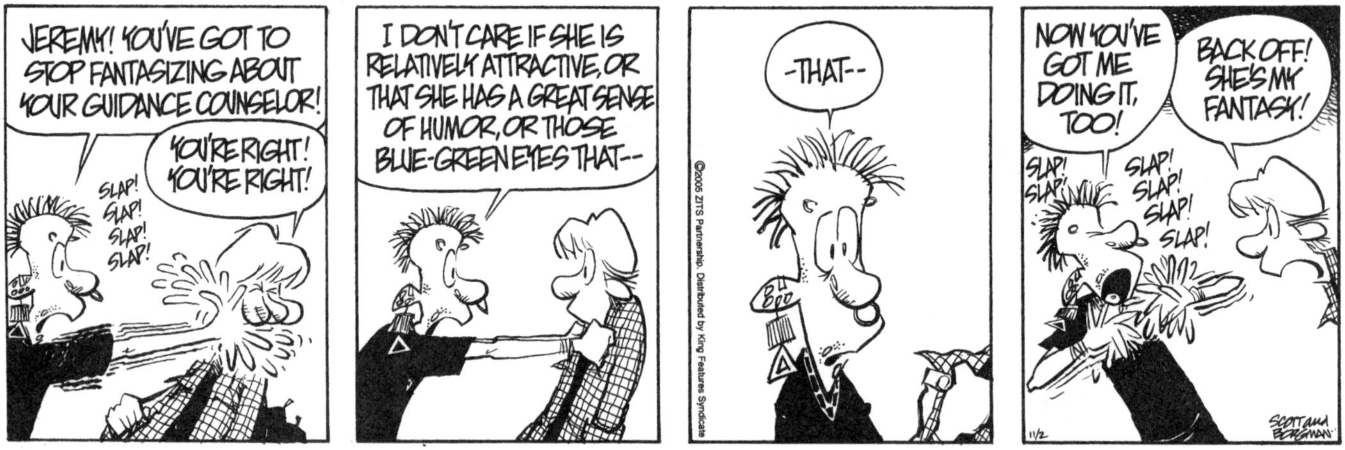
JEREMY! YOU'VE GOT TO STOP FANTASIZING ABOUT YOUR GUIDANCE COUNSELOR!
YOU'RE RIGHT! YOU'RE RIGHT!
SLAP! SLAP! SLAP! SLAP!
I DON'T CARE IF SHE IS RELATIVELY ATTRACTIVE, OR THAT SHE HAS A GREAT SENSE OF HUMOR, OR THOSE BLUE-GREEN EYES THAT--
©2005 ZITS Partnership. Distributed by King Features Syndicate
-THAT--
NOW YOU'VE GOT ME DOING IT, TOO!
BACK OFF! SHE'S MY FANTASY!
SLAP! SLAP! SLAP! SLAP! SLAP! SLAP!

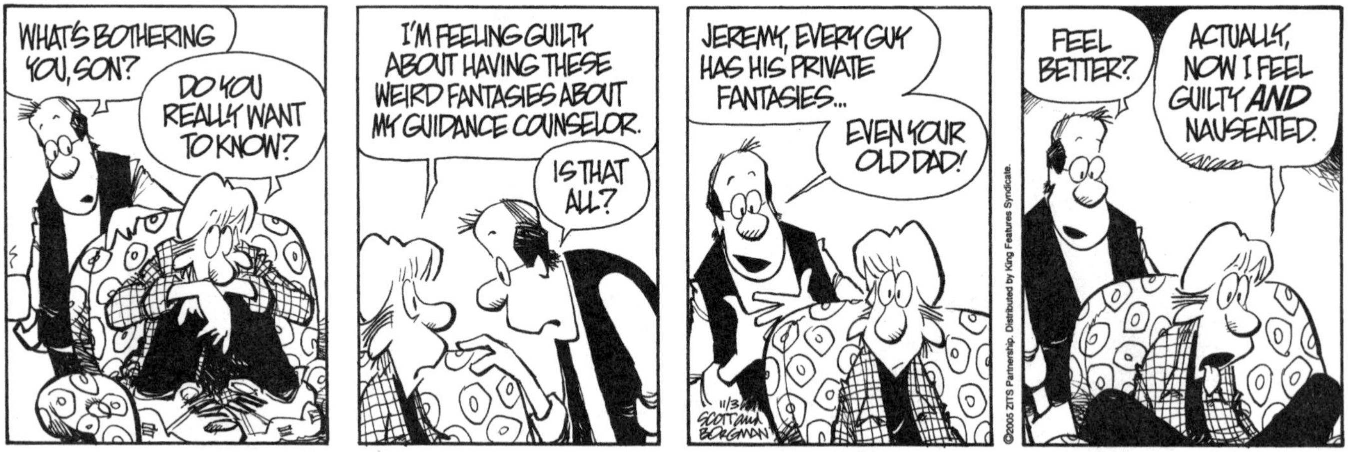
WHAT'S BOTHERING YOU, SON?
DO YOU REALLY WANT TO KNOW?
I'M FEELING GUILTY ABOUT HAVING THESE WEIRD FANTASIES ABOUT MY GUIDANCE COUNSELOR.
IS THAT ALL?
JEREMY, EVERY GUY HAS HIS PRIVATE FANTASIES...
EVEN YOUR OLD DAD!
©2005 ZITS Partnership. Distributed by King Features Syndicate.
FEEL BETTER?
ACTUALLY, NOW I FEEL GUILTY **AND** NAUSEATED.

Zits
JERRY SCOTT and
JIM BORGMAN

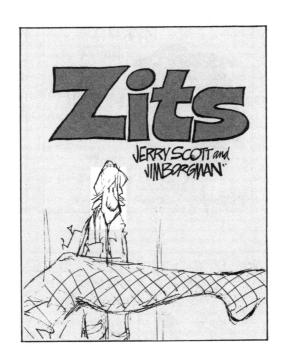

I WONDER IF OTHER PEOPLE HAVE FANTASIES ABOUT THEIR GUIDANCE COUNSELOR.
IT'S WEIRD...
...AND A LITTLE UNCOMFORTABLE.
BUT MOSTLY WEIRD.
IT'S NOT HER FAULT.
I MEAN, IT'S NOT LIKE SHE'S SUPERHOT OR ANYTHING.
SHE JUST HAS THAT ONE THING THAT HAPPENS TO TURN ME ON.
SHE'S FEMALE.
©2007 ZITS Partnership. Distributed by King Features Syndicate.
SCOTT and BORGMAN

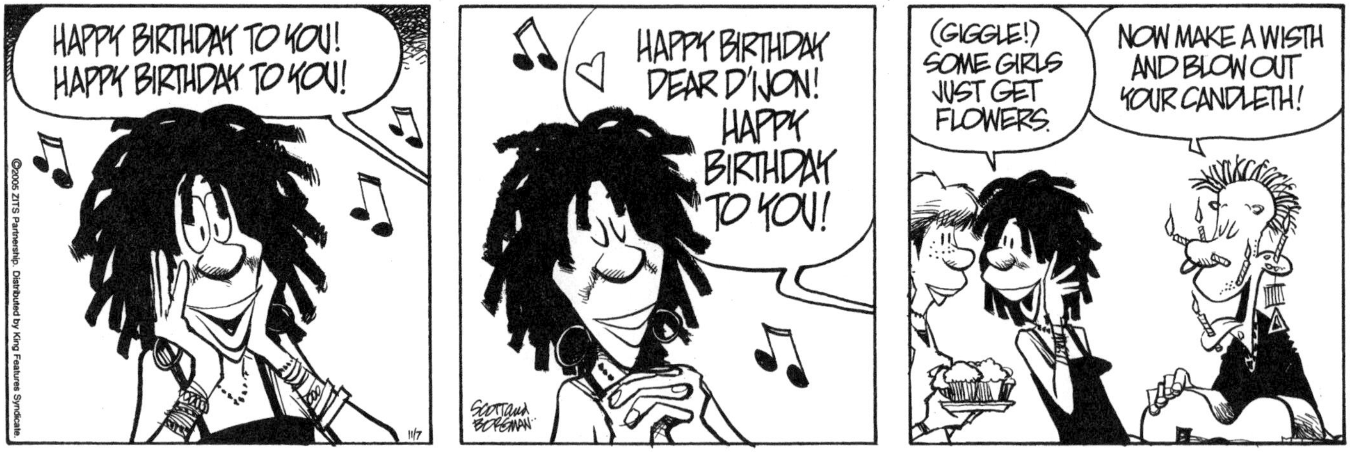
HAPPY BIRTHDAY TO YOU! HAPPY BIRTHDAY TO YOU!
HAPPY BIRTHDAY DEAR D'JON! HAPPY BIRTHDAY TO YOU!
(GIGGLE!) SOME GIRLS JUST GET FLOWERS.
NOW MAKE A WISTH AND BLOW OUT YOUR CANDLETH!
©2005 ZITS Partnership. Distributed by King Features Syndicate
SCOTT and BORGMAN

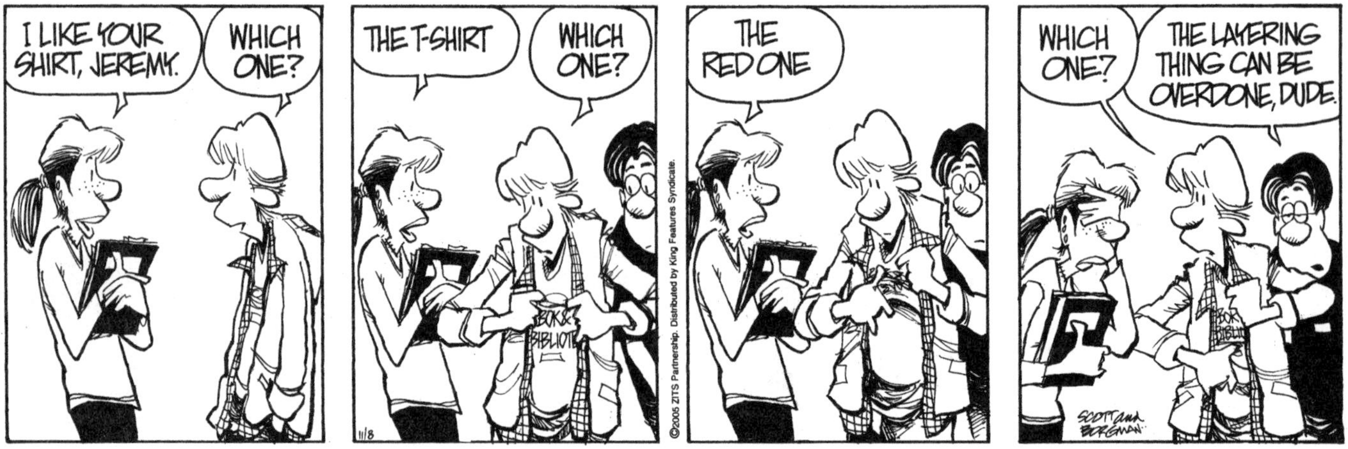
I LIKE YOUR SHIRT, JEREMY.
WHICH ONE?
THE T-SHIRT
WHICH ONE?
THE RED ONE
WHICH ONE?
THE LAYERING THING CAN BE OVERDONE, DUDE.
©2005 ZITS Partnership. Distributed by King Features Syndicate.
SCOTT and BORGMAN

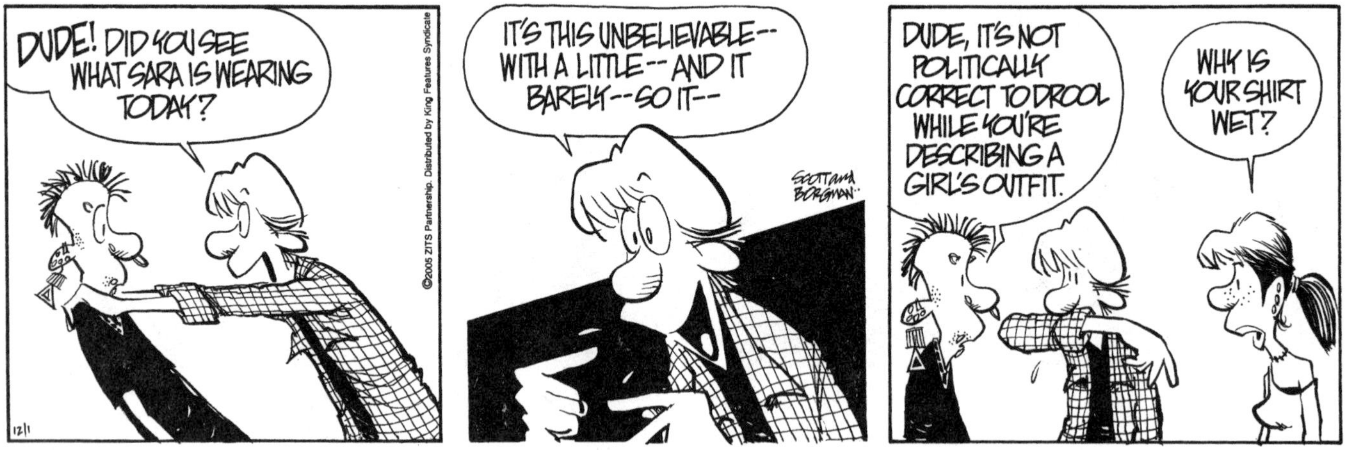
DUDE! DID YOU SEE WHAT SARA IS WEARING TODAY?
IT'S THIS UNBELIEVABLE-- WITH A LITTLE-- AND IT BARELY--SO IT--
DUDE, IT'S NOT POLITICALLY CORRECT TO DROOL WHILE YOU'RE DESCRIBING A GIRL'S OUTFIT.
WHY IS YOUR SHIRT WET?
©2005 ZITS Partnership. Distributed by King Features Syndicate
SCOTT and BORGMAN

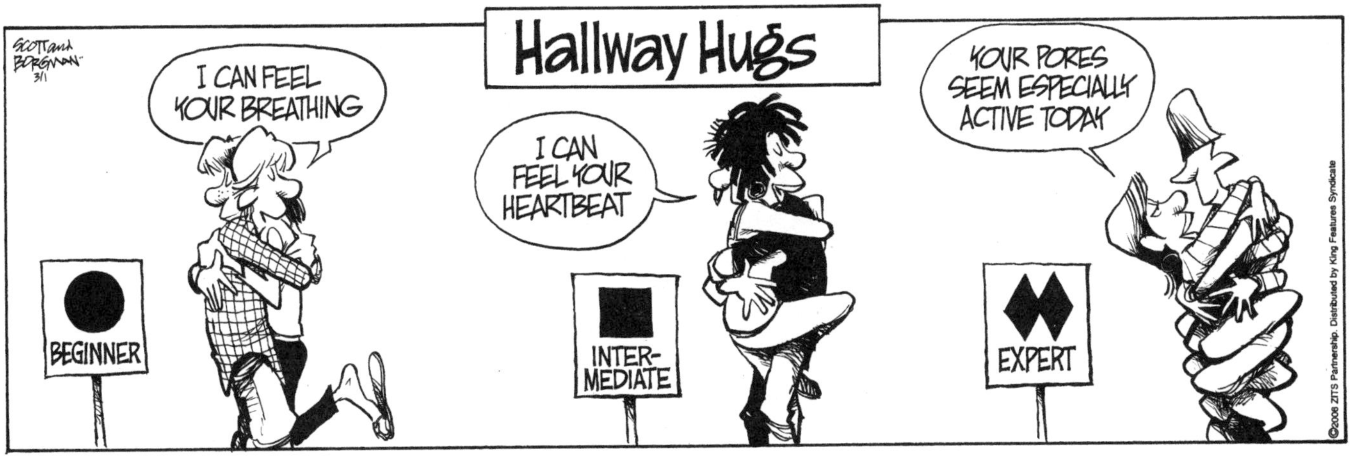
Hallway Hugs
I CAN FEEL YOUR BREATHING
BEGINNER
I CAN FEEL YOUR HEARTBEAT
INTER-MEDIATE
YOUR PORES SEEM ESPECIALLY ACTIVE TODAY
EXPERT
©2006 ZITS Partnership. Distributed by King Features Syndicate

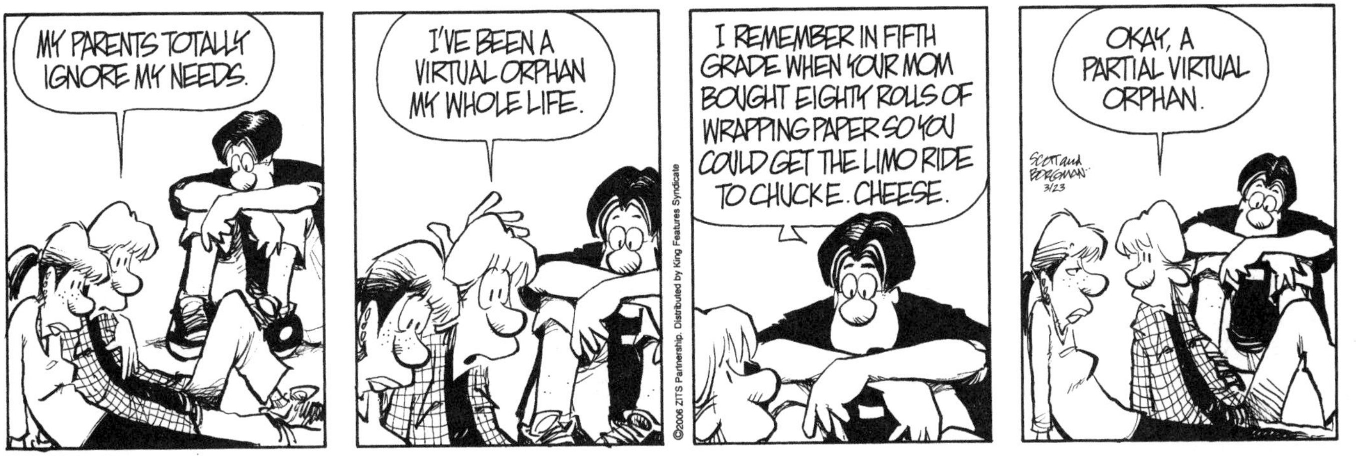
MY PARENTS TOTALLY IGNORE MY NEEDS.
I'VE BEEN A VIRTUAL ORPHAN MY WHOLE LIFE.
©2006 ZITS Partnership. Distributed by King Features Syndicate
I REMEMBER IN FIFTH GRADE WHEN YOUR MOM BOUGHT EIGHTY ROLLS OF WRAPPING PAPER SO YOU COULD GET THE LIMO RIDE TO CHUCK E. CHEESE.
OKAY, A PARTIAL VIRTUAL ORPHAN.

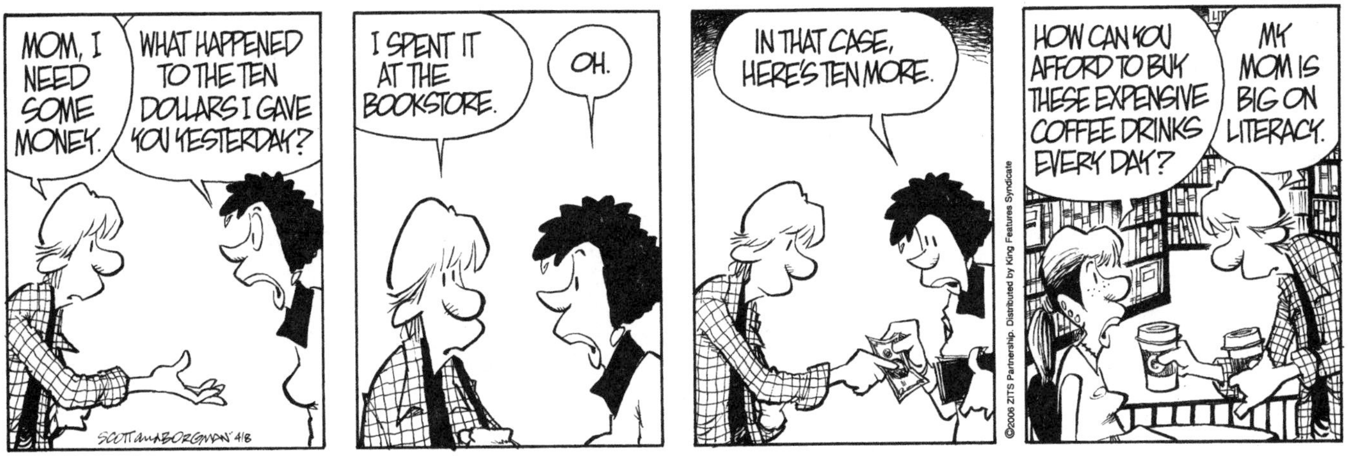
MOM, I NEED SOME MONEY.
WHAT HAPPENED TO THE TEN DOLLARS I GAVE YOU YESTERDAY?
I SPENT IT AT THE BOOKSTORE.
OH.
IN THAT CASE, HERE'S TEN MORE.
©2006 ZITS Partnership. Distributed by King Features Syndicate
HOW CAN YOU AFFORD TO BUY THESE EXPENSIVE COFFEE DRINKS EVERY DAY?
MY MOM IS BIG ON LITERACY.

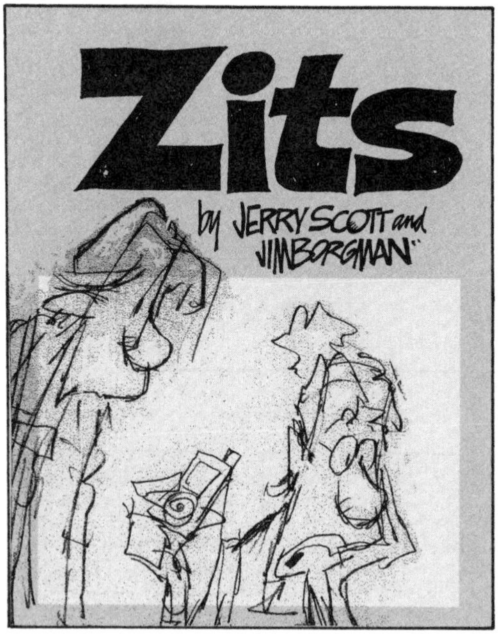
Zits
by JERRY SCOTT and JIM BORGMAN

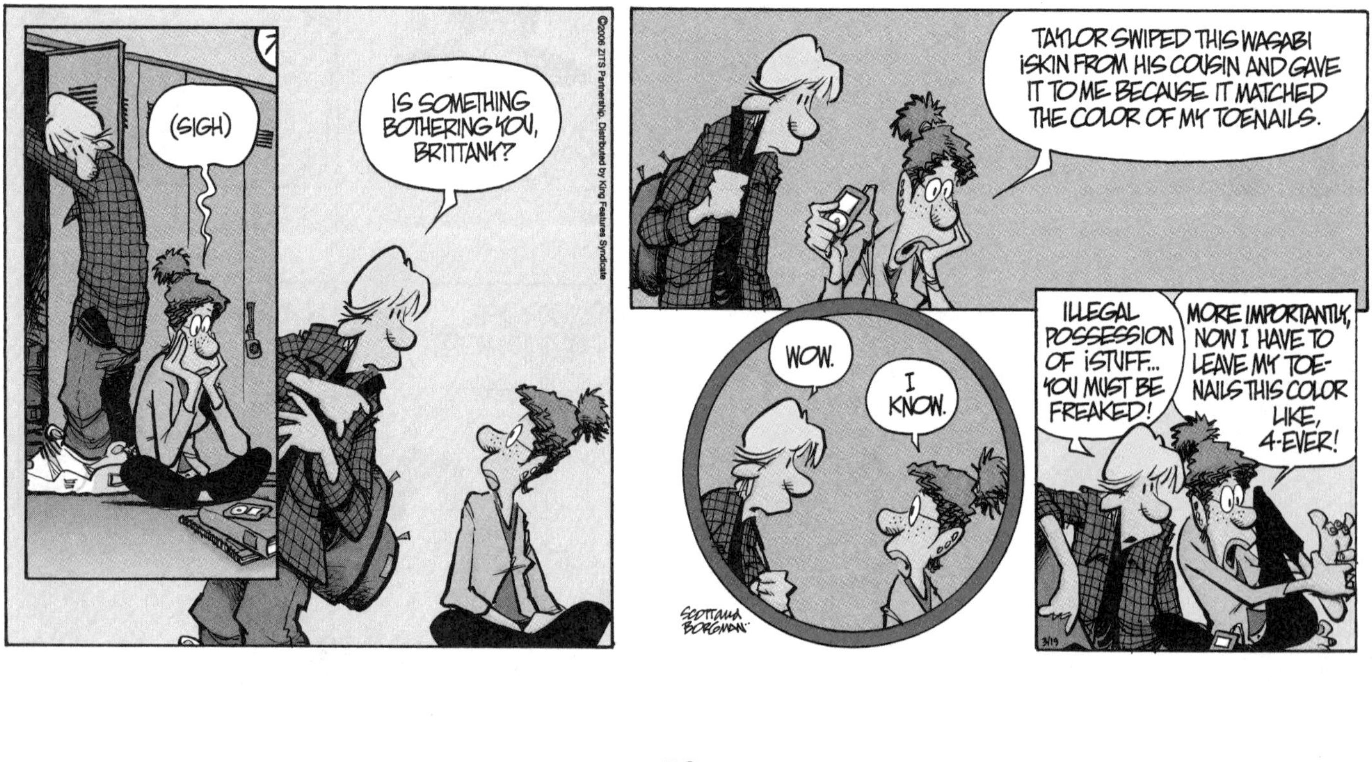
©2006 ZITS Partnership. Distributed by King Features Syndicate
(SIGH)
IS SOMETHING BOTHERING YOU, BRITTANY?
TAYLOR SWIPED THIS WASABI iSKIN FROM HIS COUSIN AND GAVE IT TO ME BECAUSE IT MATCHED THE COLOR OF MY TOENAILS.
WOW.
I KNOW.
ILLEGAL POSSESSION OF iSTUFF... YOU MUST BE FREAKED!
MORE IMPORTANTLY, NOW I HAVE TO LEAVE MY TOE-NAILS THIS COLOR LIKE, 4-EVER!
SCOTT and BORGMAN
3/19

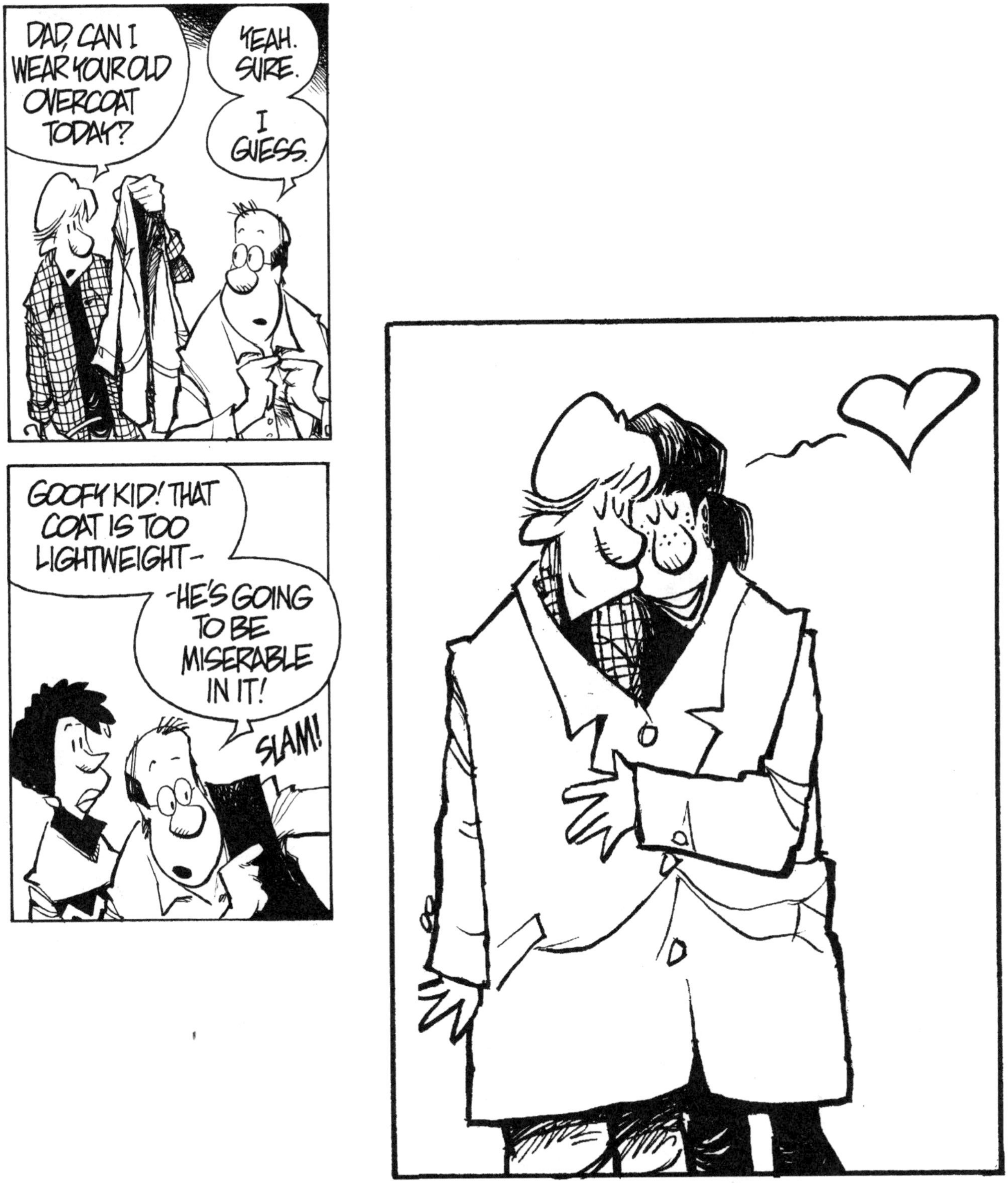
DAD, CAN I WEAR YOUR OLD OVERCOAT TODAY?
YEAH. SURE.
I GUESS.
GOOFY KID! THAT COAT IS TOO LIGHTWEIGHT-
-HE'S GOING TO BE MISERABLE IN IT!
SLAM!

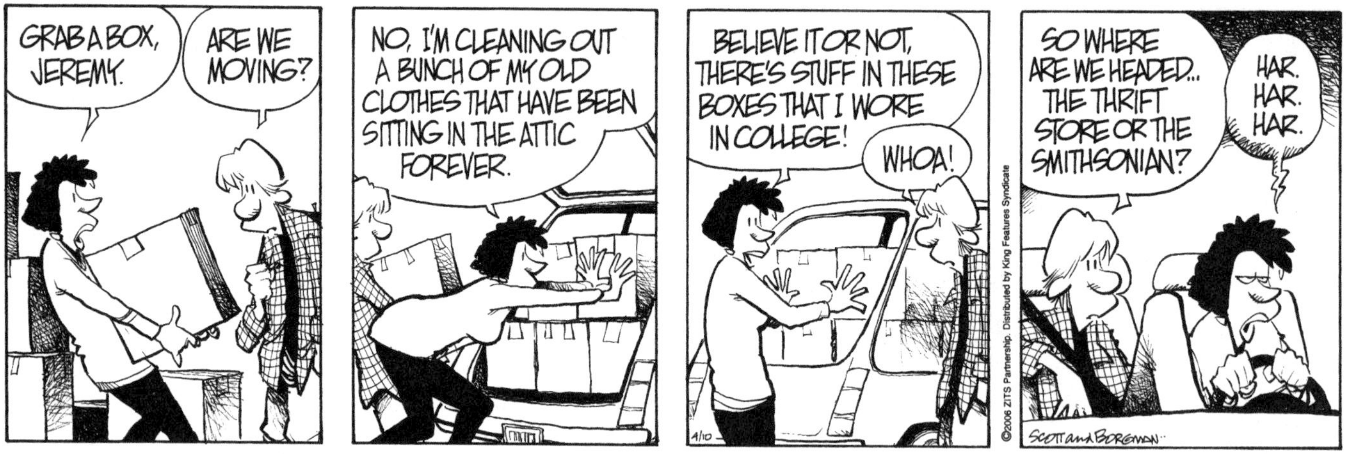
GRAB A BOX, JEREMY.
ARE WE MOVING?
NO, I'M CLEANING OUT A BUNCH OF MY OLD CLOTHES THAT HAVE BEEN SITTING IN THE ATTIC FOREVER.
BELIEVE IT OR NOT, THERE'S STUFF IN THESE BOXES THAT I WORE IN COLLEGE!
WHOA!
SO WHERE ARE WE HEADED... THE THRIFT STORE OR THE SMITHSONIAN?
HAR. HAR. HAR.
4/10
©2006 ZITS Partnership. Distributed by King Features Syndicate
SCOTT and BORGMAN

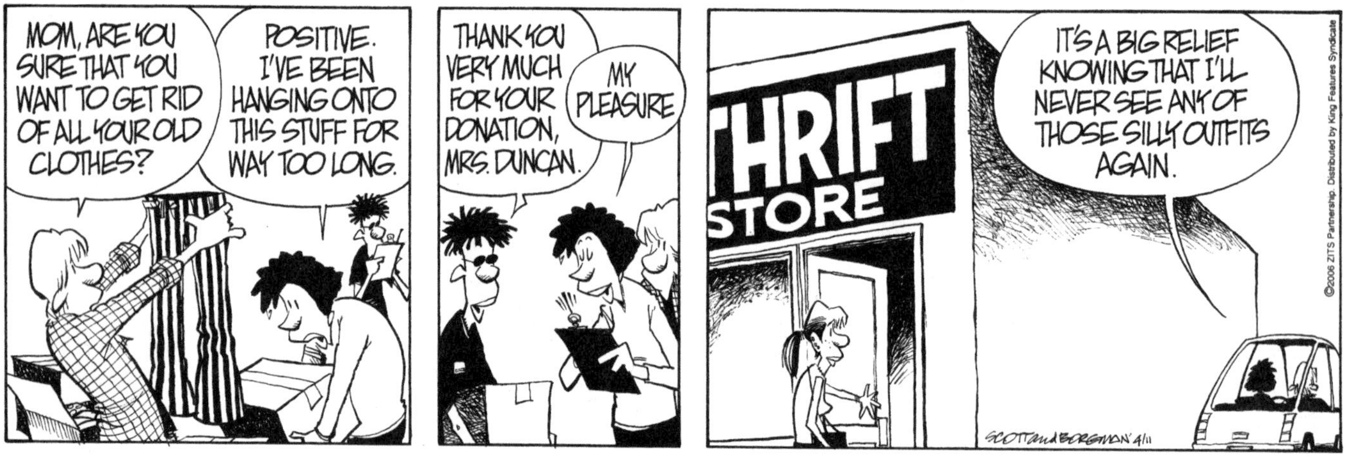
MOM, ARE YOU SURE THAT YOU WANT TO GET RID OF ALL YOUR OLD CLOTHES?
POSITIVE. I'VE BEEN HANGING ONTO THIS STUFF FOR WAY TOO LONG.
THANK YOU VERY MUCH FOR YOUR DONATION, MRS. DUNCAN.
MY PLEASURE
THRIFT STORE
IT'S A BIG RELIEF KNOWING THAT I'LL NEVER SEE ANY OF THOSE SILLY OUTFITS AGAIN.
©2006 ZITS Partnership. Distributed by King Features Syndicate
SCOTT and BORGMAN 4/11

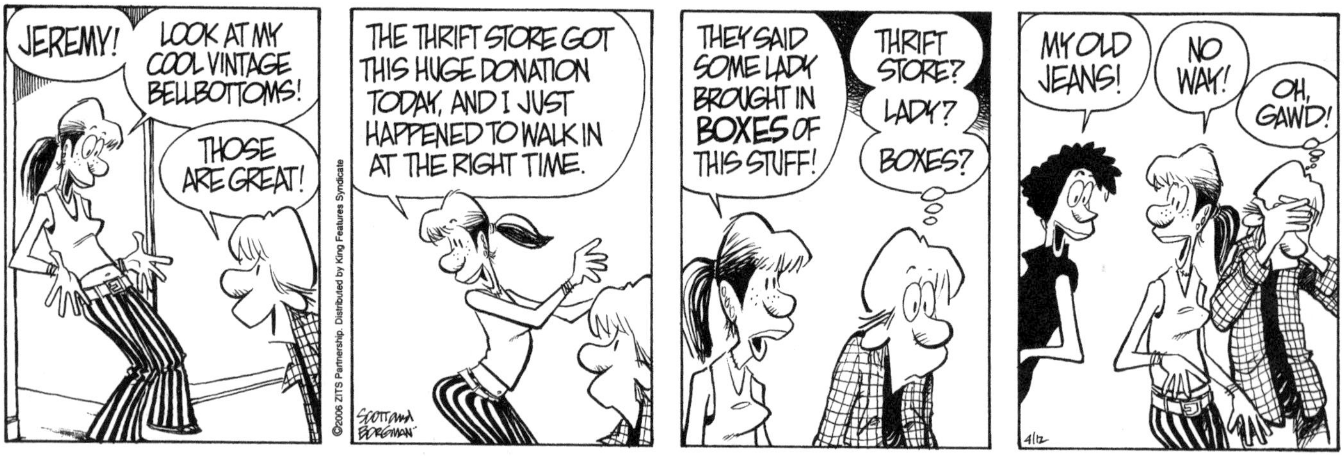
JEREMY!
LOOK AT MY COOL VINTAGE BELLBOTTOMS!
THOSE ARE GREAT!
©2006 ZITS Partnership. Distributed by King Features Syndicate
THE THRIFT STORE GOT THIS HUGE DONATION TODAY, AND I JUST HAPPENED TO WALK IN AT THE RIGHT TIME.
SCOTT and BORGMAN
THEY SAID SOME LADY BROUGHT IN BOXES OF THIS STUFF!
THRIFT STORE?
LADY?
BOXES?
4/12
MY OLD JEANS!
NO WAY!
OH, GAWD!

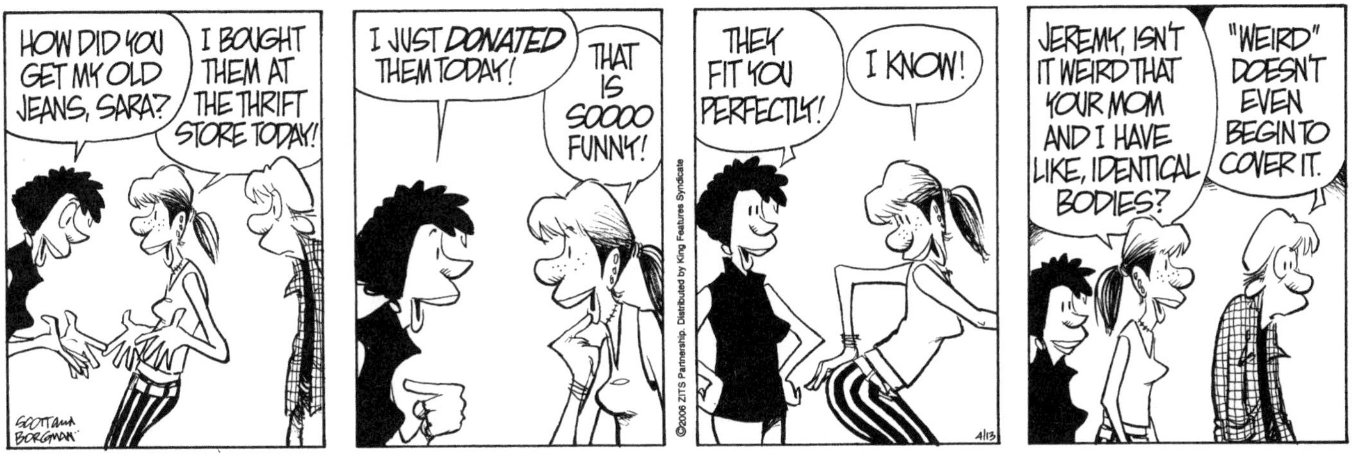
HOW DID YOU GET MY OLD JEANS, SARA?
I BOUGHT THEM AT THE THRIFT STORE TODAY!
SCOTT and BORGMAN
I JUST DONATED THEM TODAY!
THAT IS SOOOO FUNNY!
©2006 ZITS Partnership. Distributed by King Features Syndicate
THEY FIT YOU PERFECTLY!
I KNOW!
4/13
JEREMY, ISN'T IT WEIRD THAT YOUR MOM AND I HAVE LIKE, IDENTICAL BODIES?
"WEIRD" DOESN'T EVEN BEGIN TO COVER IT.

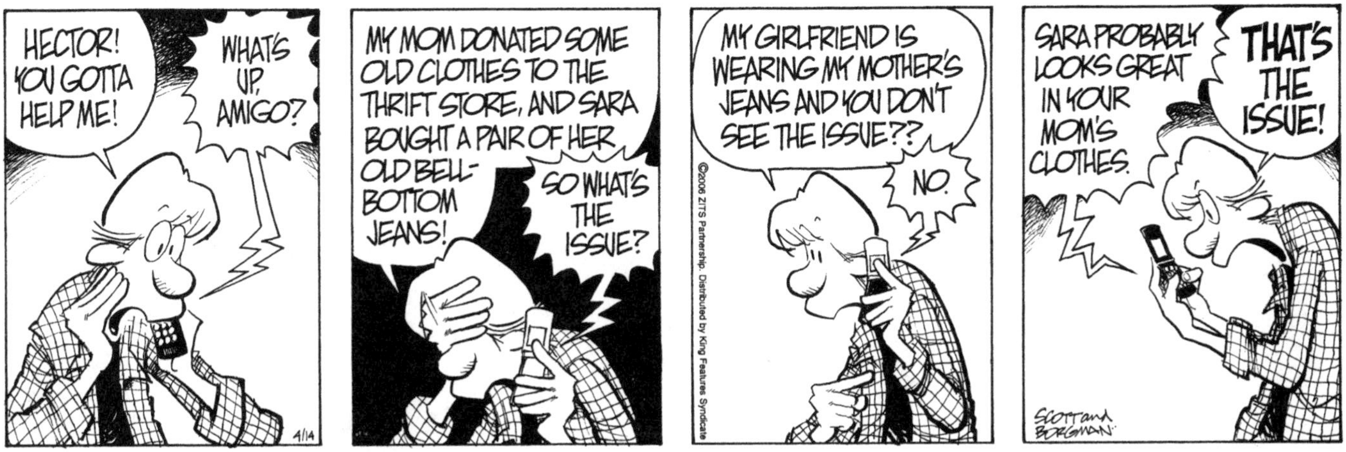
HECTOR! YOU GOTTA HELP ME!
WHAT'S UP, AMIGO?
4/14
MY MOM DONATED SOME OLD CLOTHES TO THE THRIFT STORE, AND SARA BOUGHT A PAIR OF HER OLD BELL-BOTTOM JEANS!
SO WHAT'S THE ISSUE?
©2006 ZITS Partnership. Distributed by King Features Syndicate
MY GIRLFRIEND IS WEARING MY MOTHER'S JEANS AND YOU DON'T SEE THE ISSUE??
NO.
SARA PROBABLY LOOKS GREAT IN YOUR MOM'S CLOTHES.
THAT'S THE ISSUE!
SCOTT and BORGMAN

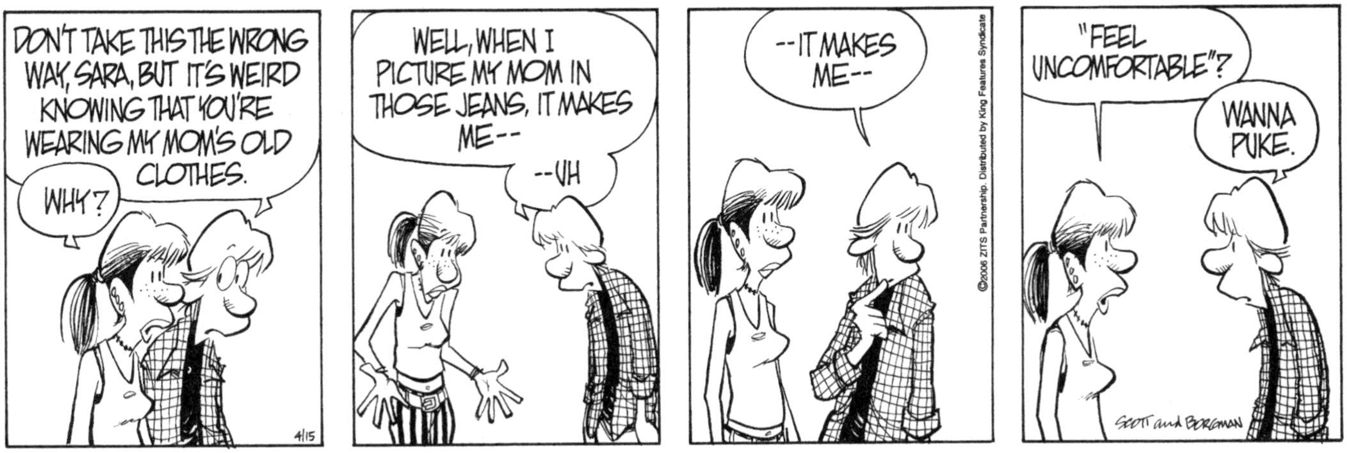
DON'T TAKE THIS THE WRONG WAY, SARA, BUT IT'S WEIRD KNOWING THAT YOU'RE WEARING MY MOM'S OLD CLOTHES.
WHY?
4/15
WELL, WHEN I PICTURE MY MOM IN THOSE JEANS, IT MAKES ME--
--UH
--IT MAKES ME--
©2006 ZITS Partnership. Distributed by King Features Syndicate
"FEEL UNCOMFORTABLE"?
WANNA PUKE.
SCOTT and BORGMAN

Zits
by
JERRY SCOTT and
JIM BORGMAN

BRILLIANT!
PHENOMENAL!
A NEW RECORD!
CUTE.
ANOTHER PERFECT QUIZ SCORE!
HOW WAS YOUR DAY, JEREMY?
SARA LIKED MY SHIRT.
SCOTT and BORGMAN
©2006 ZITS Partnership. Distributed by King Features Syndicate

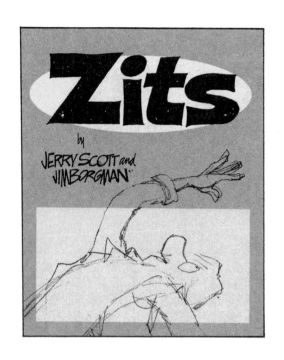

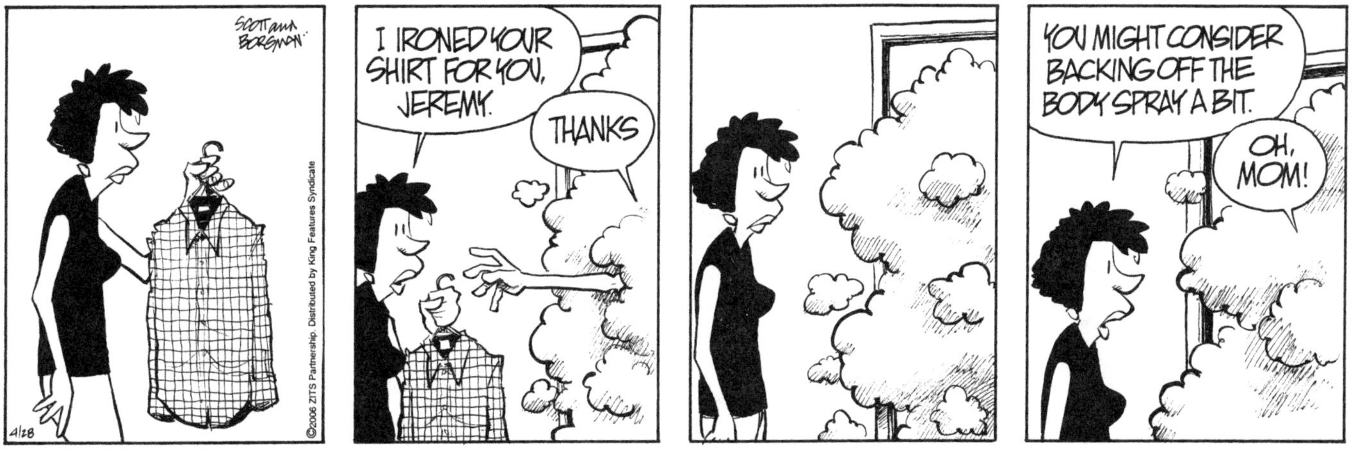
SCOTT and BORGMAN
4/28
©2006 ZITS Partnership. Distributed by King Features Syndicate
I IRONED YOUR SHIRT FOR YOU, JEREMY.
THANKS
YOU MIGHT CONSIDER BACKING OFF THE BODY SPRAY A BIT.
OH, MOM!

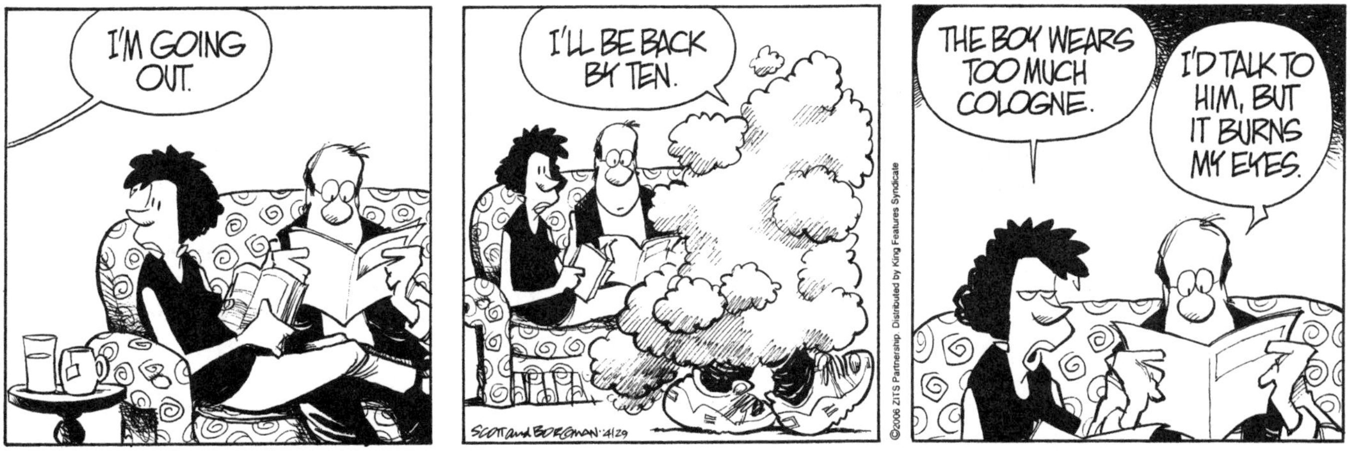
I'M GOING OUT.
I'LL BE BACK BY TEN.
SCOTT and BORGMAN 4/29
©2006 ZITS Partnership. Distributed by King Features Syndicate
THE BOY WEARS TOO MUCH COLOGNE.
I'D TALK TO HIM, BUT IT BURNS MY EYES.

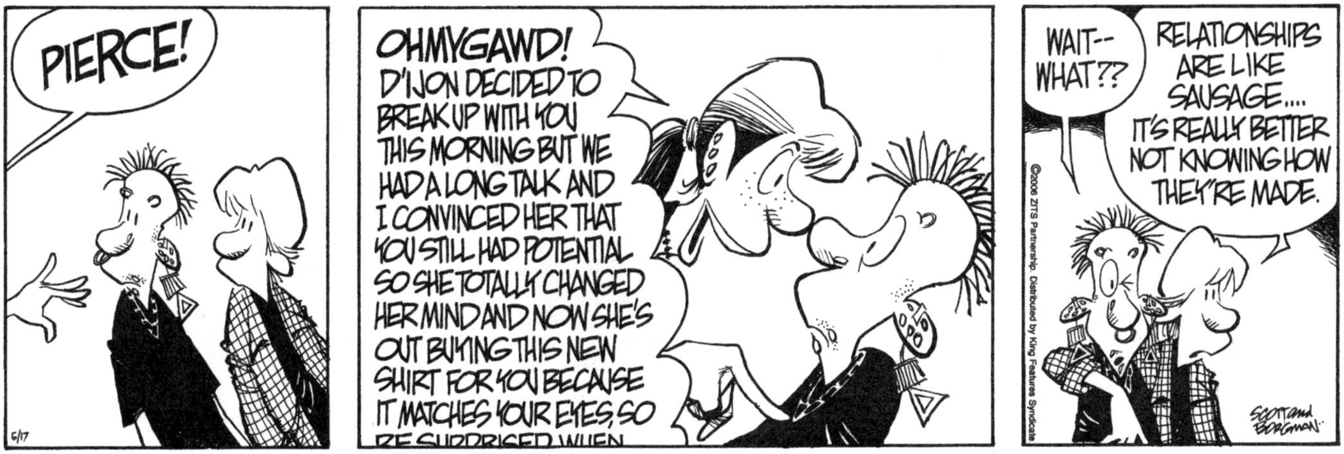
PIERCE!
5/17
OHMYGAWD! D'JON DECIDED TO BREAK UP WITH YOU THIS MORNING BUT WE HAD A LONG TALK AND I CONVINCED HER THAT YOU STILL HAD POTENTIAL SO SHE TOTALLY CHANGED HER MIND AND NOW SHE'S OUT BUYING THIS NEW SHIRT FOR YOU BECAUSE IT MATCHES YOUR EYES, SO
WAIT-- WHAT??
RELATIONSHIPS ARE LIKE SAUSAGE.... IT'S REALLY BETTER NOT KNOWING HOW THEY'RE MADE.
©2006 ZITS Partnership. Distributed by King Features Syndicate
SCOTT and BORGMAN

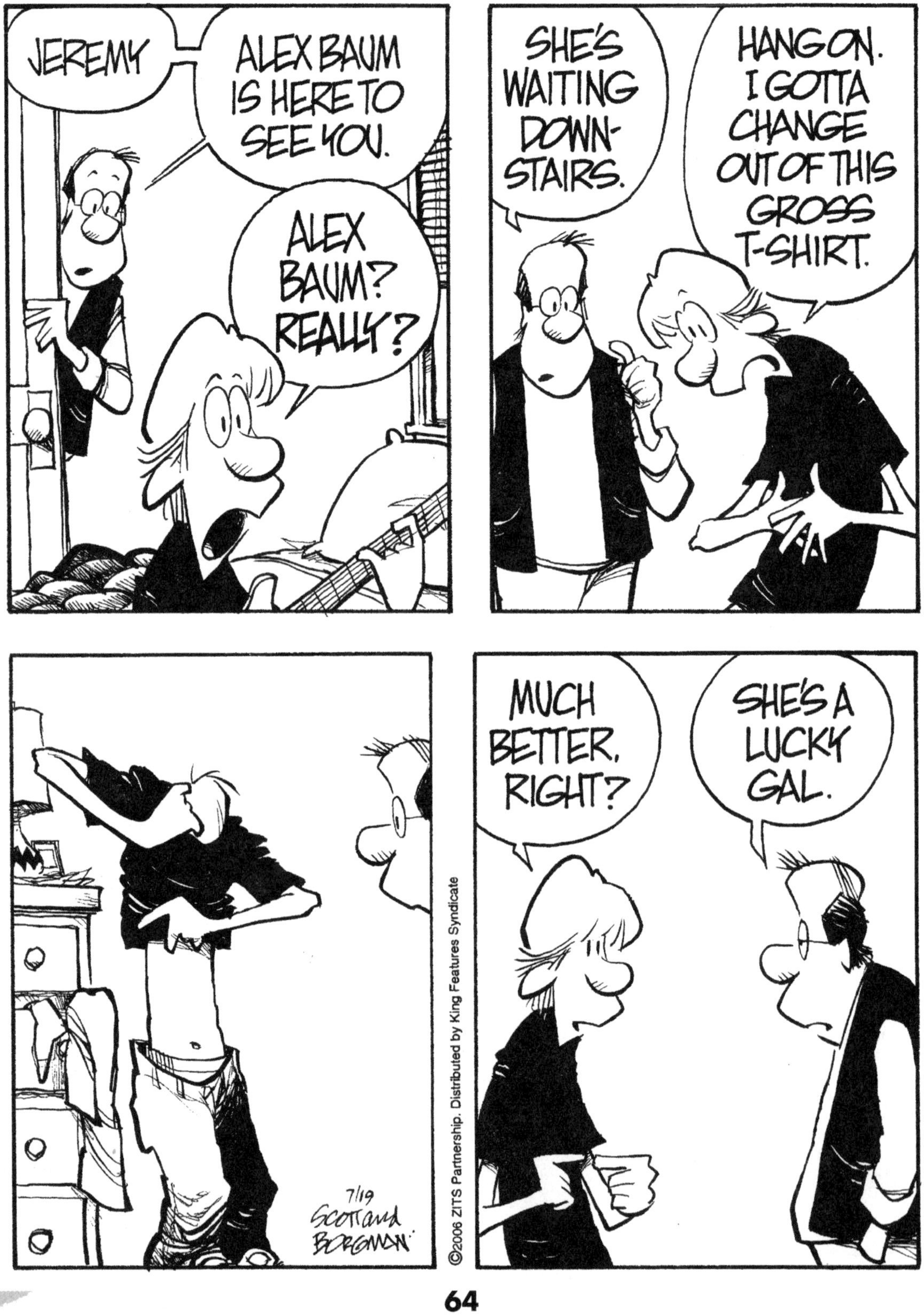
JEREMY
ALEX BAUM IS HERE TO SEE YOU.
ALEX BAUM? REALLY?
SHE'S WAITING DOWN-STAIRS.
HANG ON. I GOTTA CHANGE OUT OF THIS GROSS T-SHIRT.
7/19 SCOTT AND BORGMAN
©2006 ZITS Partnership. Distributed by King Features Syndicate
MUCH BETTER, RIGHT?
SHE'S A LUCKY GAL.

Zits
by
JERRY SCOTT and
JIM BORGMAN

HEY.
THERE GOES SARA.
6/4
SARA!
HEY SARA!
SA-RA!
YO!
SCOTT and BORGMAN
©2006 ZITS Partnership. Distributed by King Features Syndicate
SARA!
SARA!
SARA TOOMEY!
FWEEEEEET!
OH, HI JEREMY.
SOMETIMES I FEEL SMOTHERED IN THIS RELATIONSHIP.

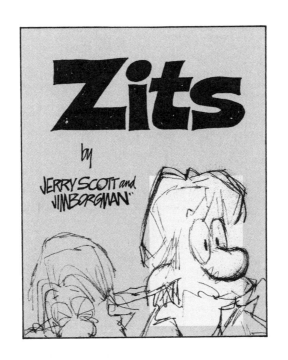

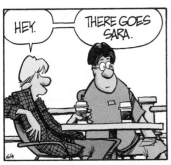

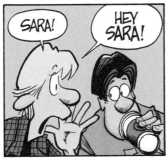

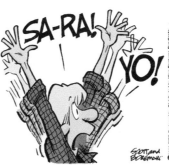

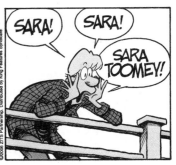

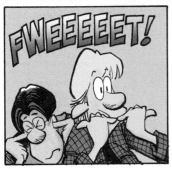

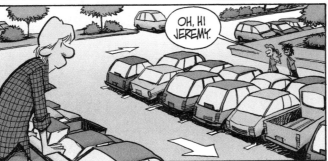

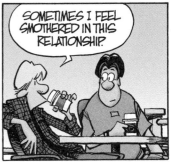

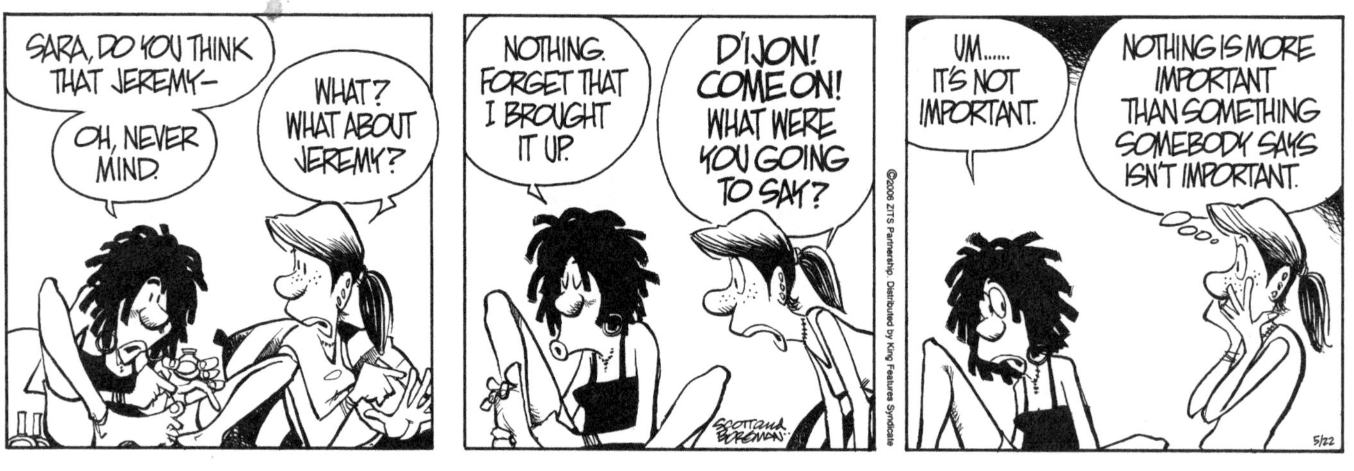
SARA, DO YOU THINK THAT JEREMY–
OH, NEVER MIND.
WHAT? WHAT ABOUT JEREMY?
NOTHING. FORGET THAT I BROUGHT IT UP.
D'JON! COME ON! WHAT WERE YOU GOING TO SAY?
©2006 ZITS Partnership. Distributed by King Features Syndicate
SCOTT and BORGMAN
UM...... IT'S NOT IMPORTANT.
NOTHING IS MORE IMPORTANT THAN SOMETHING SOMEBODY SAYS ISN'T IMPORTANT.
5/22

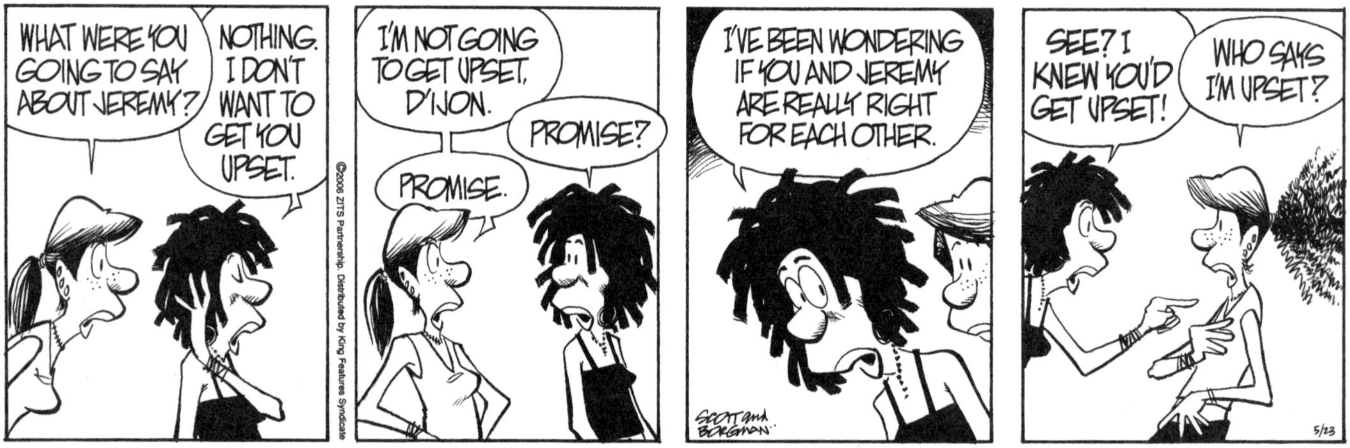
WHAT WERE YOU GOING TO SAY ABOUT JEREMY?
NOTHING. I DON'T WANT TO GET YOU UPSET.
©2006 ZITS Partnership. Distributed by King Features Syndicate
I'M NOT GOING TO GET UPSET, D'JON.
PROMISE?
PROMISE.
I'VE BEEN WONDERING IF YOU AND JEREMY ARE REALLY RIGHT FOR EACH OTHER.
SCOTT and BORGMAN
SEE? I KNEW YOU'D GET UPSET!
WHO SAYS I'M UPSET?
5/23

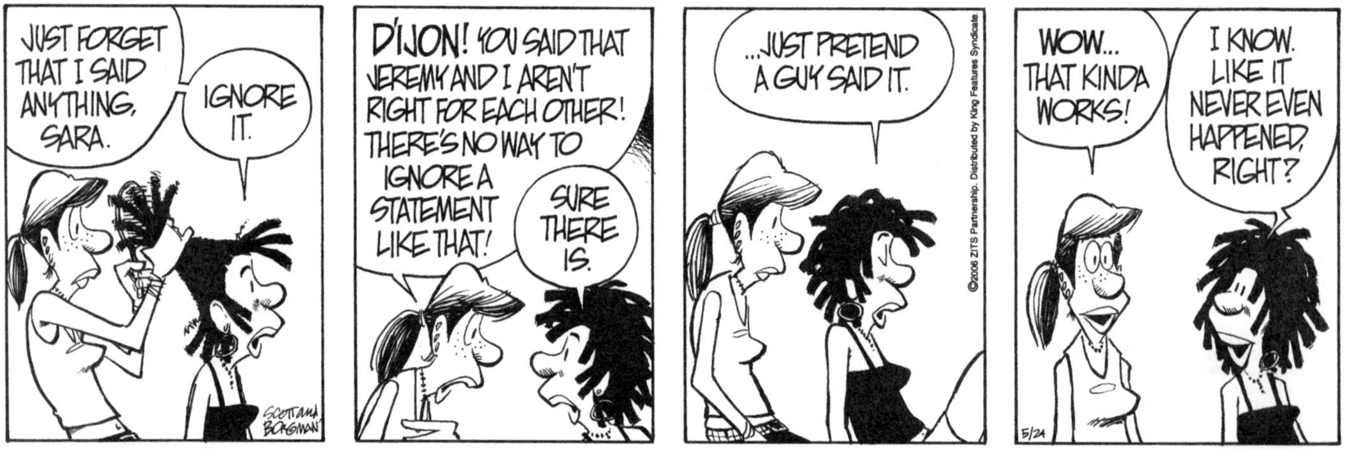
JUST FORGET THAT I SAID ANYTHING, SARA.
IGNORE IT.
SCOTT and BORGMAN
D'JON! YOU SAID THAT JEREMY AND I AREN'T RIGHT FOR EACH OTHER! THERE'S NO WAY TO IGNORE A STATEMENT LIKE THAT!
SURE THERE IS.
...JUST PRETEND A GUY SAID IT.
©2006 ZITS Partnership. Distributed by King Features Syndicate
WOW... THAT KINDA WORKS!
I KNOW. LIKE IT NEVER EVEN HAPPENED, RIGHT?
5/24

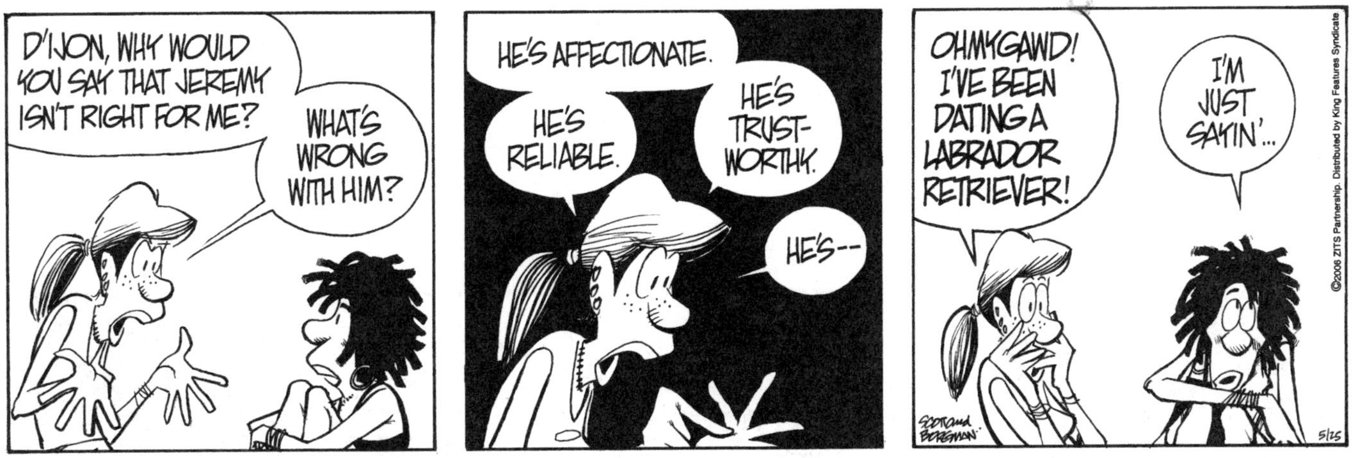

D'IJON, WHY WOULD YOU SAY THAT JEREMY ISN'T RIGHT FOR ME?
WHAT'S WRONG WITH HIM?
HE'S AFFECTIONATE.
HE'S RELIABLE.
HE'S TRUST-WORTHY.
HE'S--
OHMYGAWD! I'VE BEEN DATING A LABRADOR RETRIEVER!
I'M JUST SAYIN'...
©2006 ZITS Partnership. Distributed by King Features Syndicate
SCOTT and BORGMAN
5/25

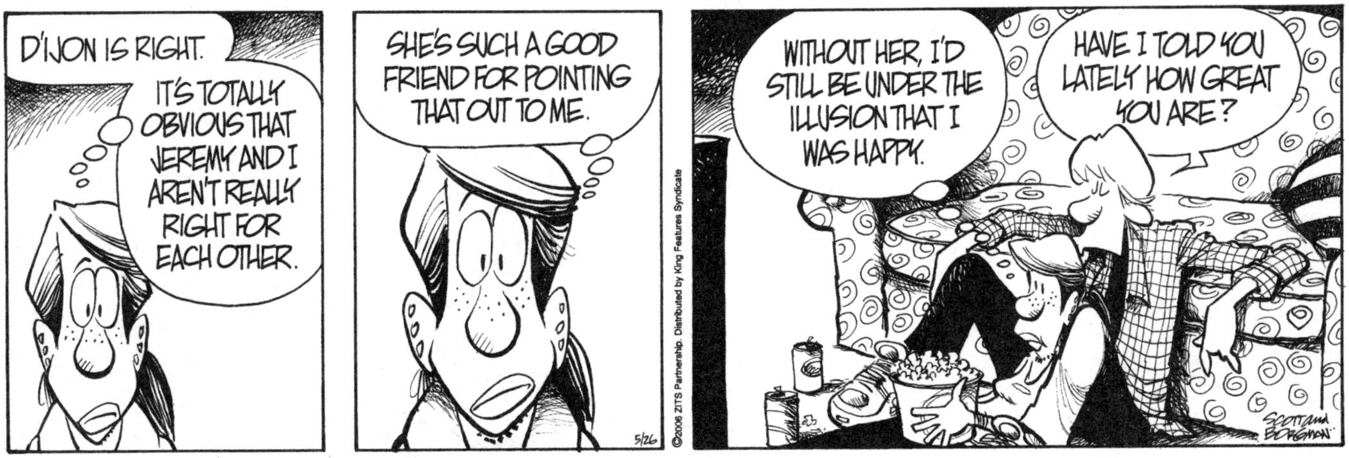

D'IJON IS RIGHT.
IT'S TOTALLY OBVIOUS THAT JEREMY AND I AREN'T REALLY RIGHT FOR EACH OTHER.
SHE'S SUCH A GOOD FRIEND FOR POINTING THAT OUT TO ME.
5/26
©2006 ZITS Partnership. Distributed by King Features Syndicate
WITHOUT HER, I'D STILL BE UNDER THE ILLUSION THAT I WAS HAPPY.
HAVE I TOLD YOU LATELY HOW GREAT YOU ARE?
SCOTT and BORGMAN

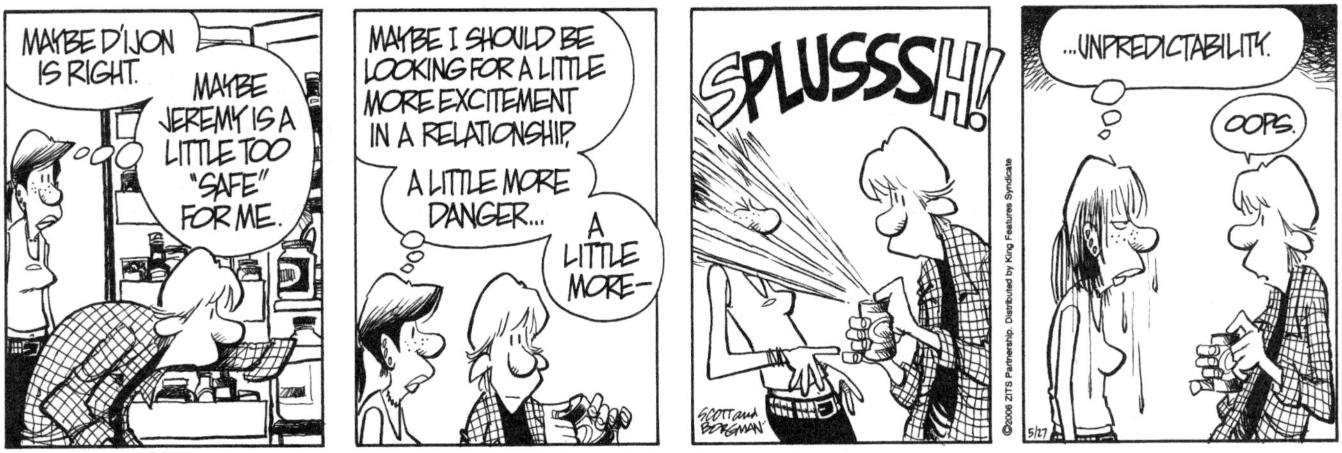

MAYBE D'IJON IS RIGHT.
MAYBE JEREMY IS A LITTLE TOO "SAFE" FOR ME.
MAYBE I SHOULD BE LOOKING FOR A LITTLE MORE EXCITEMENT IN A RELATIONSHIP,
A LITTLE MORE DANGER...
A LITTLE MORE-
SPLUSSSH!
SCOTT and BORGMAN
©2006 ZITS Partnership. Distributed by King Features Syndicate
...UNPREDICTABILITY.
OOPS.
5/27

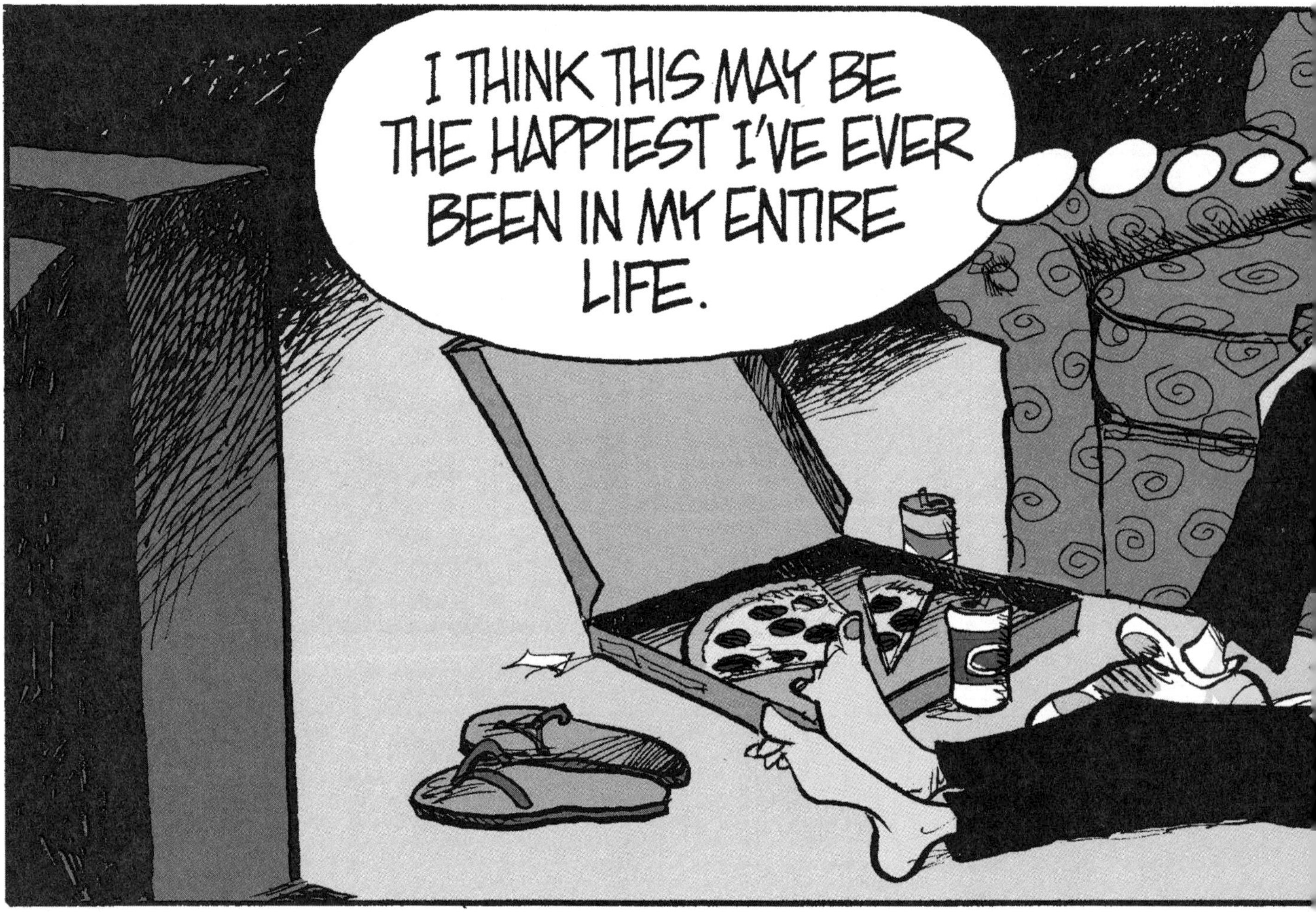
I THINK THIS MAY BE THE HAPPIEST I'VE EVER BEEN IN MY ENTIRE LIFE.

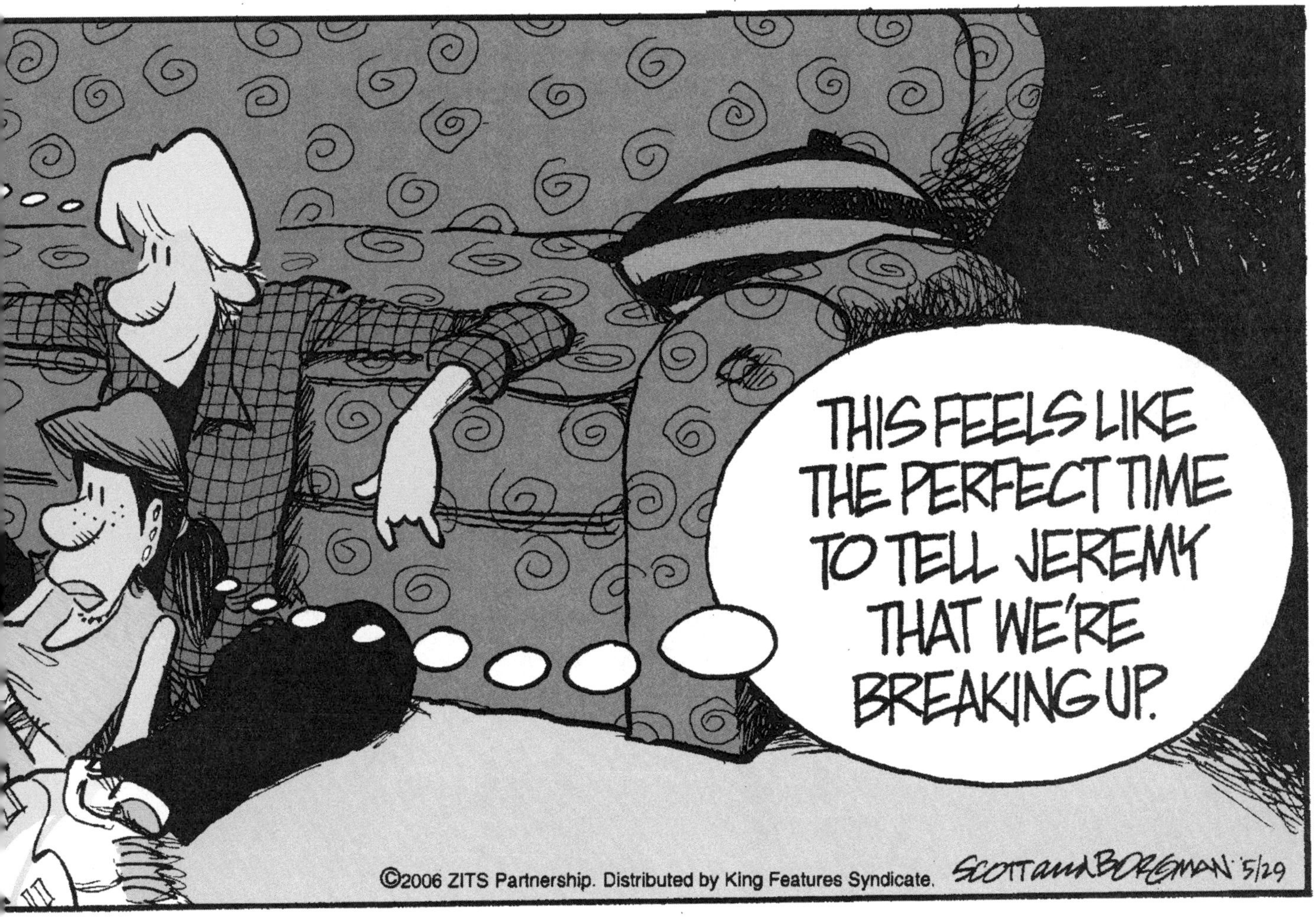
THIS FEELS LIKE THE PERFECT TIME TO TELL JEREMY THAT WE'RE BREAKING UP.
©2006 ZITS Partnership. Distributed by King Features Syndicate.
SCOTT and BORGMAN 5/29

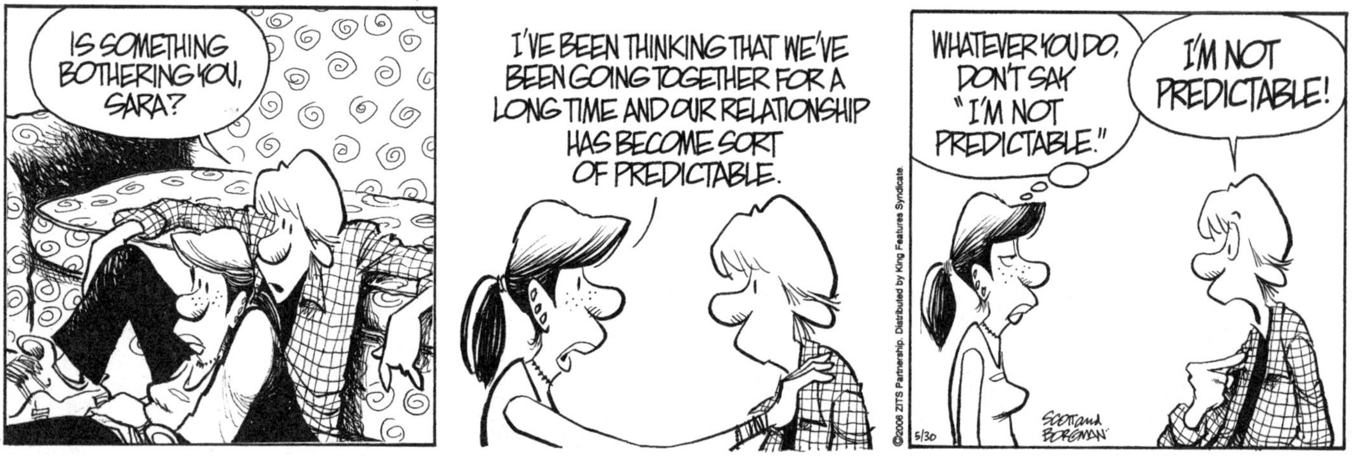
IS SOMETHING BOTHERING YOU, SARA?
I'VE BEEN THINKING THAT WE'VE BEEN GOING TOGETHER FOR A LONG TIME AND OUR RELATIONSHIP HAS BECOME SORT OF PREDICTABLE.
WHATEVER YOU DO, DON'T SAY "I'M NOT PREDICTABLE."
I'M NOT PREDICTABLE!
©2006 ZITS Partnership. Distributed by King Features Syndicate.
5/30
SCOTT and BORGMAN

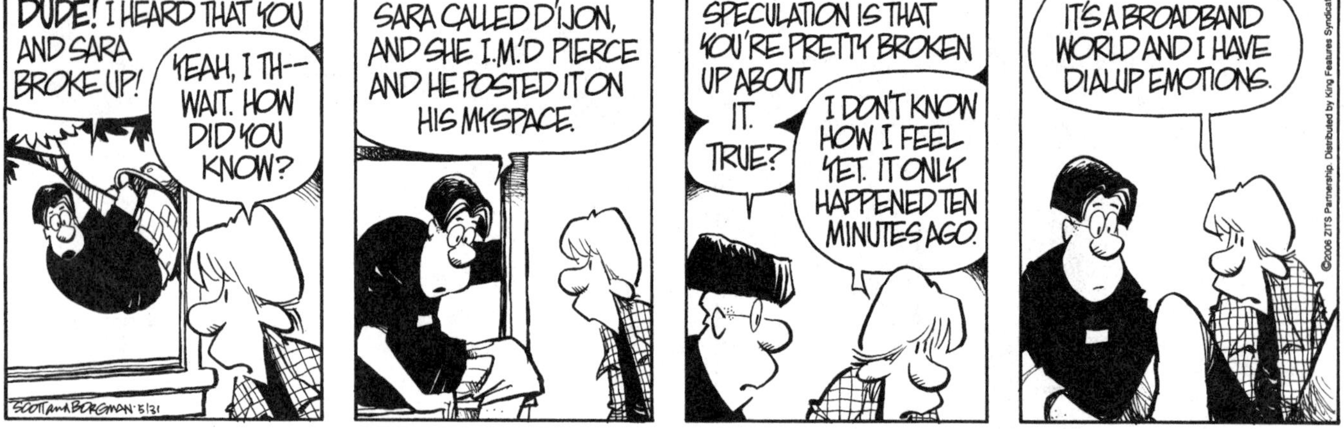
DUDE! I HEARD THAT YOU AND SARA BROKE UP!
YEAH, I TH-- WAIT. HOW DID YOU KNOW?
SCOTT and BORGMAN 5/31
SARA CALLED D'IJON, AND SHE I.M.'D PIERCE AND HE POSTED IT ON HIS MYSPACE.
SPECULATION IS THAT YOU'RE PRETTY BROKEN UP ABOUT IT. TRUE?
I DON'T KNOW HOW I FEEL YET. IT ONLY HAPPENED TEN MINUTES AGO.
IT'S A BROADBAND WORLD AND I HAVE DIALUP EMOTIONS.
©2006 ZITS Partnership. Distributed by King Features Syndicate.

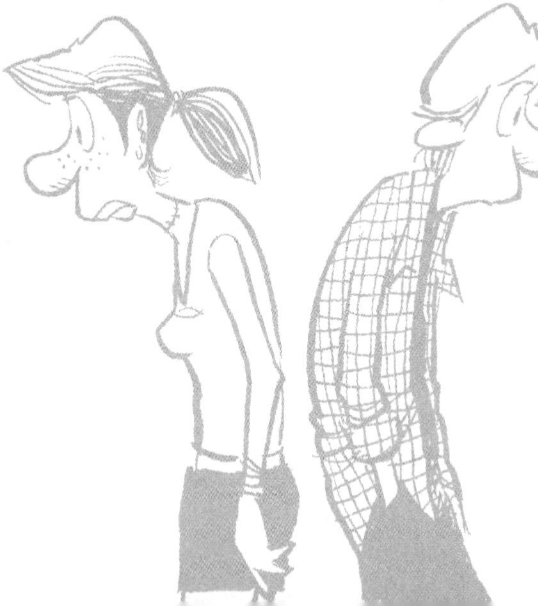

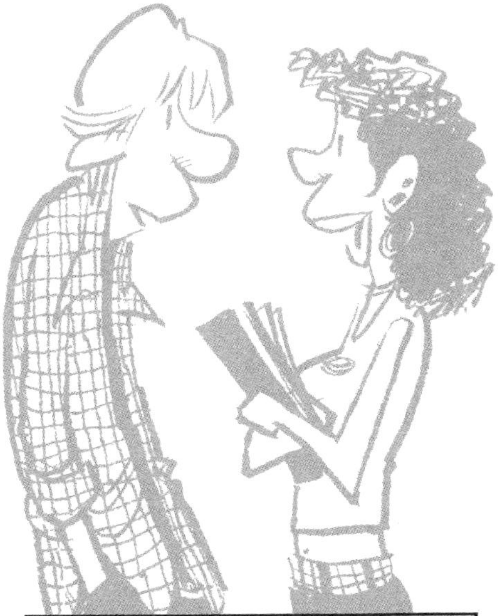

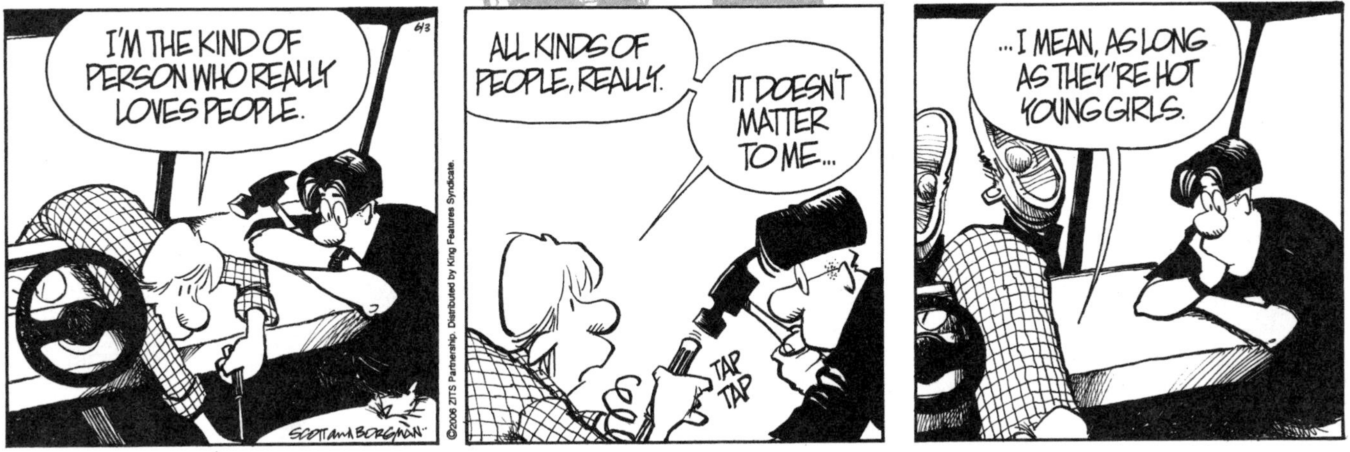
6/3
I'M THE KIND OF PERSON WHO REALLY LOVES PEOPLE.
SCOTT and BORGMAN
©2006 ZITS Partnership. Distributed by King Features Syndicate.
ALL KINDS OF PEOPLE, REALLY.
IT DOESN'T MATTER TO ME...
TAP TAP
...I MEAN, AS LONG AS THEY'RE HOT YOUNG GIRLS.

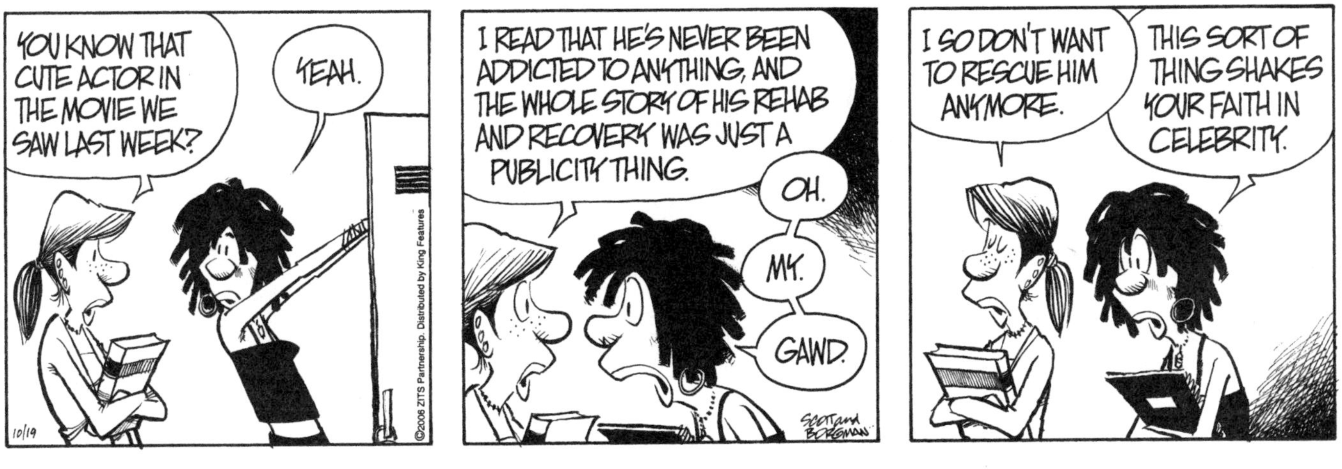
YOU KNOW THAT CUTE ACTOR IN THE MOVIE WE SAW LAST WEEK?
YEAH.
10/19
©2006 ZITS Partnership. Distributed by King Features
I READ THAT HE'S NEVER BEEN ADDICTED TO ANYTHING, AND THE WHOLE STORY OF HIS REHAB AND RECOVERY WAS JUST A PUBLICITY THING.
OH.
MY.
GAWD.
SCOTT and BORGMAN
I SO DON'T WANT TO RESCUE HIM ANYMORE.
THIS SORT OF THING SHAKES YOUR FAITH IN CELEBRITY.

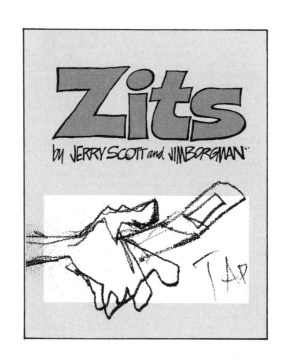

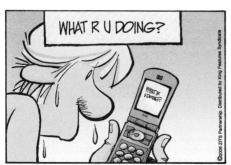

Zits
by JERRY SCOTT and JIM BORGMAN
TAP

WHAT R U DOING?
WHAT R U DOING?
©2006 ZITS Partnership. Distributed by King Features Syndicate
NUTHN. JST TKNG A SHWR.
TAP! TAP! TAP! TAP! TAP! TAP! TAP!
NOW I M BRSHNG MY TEETH
TAP! TAP! TAP! TAP!
THNKNG ABT GNG 2 BED
TAP! TAP! TAP! TAP! TAP! TAP! TAP!
TRNG OUT LGHT. NITE.
TAP! TAP! TAP! TAP!
ZZZZZZZZZZZZZZZZZZZZZZ
TAP! TAP! TAP! TAP! TAP! TAP! TAP! TAP! TAP! TAP! TAP! TAP! TAP! TAP! TAP! TAP! TAP!

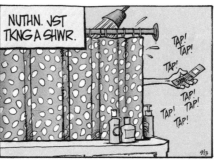

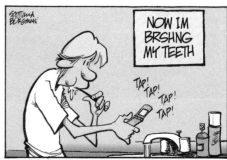

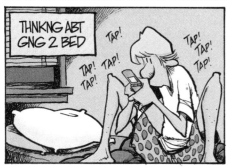

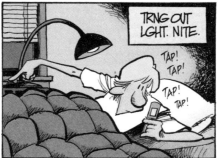

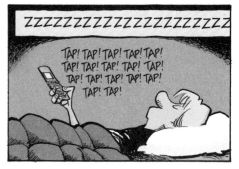

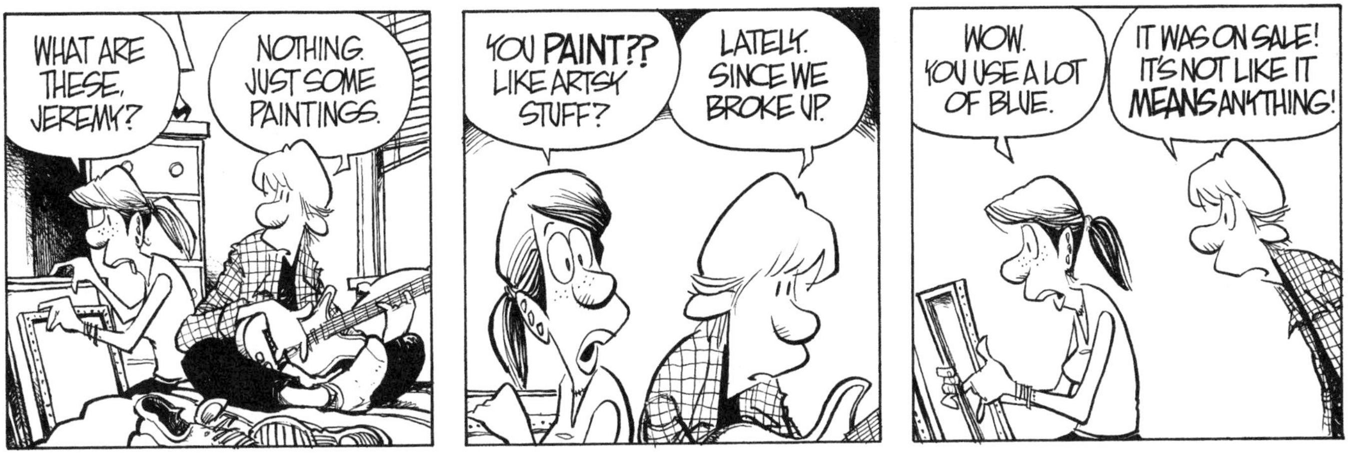
WHAT ARE THESE, JEREMY?
NOTHING. JUST SOME PAINTINGS.
YOU PAINT?? LIKE ARTSY STUFF?
LATELY. SINCE WE BROKE UP.
WOW. YOU USE A LOT OF BLUE.
IT WAS ON SALE! IT'S NOT LIKE IT MEANS ANYTHING!

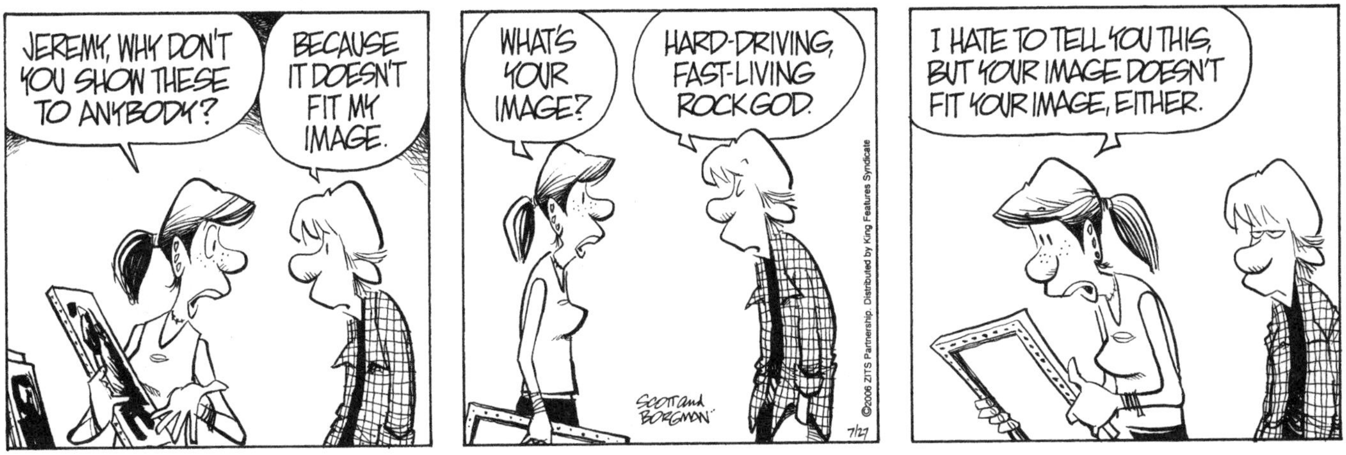
JEREMY, WHY DON'T YOU SHOW THESE TO ANYBODY?
BECAUSE IT DOESN'T FIT MY IMAGE.
WHAT'S YOUR IMAGE?
HARD-DRIVING, FAST-LIVING ROCK GOD.
SCOTT and BORGMAN
©2006 ZITS Partnership. Distributed by King Features Syndicate
7/27
I HATE TO TELL YOU THIS, BUT YOUR IMAGE DOESN'T FIT YOUR IMAGE, EITHER.

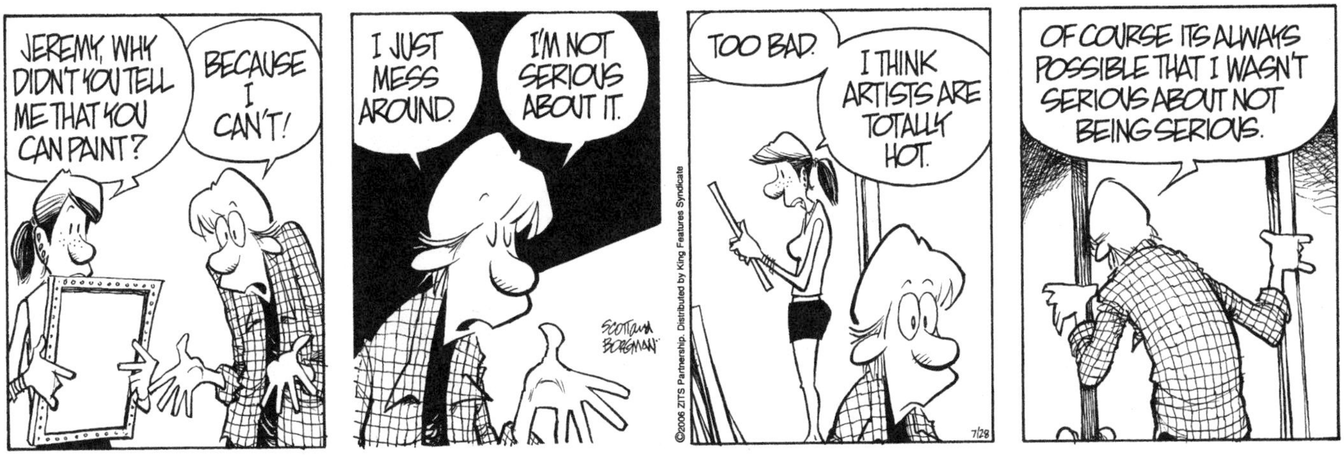
JEREMY, WHY DIDN'T YOU TELL ME THAT YOU CAN PAINT?
BECAUSE I CAN'T!
I JUST MESS AROUND.
I'M NOT SERIOUS ABOUT IT.
SCOTT and BORGMAN
©2006 ZITS Partnership. Distributed by King Features Syndicate
TOO BAD.
I THINK ARTISTS ARE TOTALLY HOT.
7/28
OF COURSE ITS ALWAYS POSSIBLE THAT I WASN'T SERIOUS ABOUT NOT BEING SERIOUS.

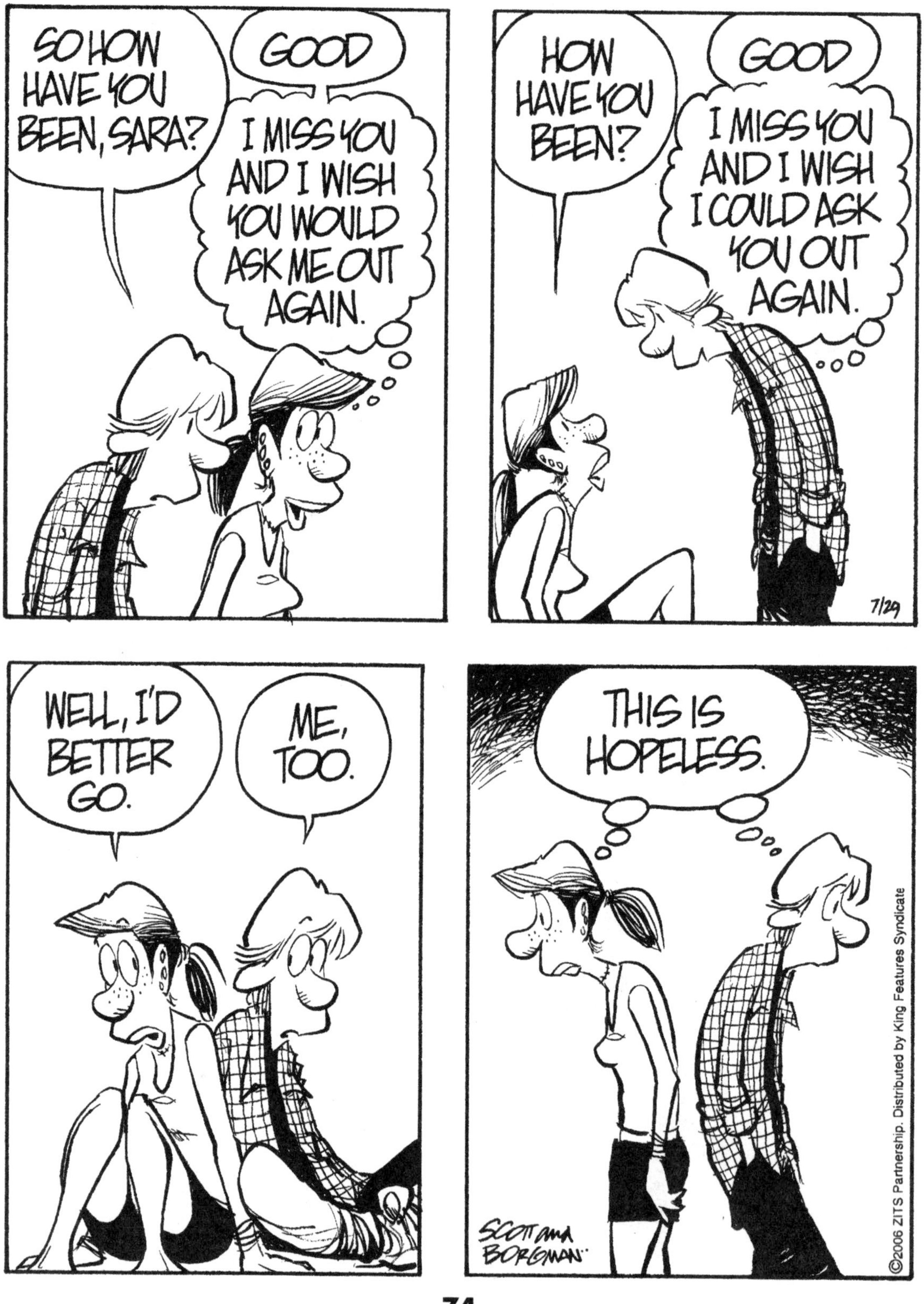

SO HOW HAVE YOU BEEN, SARA?
GOOD
I MISS YOU AND I WISH YOU WOULD ASK ME OUT AGAIN.
HOW HAVE YOU BEEN?
GOOD
I MISS YOU AND I WISH I COULD ASK YOU OUT AGAIN.
7/29
WELL, I'D BETTER GO.
ME, TOO.
THIS IS HOPELESS.
SCOTT AND BORGMAN
©2006 ZITS Partnership. Distributed by King Features Syndicate

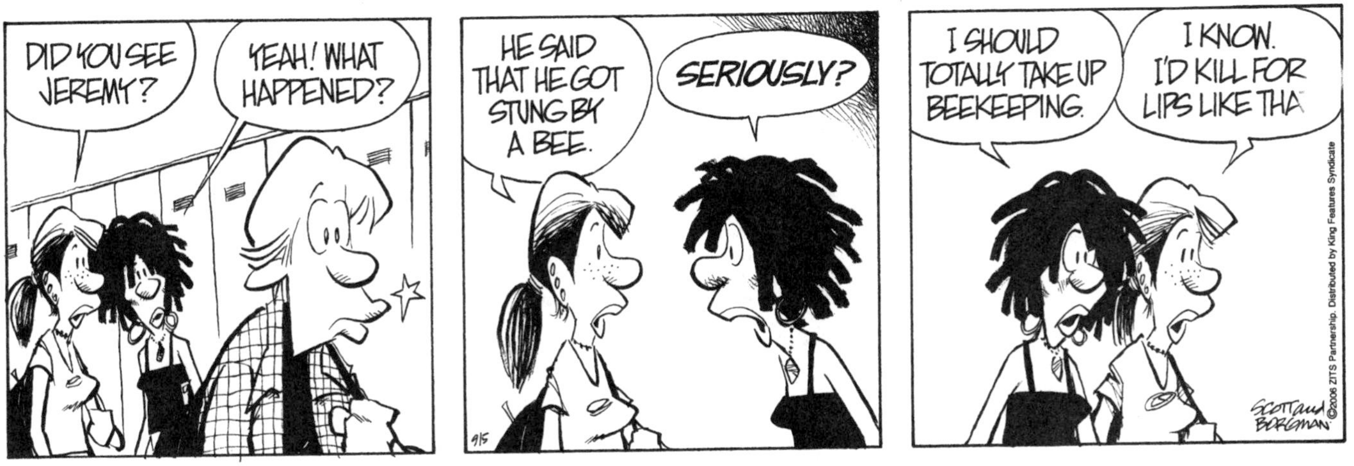
DID YOU SEE JEREMY?
YEAH! WHAT HAPPENED?
HE SAID THAT HE GOT STUNG BY A BEE.
SERIOUSLY?
I SHOULD TOTALLY TAKE UP BEEKEEPING.
I KNOW. I'D KILL FOR LIPS LIKE THA
9/5
SCOTT and BORGMAN
©2006 ZITS Partnership. Distributed by King Features Syndicate

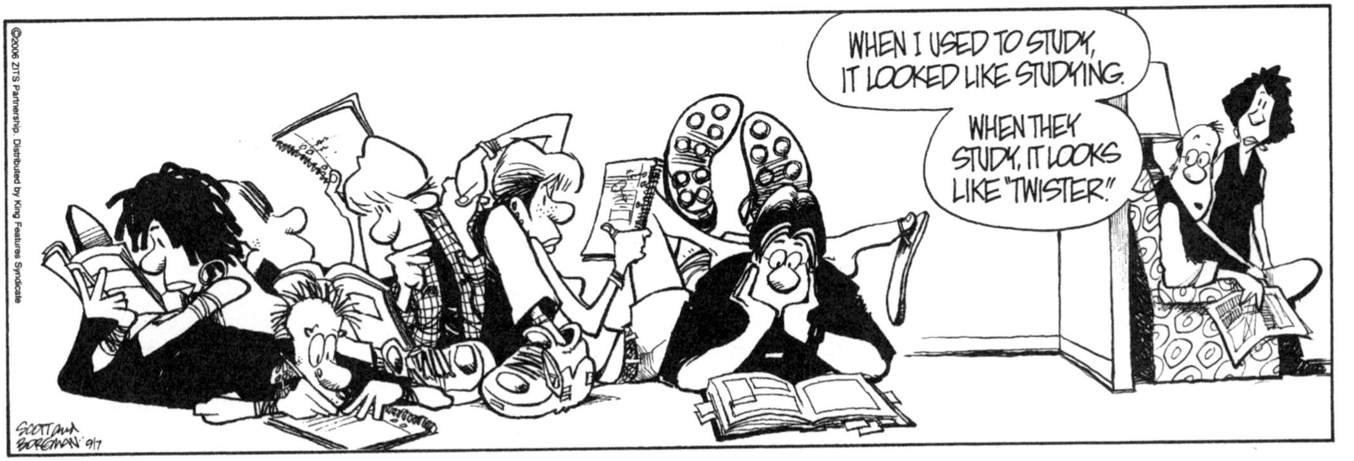
WHEN I USED TO STUDY, IT LOOKED LIKE STUDYING.
WHEN THEY STUDY, IT LOOKS LIKE "TWISTER."
SCOTT and BORGMAN 9/7
©2006 ZITS Partnership. Distributed by King Features Syndicate

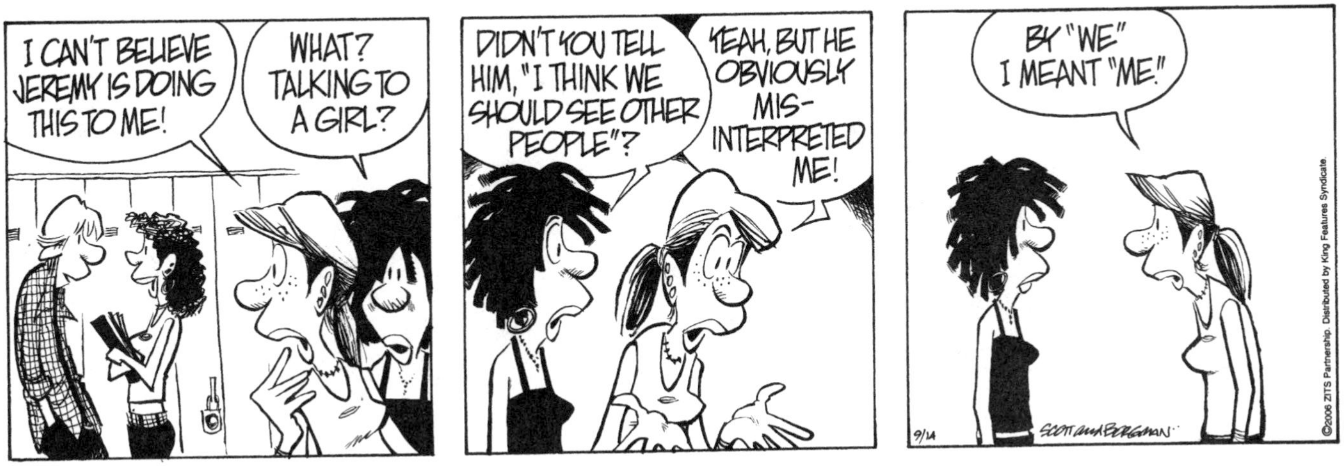
I CAN'T BELIEVE JEREMY IS DOING THIS TO ME!
WHAT? TALKING TO A GIRL?
DIDN'T YOU TELL HIM, "I THINK WE SHOULD SEE OTHER PEOPLE"?
YEAH, BUT HE OBVIOUSLY MIS-INTERPRETED ME!
BY "WE" I MEANT "ME."
9/14
SCOTT and BORGMAN
©2006 ZITS Partnership. Distributed by King Features Syndicate.

Zits
by JERRY SCOTT and JIM BORGMAN

Winter Mixer
GUIDELINES
PROVOCATIVE DRESS AND LEWD BEHAVIOR ARE DISCOURAGED.
GRINDING, BUMPING, MOSHING, MASHING, LICKING, SQUEANING, SHOVING, SLEDGING, ROLLING, KICKING, WALLOWING, FREAKING, PRONKING, BOOTY DANCING, FONDLING, AND WHOLE OR HALF-BODY KNURLING WILL NOT BE PERMITTED.
HIGH SCHOOL DANCES HAVE CHANGED.
AND I WAS WORRIED ABOUT JEREMY'S TIE MATCHING HIS PANTS.
SCOTT and BORGMAN
©2006 ZITS Partnership. Distributed by King Features Syndicate.

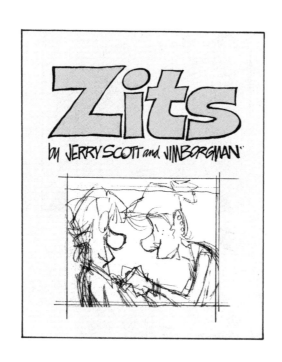

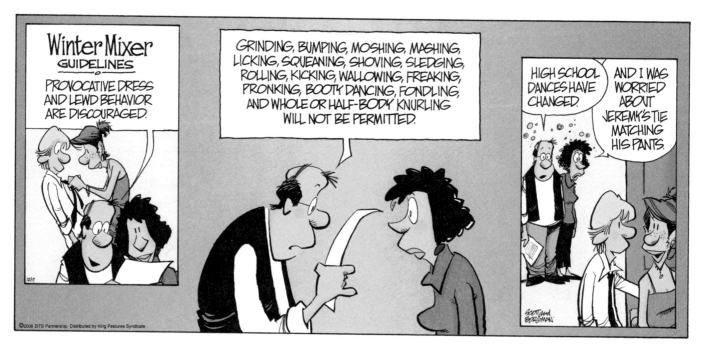

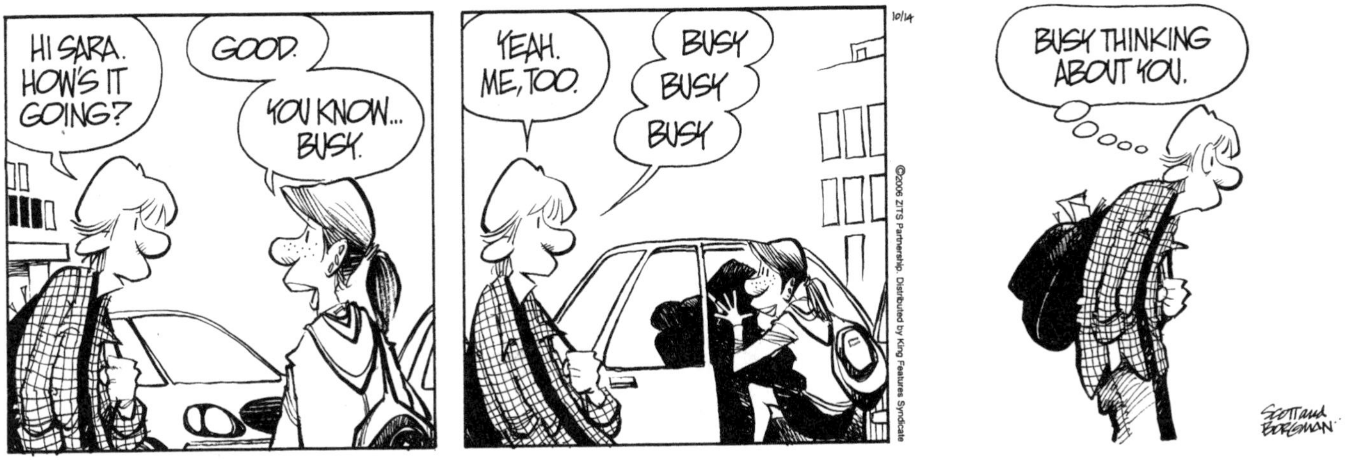
HI SARA. HOW'S IT GOING?
GOOD.
YOU KNOW... BUSY.
10/14
YEAH. ME, TOO.
BUSY
BUSY
BUSY
©2006 ZITS Partnership. Distributed by King Features Syndicate
BUSY THINKING ABOUT YOU.
SCOTT and BORGMAN

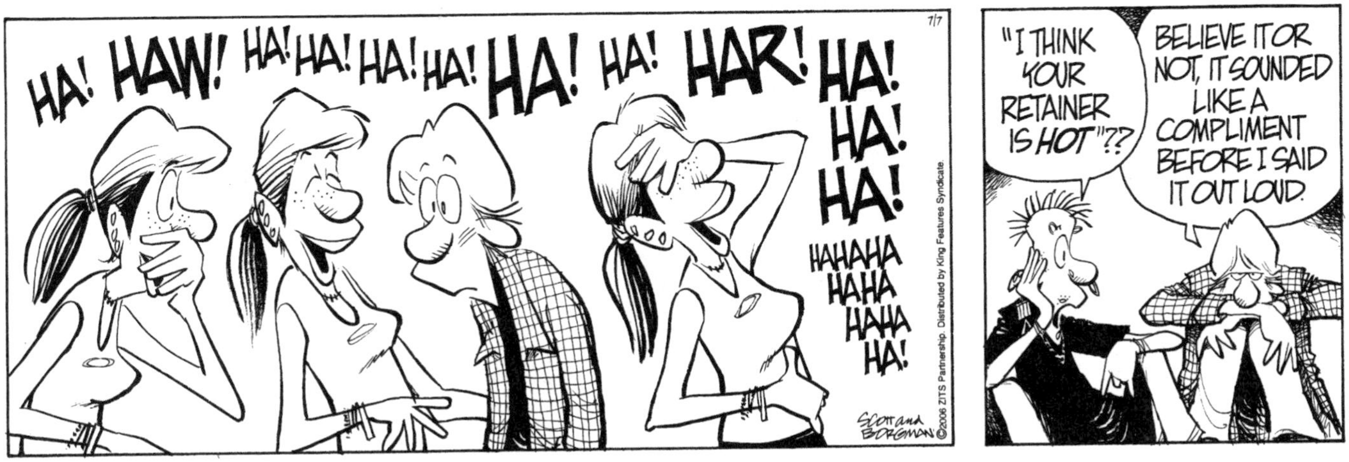
7/7
HA! HAW! HA! HA! HA! HA! HA! HA! HAR! HA! HA! HA!
HAHAHA HAHA HAHA HA!
SCOTT and BORGMAN
©2006 ZITS Partnership. Distributed by King Features Syndicate
"I THINK YOUR RETAINER IS *HOT*"??
BELIEVE IT OR NOT, IT SOUNDED LIKE A COMPLIMENT BEFORE I SAID IT OUT LOUD.

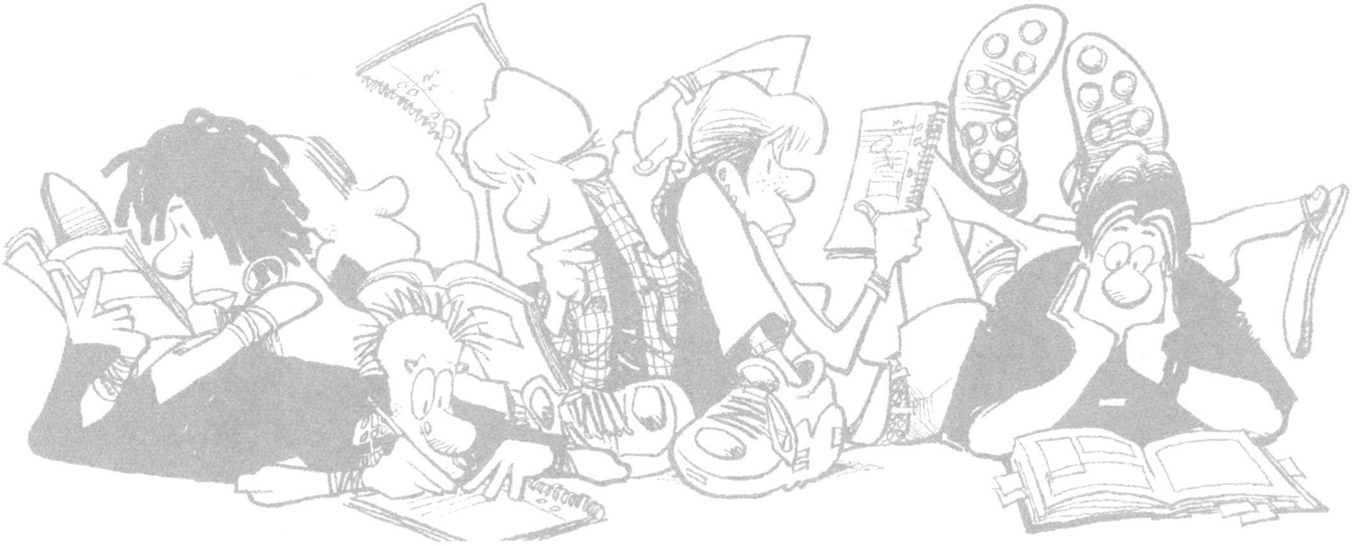

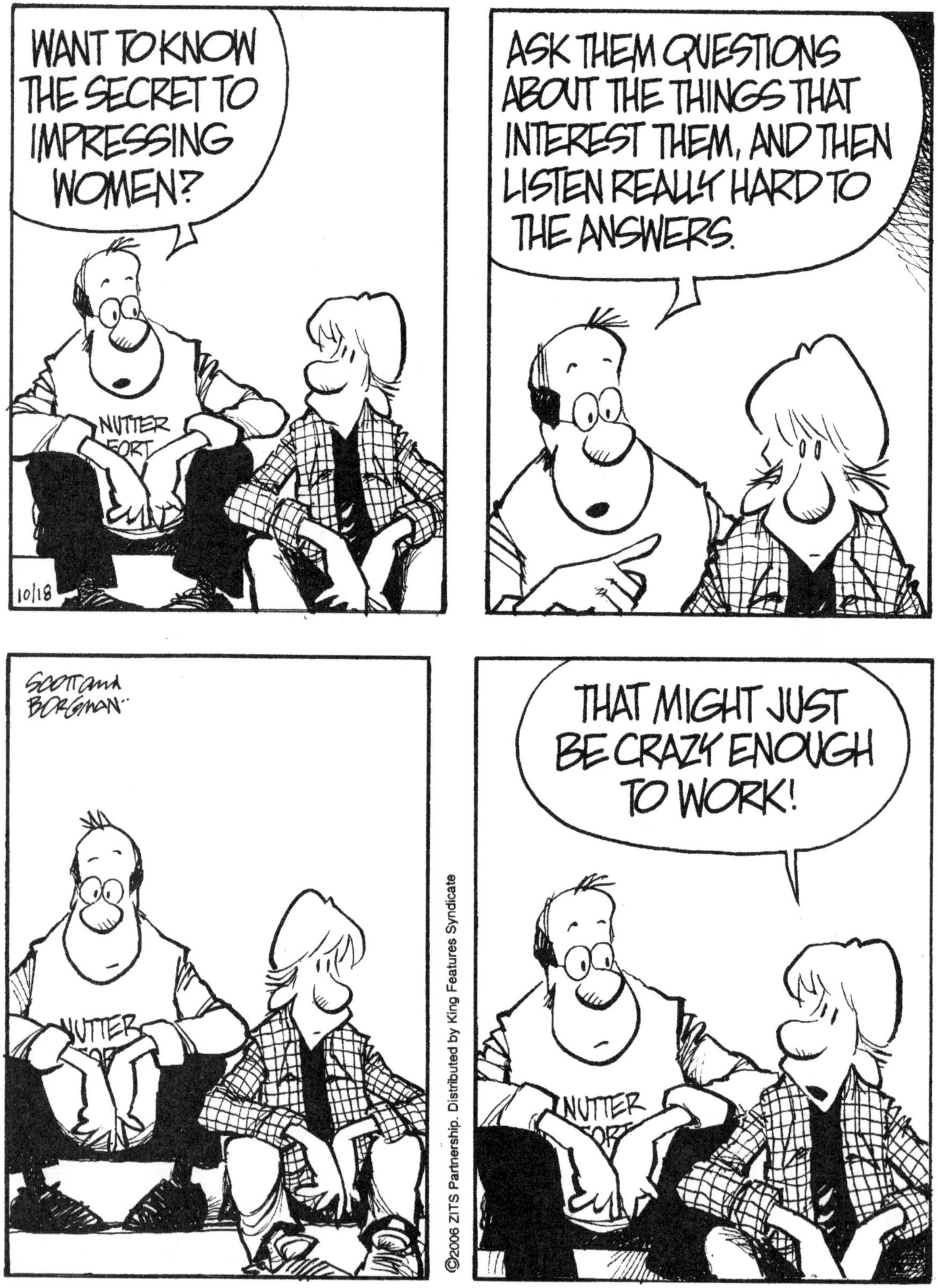
WANT TO KNOW THE SECRET TO IMPRESSING WOMEN?
NUTTER FORT
10/18
ASK THEM QUESTIONS ABOUT THE THINGS THAT INTEREST THEM, AND THEN LISTEN REALLY HARD TO THE ANSWERS.
SCOTT and BORGMAN
NUTTER
©2006 ZITS Partnership. Distributed by King Features Syndicate
THAT MIGHT JUST BE CRAZY ENOUGH TO WORK!
NUTTER

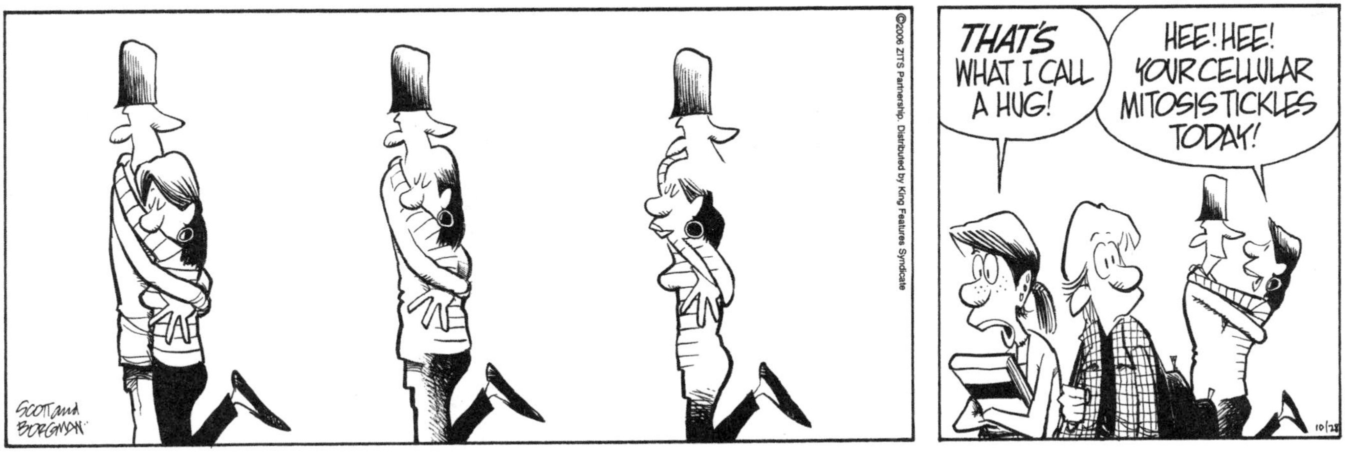
©2006 ZITS Partnership. Distributed by King Features Syndicate
SCOTT and BORGMAN
THAT'S WHAT I CALL A HUG!
HEE! HEE! YOUR CELLULAR MITOSIS TICKLES TODAY!
10/28

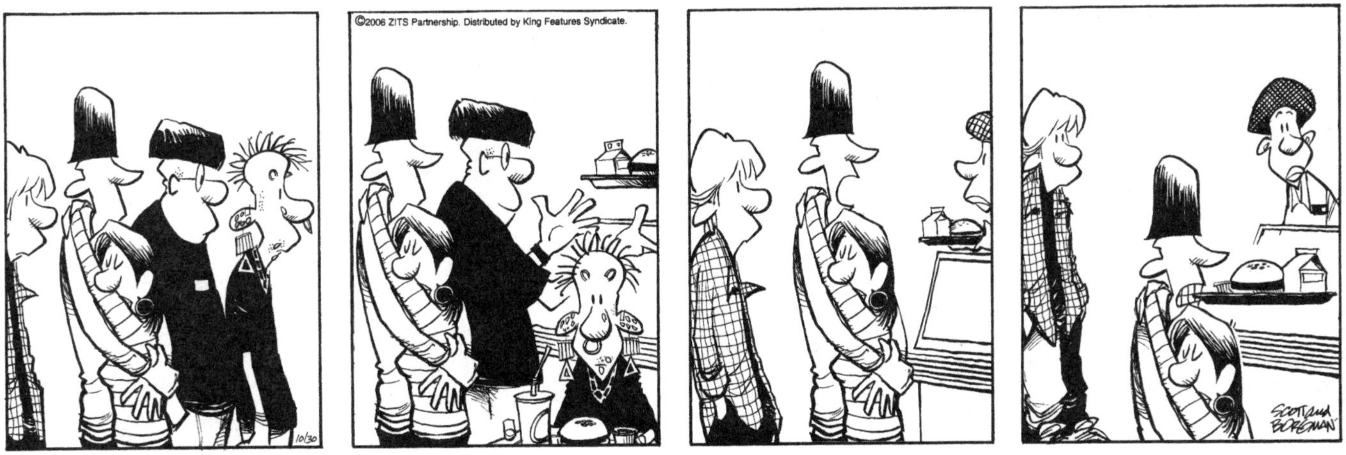
10/30
©2006 ZITS Partnership. Distributed by King Features Syndicate.
SCOTT and BORGMAN

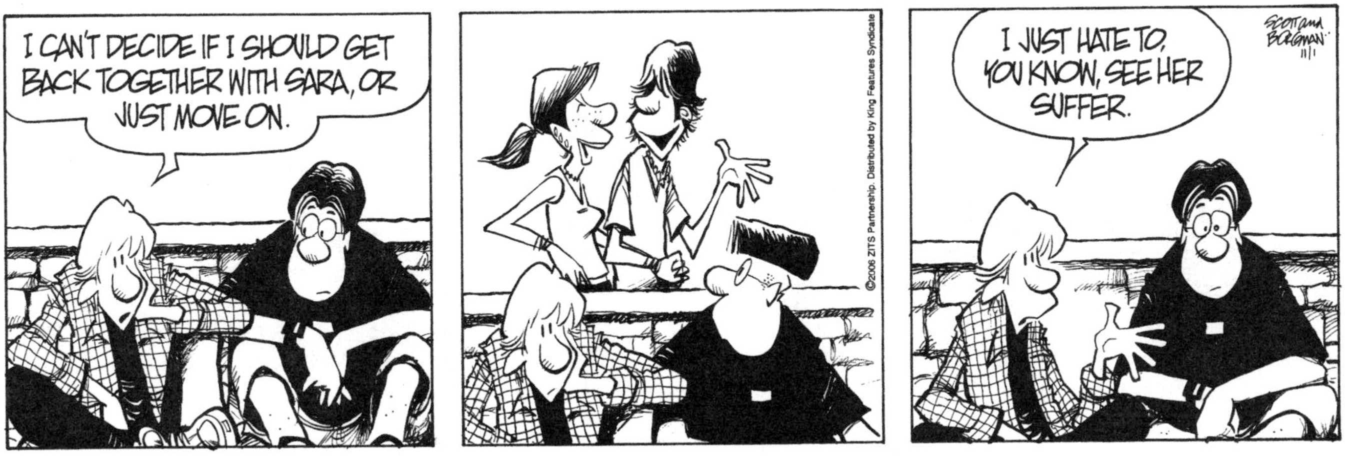
I CAN'T DECIDE IF I SHOULD GET BACK TOGETHER WITH SARA, OR JUST MOVE ON.
©2006 ZITS Partnership. Distributed by King Features Syndicate
SCOTT and BORGMAN 11/1
I JUST HATE TO, YOU KNOW, SEE HER SUFFER.

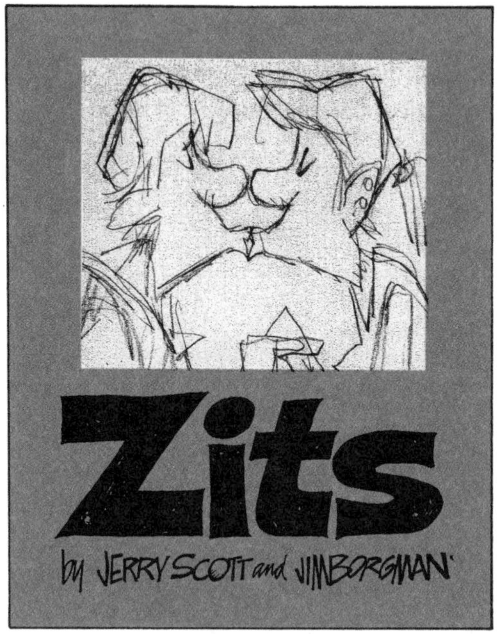
Zits
by JERRY SCOTT and JIM BORGMAN

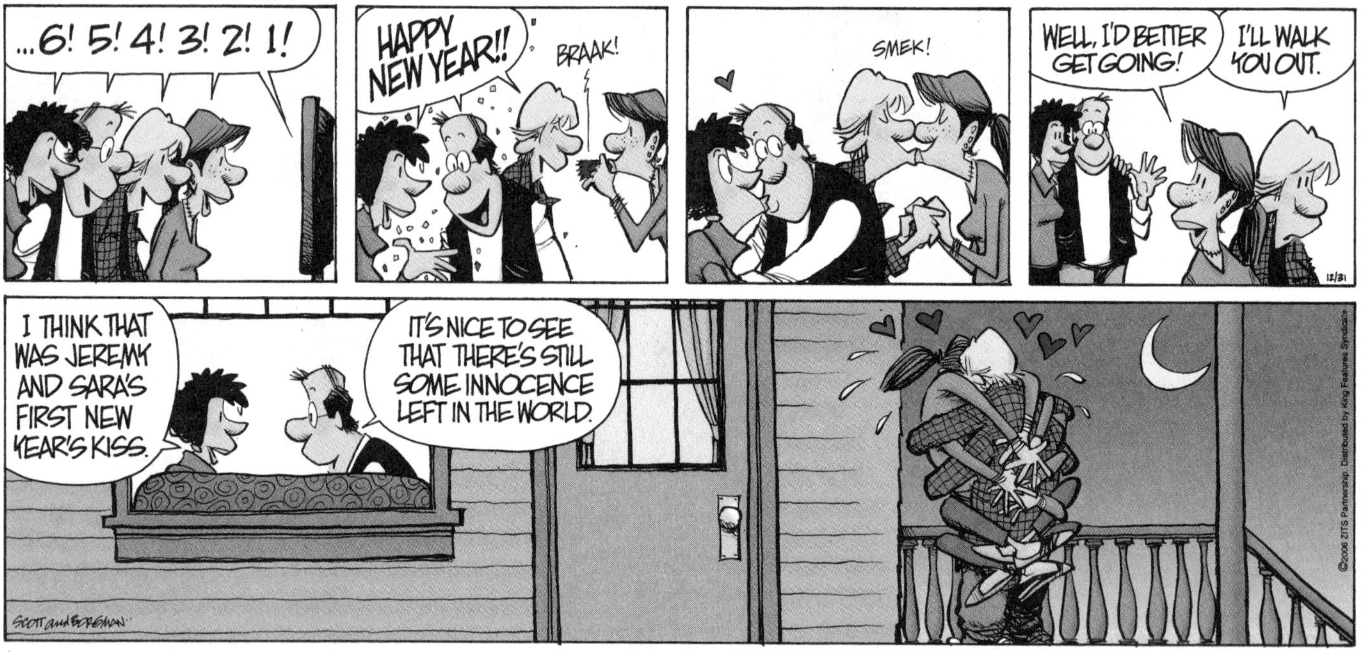
...6! 5! 4! 3! 2! 1!
HAPPY NEW YEAR!!
BRAAK!
SMEK!
WELL, I'D BETTER GET GOING!
I'LL WALK YOU OUT.
12/31
I THINK THAT WAS JEREMY AND SARA'S FIRST NEW YEAR'S KISS.
IT'S NICE TO SEE THAT THERE'S STILL SOME INNOCENCE LEFT IN THE WORLD.
SCOTT and BORGMAN
©2006 ZITS Partnership. Distributed by King Features Syndicate

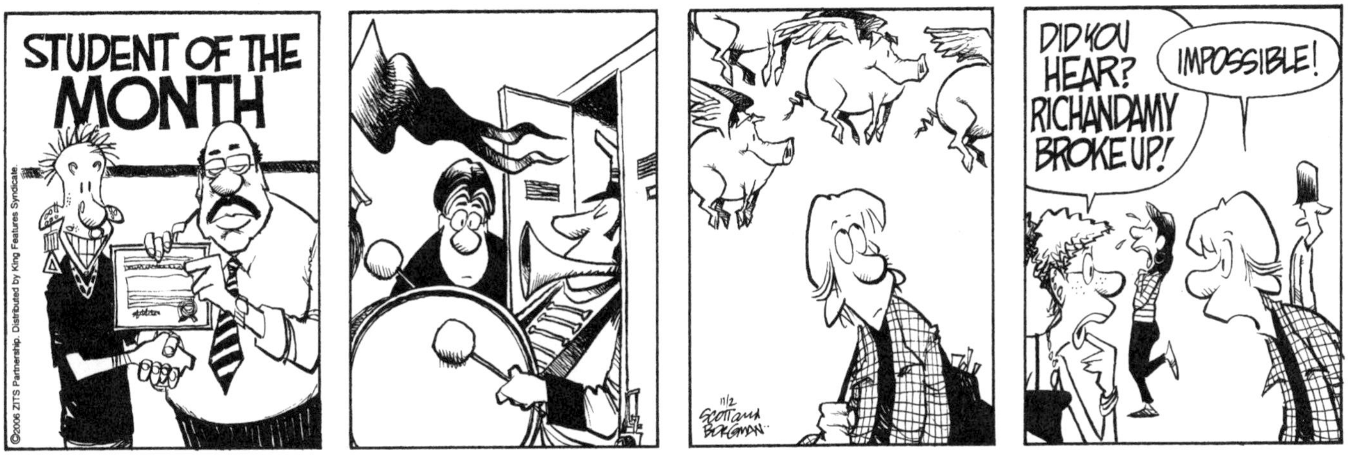
STUDENT OF THE MONTH
DID YOU HEAR? RICHANDAMY BROKE UP!
IMPOSSIBLE!
11/2 SCOTT and BORGMAN
©2006 ZITS Partnership. Distributed by King Features Syndicate.

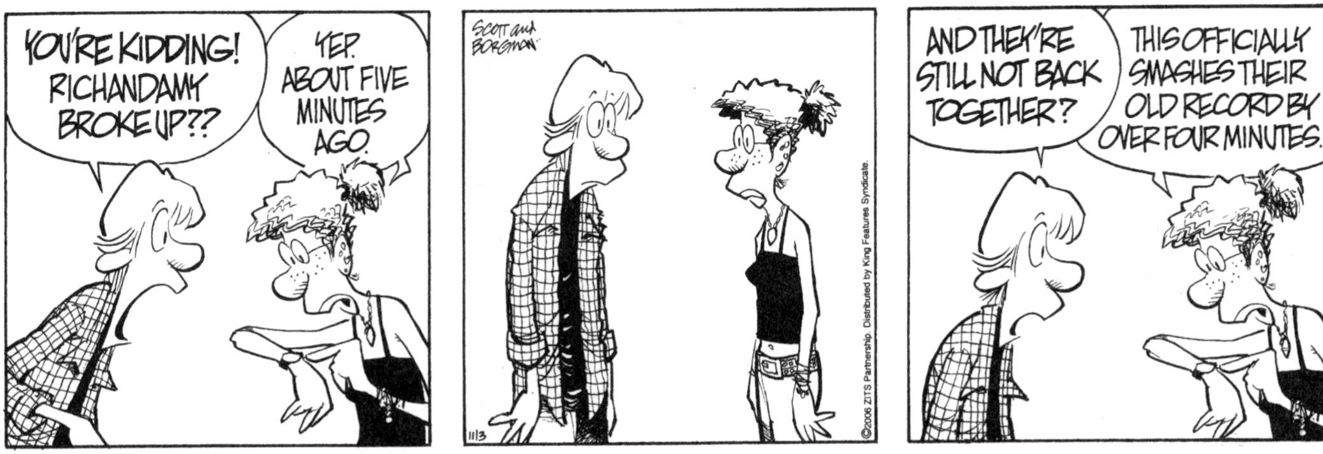
YOU'RE KIDDING! RICHANDAMY BROKE UP??
YEP. ABOUT FIVE MINUTES AGO.
SCOTT and BORGMAN 11/3
©2006 ZITS Partnership. Distributed by King Features Syndicate.
AND THEY'RE STILL NOT BACK TOGETHER?
THIS OFFICIALLY SMASHES THEIR OLD RECORD BY OVER FOUR MINUTES.

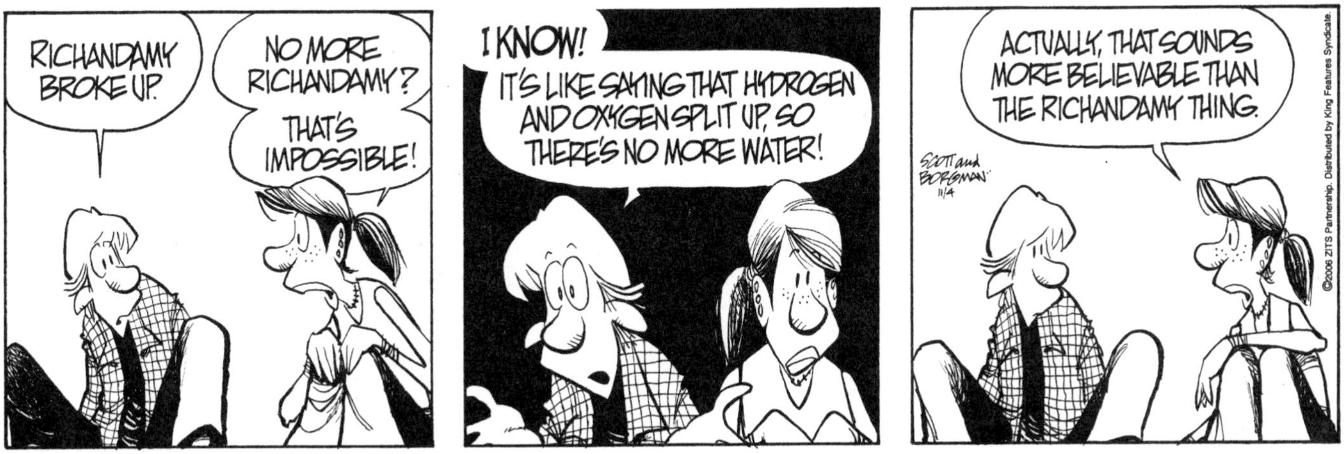
RICHANDAMY BROKE UP.
NO MORE RICHANDAMY?
THAT'S IMPOSSIBLE!
I KNOW!
IT'S LIKE SAYING THAT HYDROGEN AND OXYGEN SPLIT UP, SO THERE'S NO MORE WATER!
SCOTT and BORGMAN 11/4
ACTUALLY, THAT SOUNDS MORE BELIEVABLE THAN THE RICHANDAMY THING.
©2006 ZITS Partnership. Distributed by King Features Syndicate.

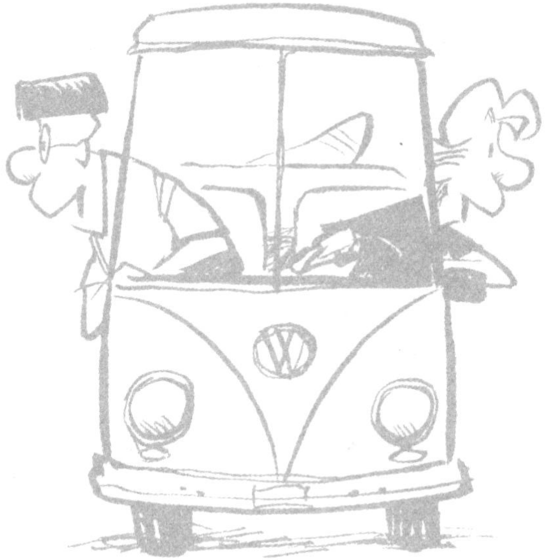

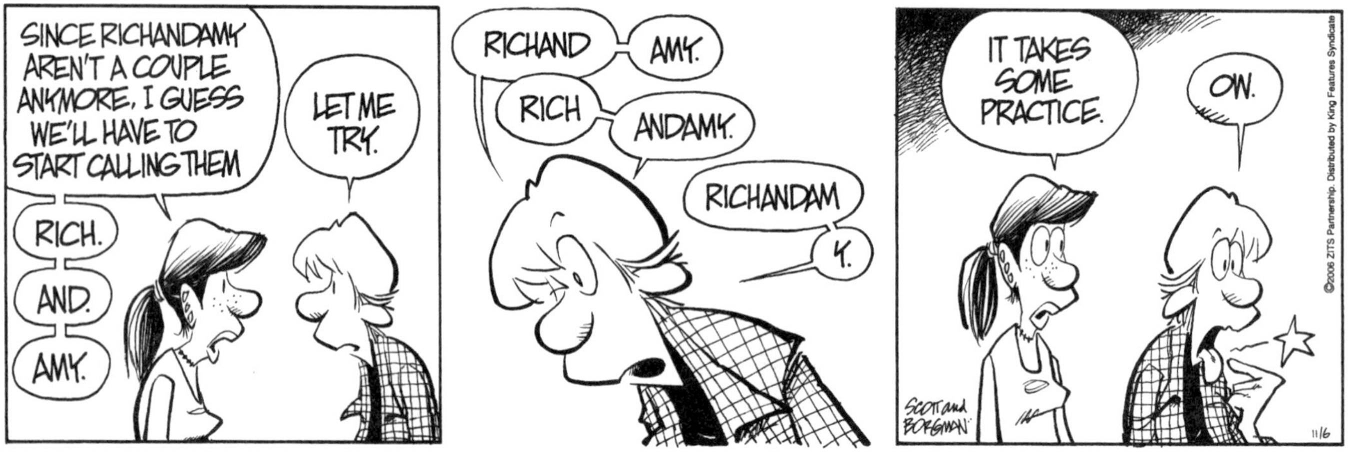

SINCE RICHANDAMY AREN'T A COUPLE ANYMORE, I GUESS WE'LL HAVE TO START CALLING THEM
RICH.
AND.
AMY.
LET ME TRY.
RICHAND
AMY.
RICH
ANDAMY.
RICHANDAM
Y.
IT TAKES SOME PRACTICE.
OW.
SCOTT and BORGMAN
11/6
©2006 ZITS Partnership. Distributed by King Features Syndicate

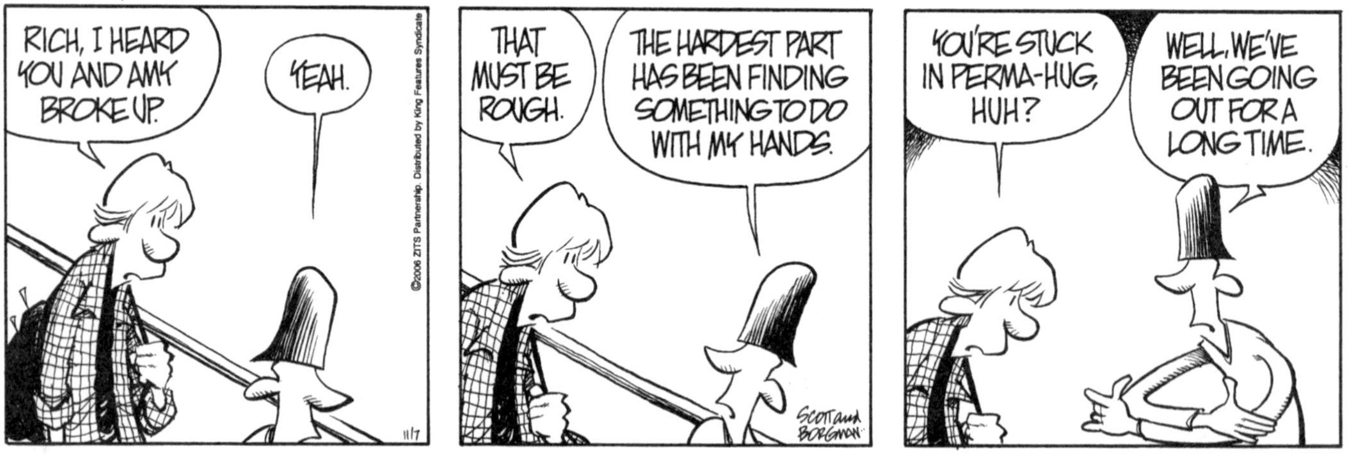

RICH, I HEARD YOU AND AMY BROKE UP.
YEAH.
11/7
©2006 ZITS Partnership. Distributed by King Features Syndicate
THAT MUST BE ROUGH.
THE HARDEST PART HAS BEEN FINDING SOMETHING TO DO WITH MY HANDS.
SCOTT and BORGMAN
YOU'RE STUCK IN PERMA-HUG, HUH?
WELL, WE'VE BEEN GOING OUT FOR A LONG TIME.

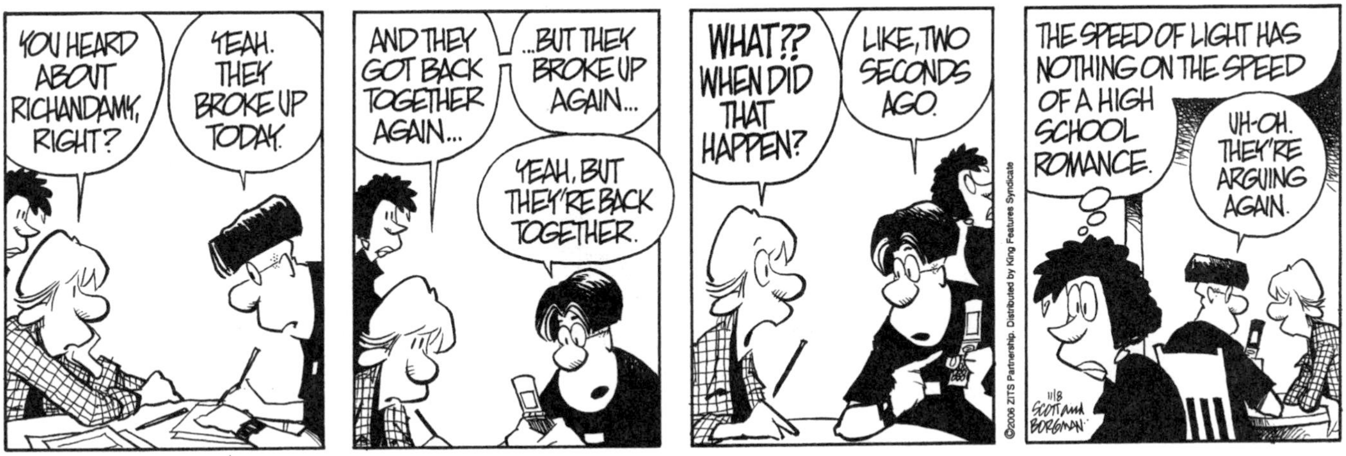
YOU HEARD ABOUT RICHANDAMY, RIGHT?
YEAH. THEY BROKE UP TODAY.
AND THEY GOT BACK TOGETHER AGAIN...
...BUT THEY BROKE UP AGAIN...
YEAH, BUT THEY'RE BACK TOGETHER.
WHAT?? WHEN DID THAT HAPPEN?
LIKE, TWO SECONDS AGO.
©2006 ZITS Partnership. Distributed by King Features Syndicate
THE SPEED OF LIGHT HAS NOTHING ON THE SPEED OF A HIGH SCHOOL ROMANCE.
UH-OH. THEY'RE ARGUING AGAIN.

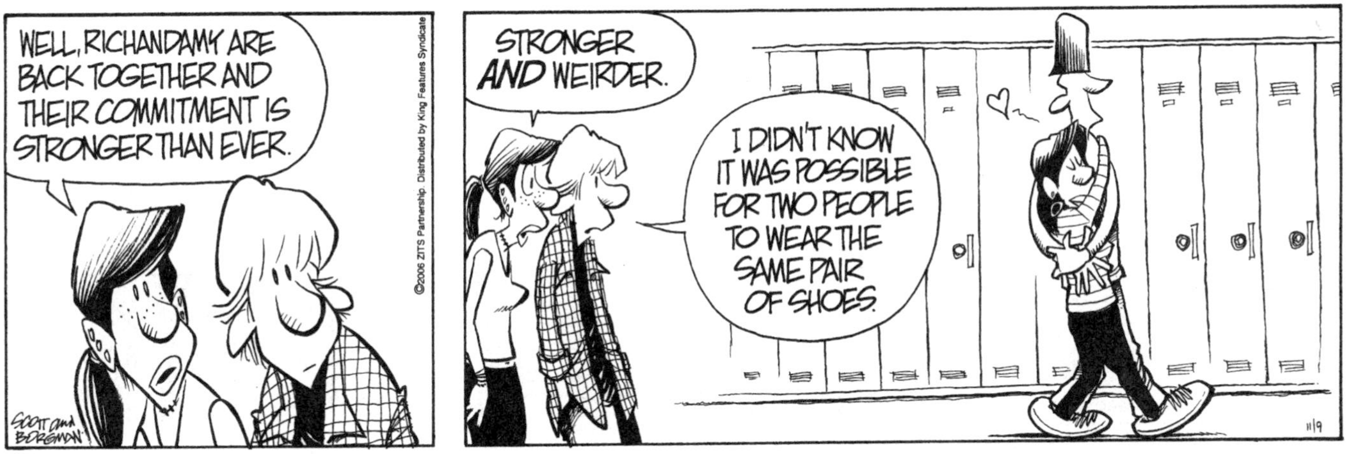
WELL, RICHANDAMY ARE BACK TOGETHER AND THEIR COMMITMENT IS STRONGER THAN EVER.
©2006 ZITS Partnership. Distributed by King Features Syndicate
STRONGER AND WEIRDER.
I DIDN'T KNOW IT WAS POSSIBLE FOR TWO PEOPLE TO WEAR THE SAME PAIR OF SHOES.

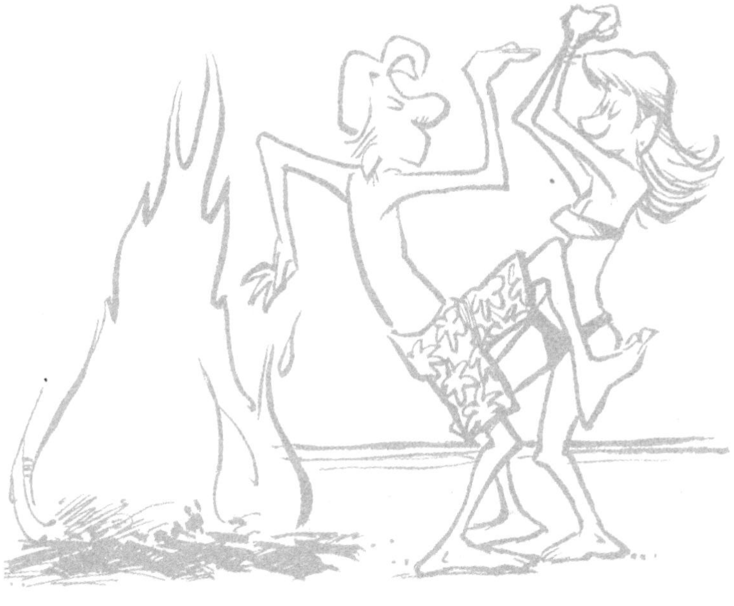

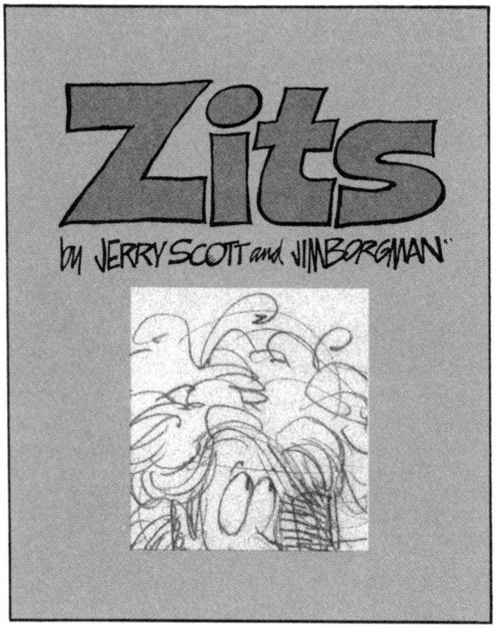
Zits
by JERRY SCOTT and JIM BORGMAN

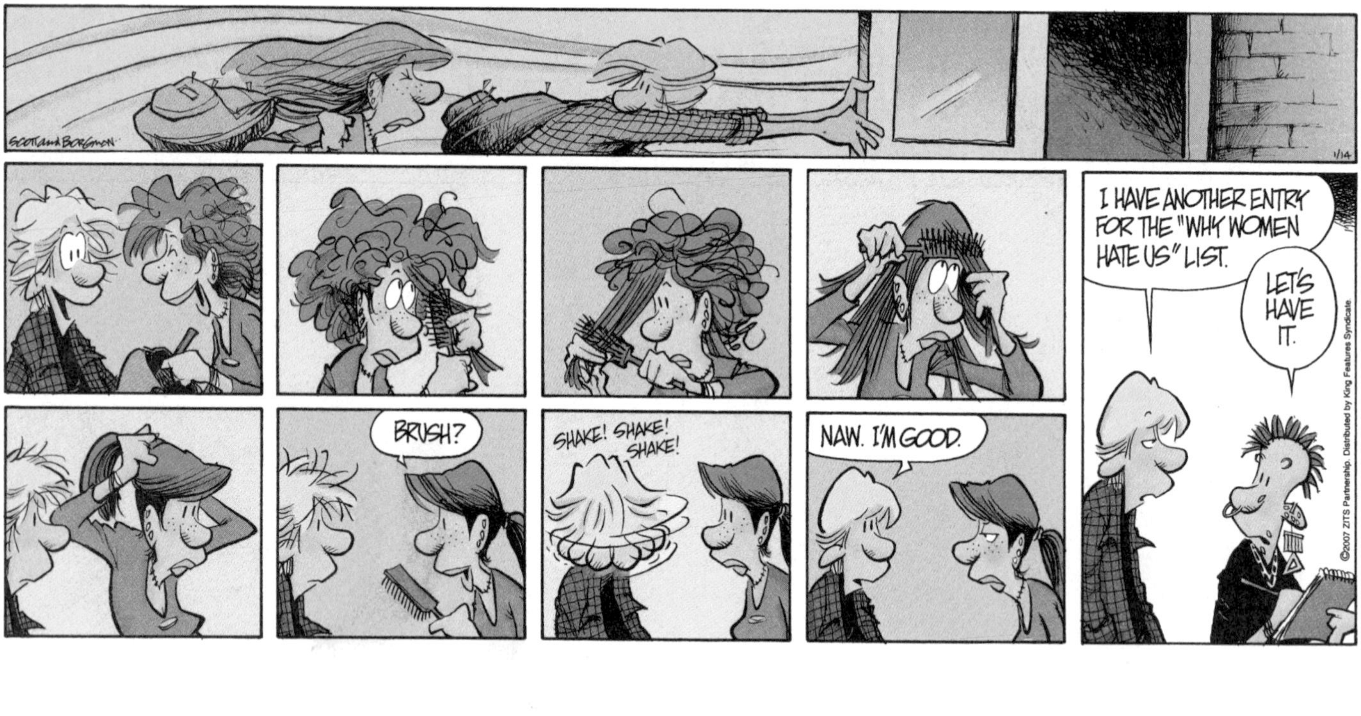
SCOTT and BORGMAN
1/14
BRUSH?
SHAKE! SHAKE! SHAKE!
NAW. I'M GOOD.
I HAVE ANOTHER ENTRY FOR THE "WHY WOMEN HATE US" LIST.
LET'S HAVE IT.
©2007 ZITS Partnership. Distributed by King Features Syndicate.

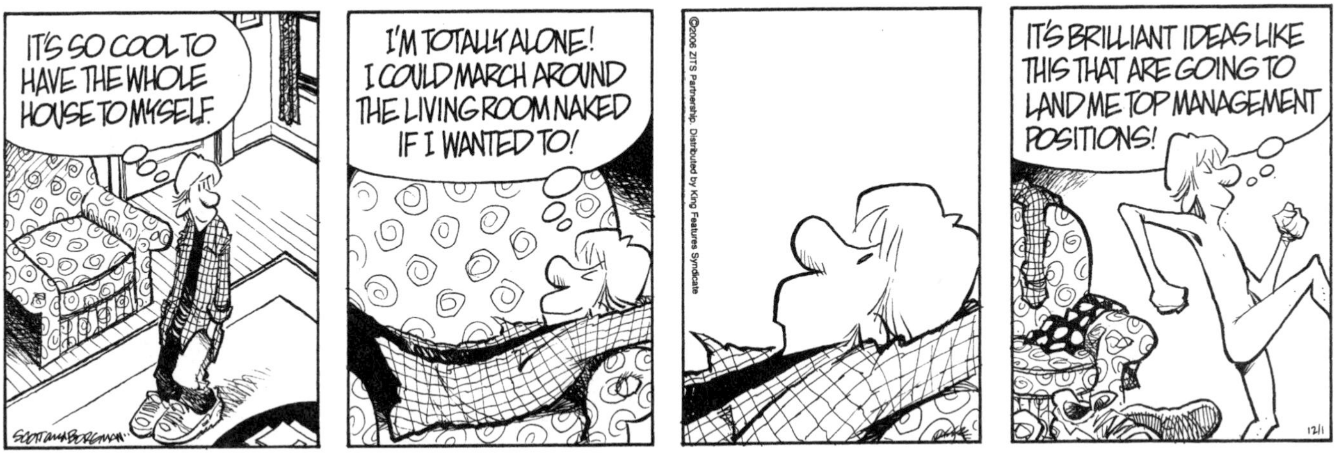
IT'S SO COOL TO HAVE THE WHOLE HOUSE TO MYSELF.
SCOTT and BORGMAN
I'M TOTALLY ALONE! I COULD MARCH AROUND THE LIVING ROOM NAKED IF I WANTED TO!
©2006 ZITS Partnership. Distributed by King Features Syndicate
IT'S BRILLIANT IDEAS LIKE THIS THAT ARE GOING TO LAND ME TOP MANAGEMENT POSITIONS!
12/1

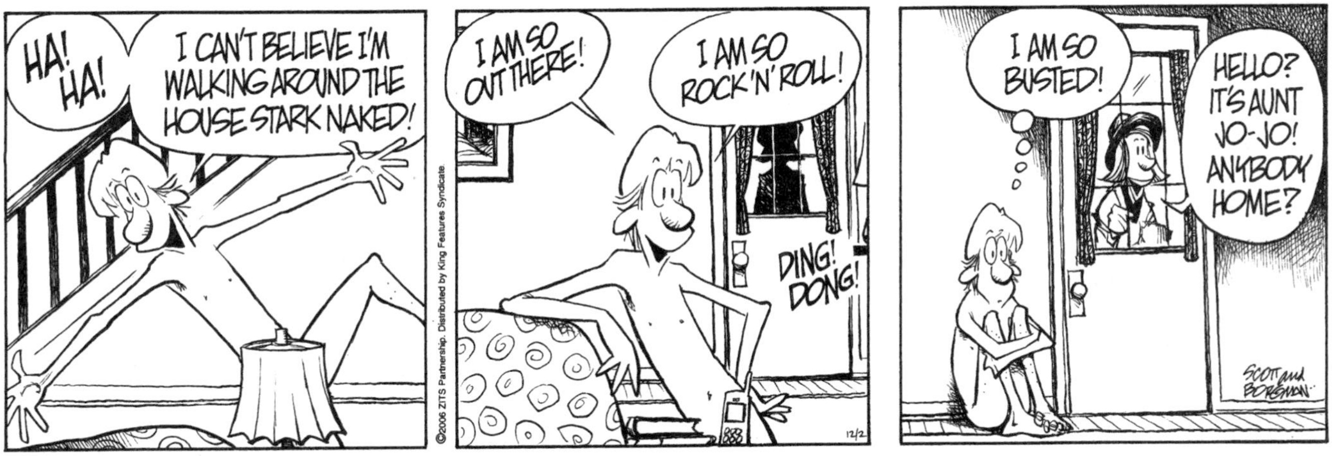
HA! HA!
I CAN'T BELIEVE I'M WALKING AROUND THE HOUSE STARK NAKED!
©2006 ZITS Partnership. Distributed by King Features Syndicate
I AM SO OUT THERE!
I AM SO ROCK 'N' ROLL!
DING! DONG!
12/2
I AM SO BUSTED!
HELLO? IT'S AUNT JO-JO! ANYBODY HOME?
SCOTT and BORGMAN

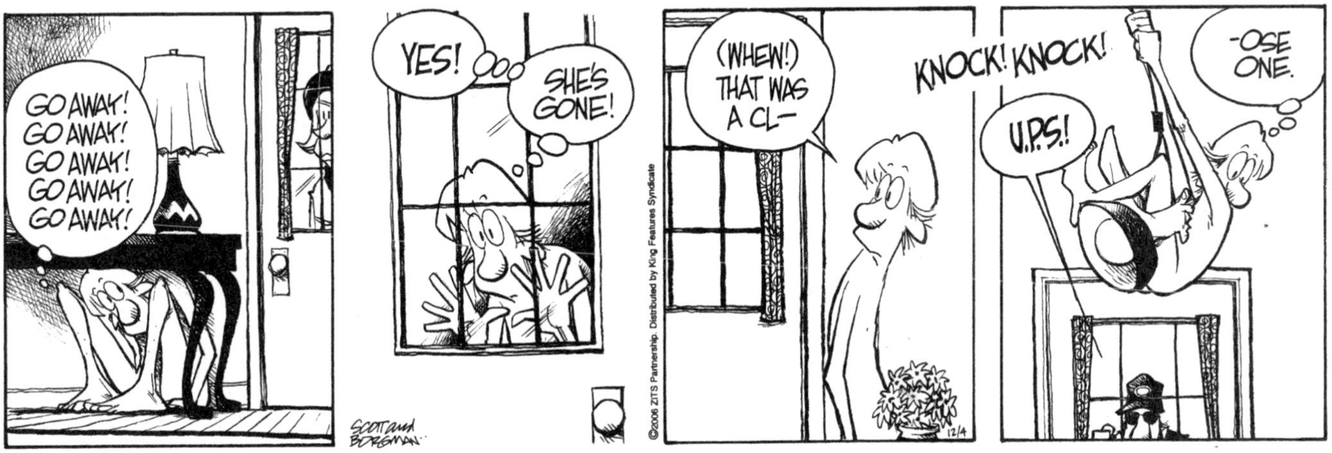
GO AWAY! GO AWAY! GO AWAY! GO AWAY! GO AWAY!
SCOTT and BORGMAN
YES!
SHE'S GONE!
©2006 ZITS Partnership. Distributed by King Features Syndicate
(WHEW!) THAT WAS A CL—
12/4
KNOCK! KNOCK!
U.P.S.!
-OSE ONE.

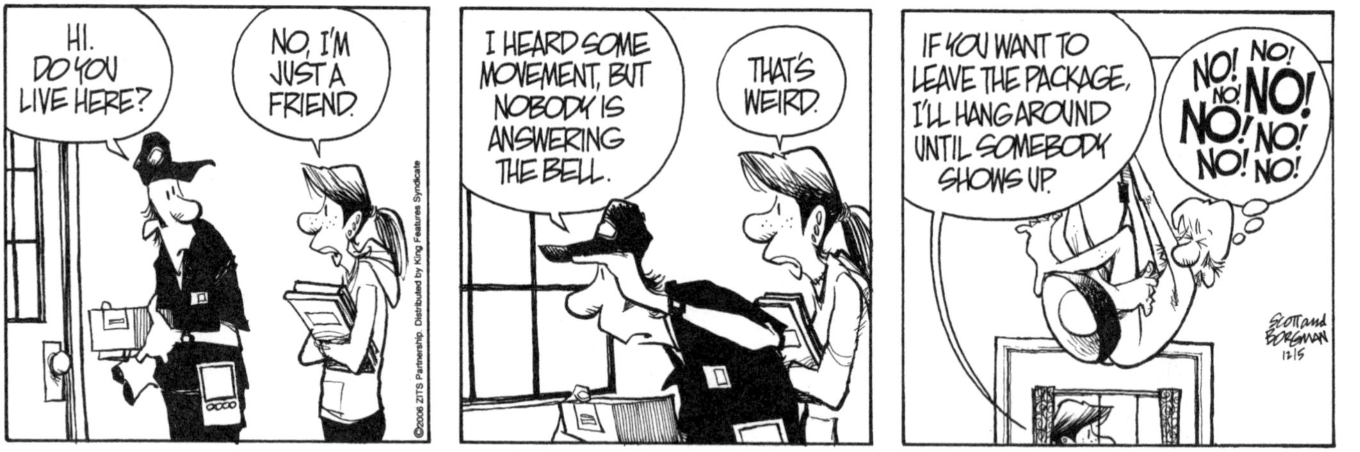
HI. DO YOU LIVE HERE?
NO, I'M JUST A FRIEND.
©2006 ZITS Partnership. Distributed by King Features Syndicate
I HEARD SOME MOVEMENT, BUT NOBODY IS ANSWERING THE BELL.
THAT'S WEIRD.
IF YOU WANT TO LEAVE THE PACKAGE, I'LL HANG AROUND UNTIL SOMEBODY SHOWS UP.
NO! NO! NO! NO! NO! NO! NO! NO!
SCOTT and BORGMAN 12/5

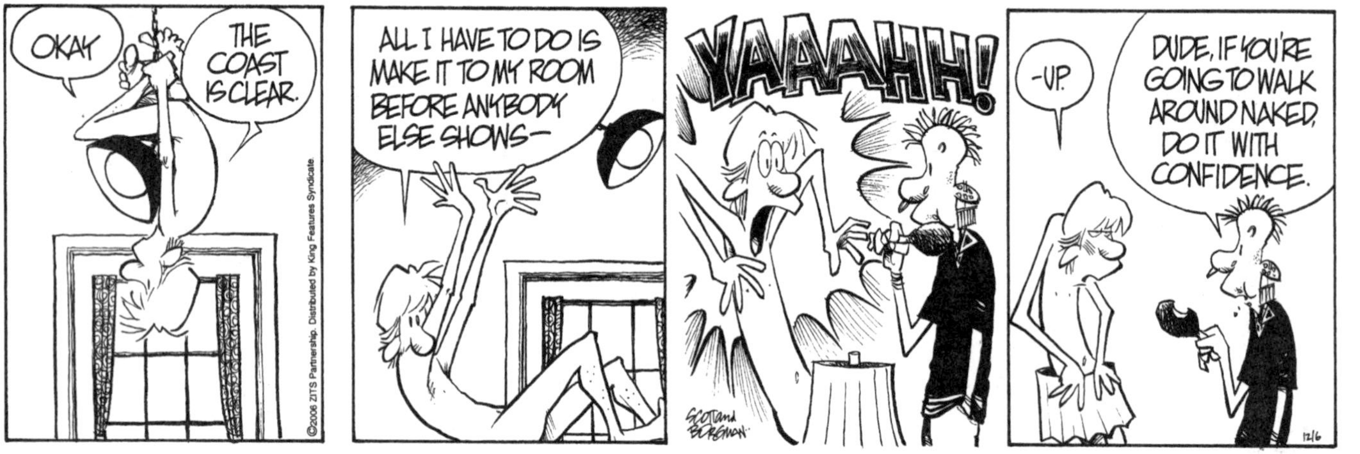
OKAY
THE COAST IS CLEAR.
©2006 ZITS Partnership. Distributed by King Features Syndicate
ALL I HAVE TO DO IS MAKE IT TO MY ROOM BEFORE ANYBODY ELSE SHOWS—
YAAAHH!
SCOTT and BORGMAN
-UP.
DUDE, IF YOU'RE GOING TO WALK AROUND NAKED, DO IT WITH CONFIDENCE.
12/6

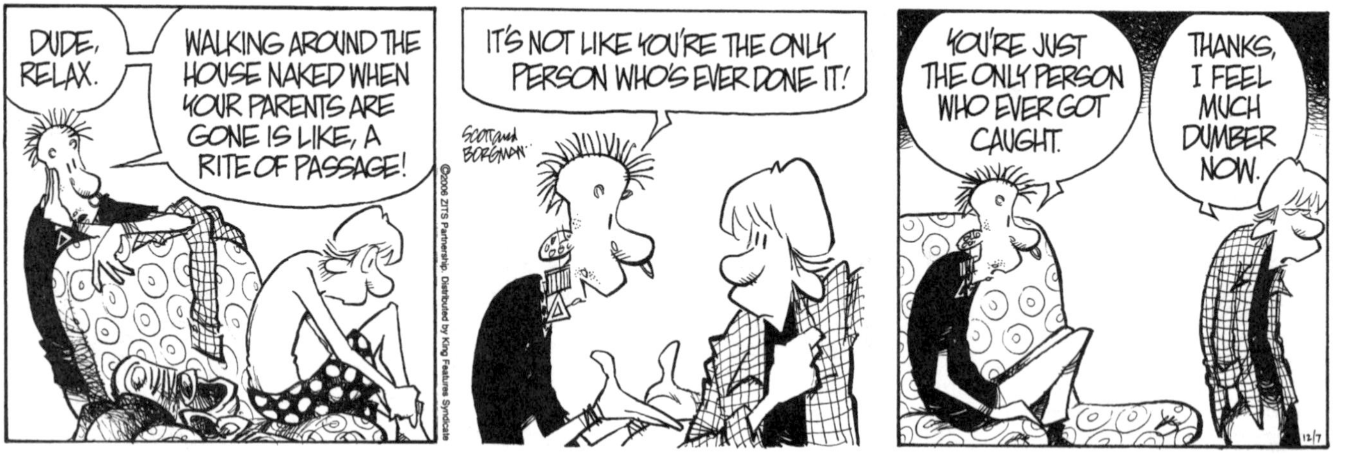
DUDE, RELAX.
WALKING AROUND THE HOUSE NAKED WHEN YOUR PARENTS ARE GONE IS LIKE, A RITE OF PASSAGE!
©2006 ZITS Partnership. Distributed by King Features Syndicate
IT'S NOT LIKE YOU'RE THE ONLY PERSON WHO'S EVER DONE IT!
SCOTT and BORGMAN
YOU'RE JUST THE ONLY PERSON WHO EVER GOT CAUGHT.
THANKS, I FEEL MUCH DUMBER NOW.
12/7

Zits
by
JERRY SCOTT and
JIM BORGMAN

HI MOM.
GAAAAA!
ARE YOU OKAY?
YES.
SORRY.
I GUESS I'M JUST A LITTLE ON EDGE.
HI SARA.
IT'S ONE OF THOSE DAYS WHEN THE SLIGHTEST THING COULD SET ME OFF.
©2007 ZITS Partnership. Distributed by King Features Syndicate
SARA AND I GOT MARRIED.
WE DID NOT!
I KNOW. I JUST WANTED TO SEE HOW HIGH SHE COULD GO.
WHAP!

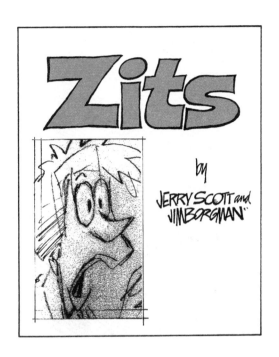

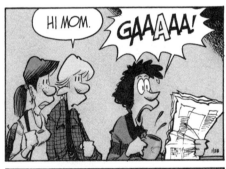

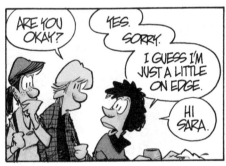

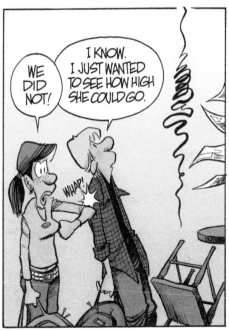

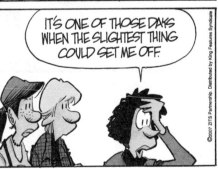

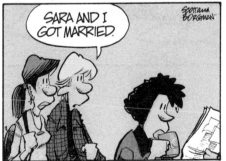

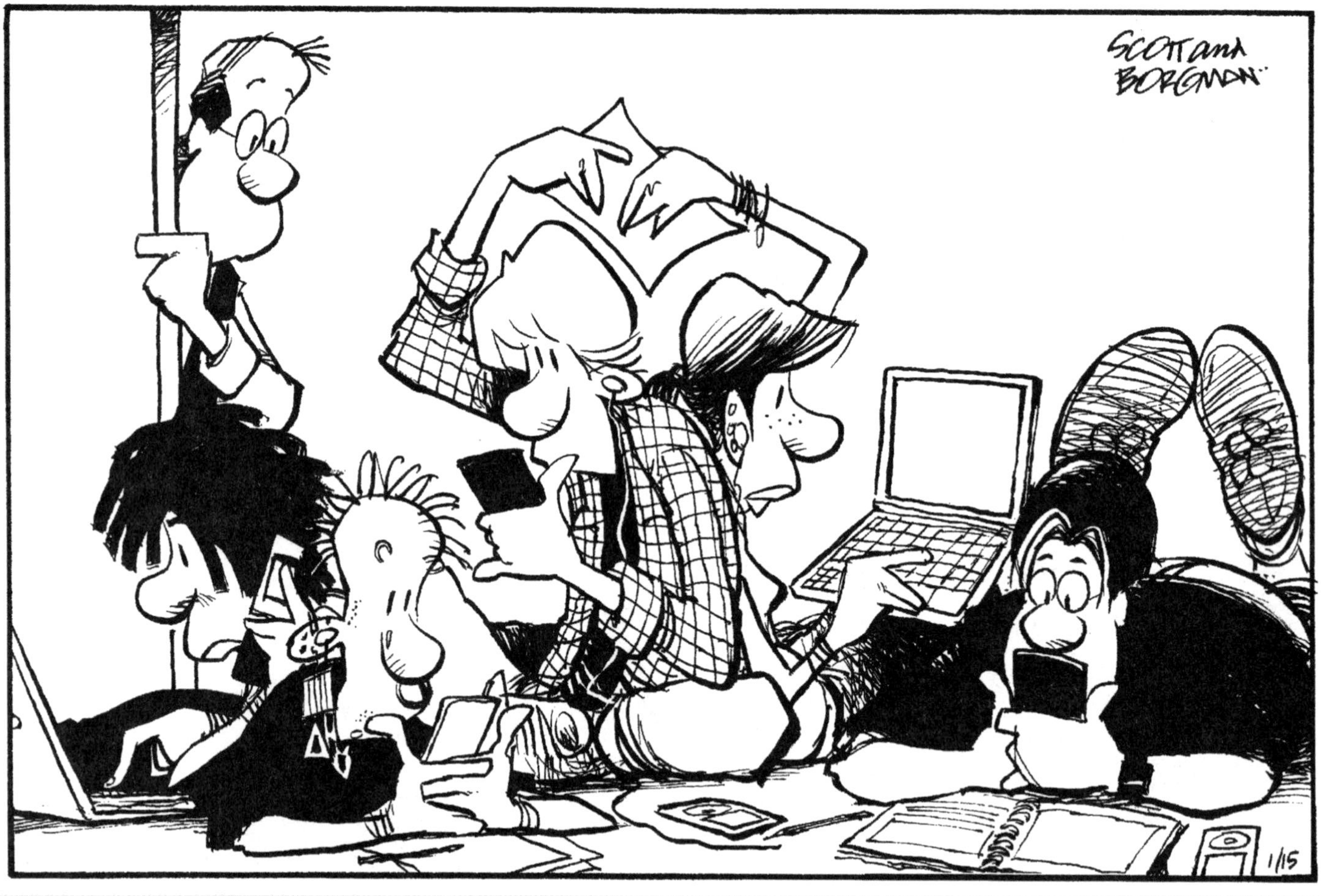
SCOTT and BORGMAN
1/15

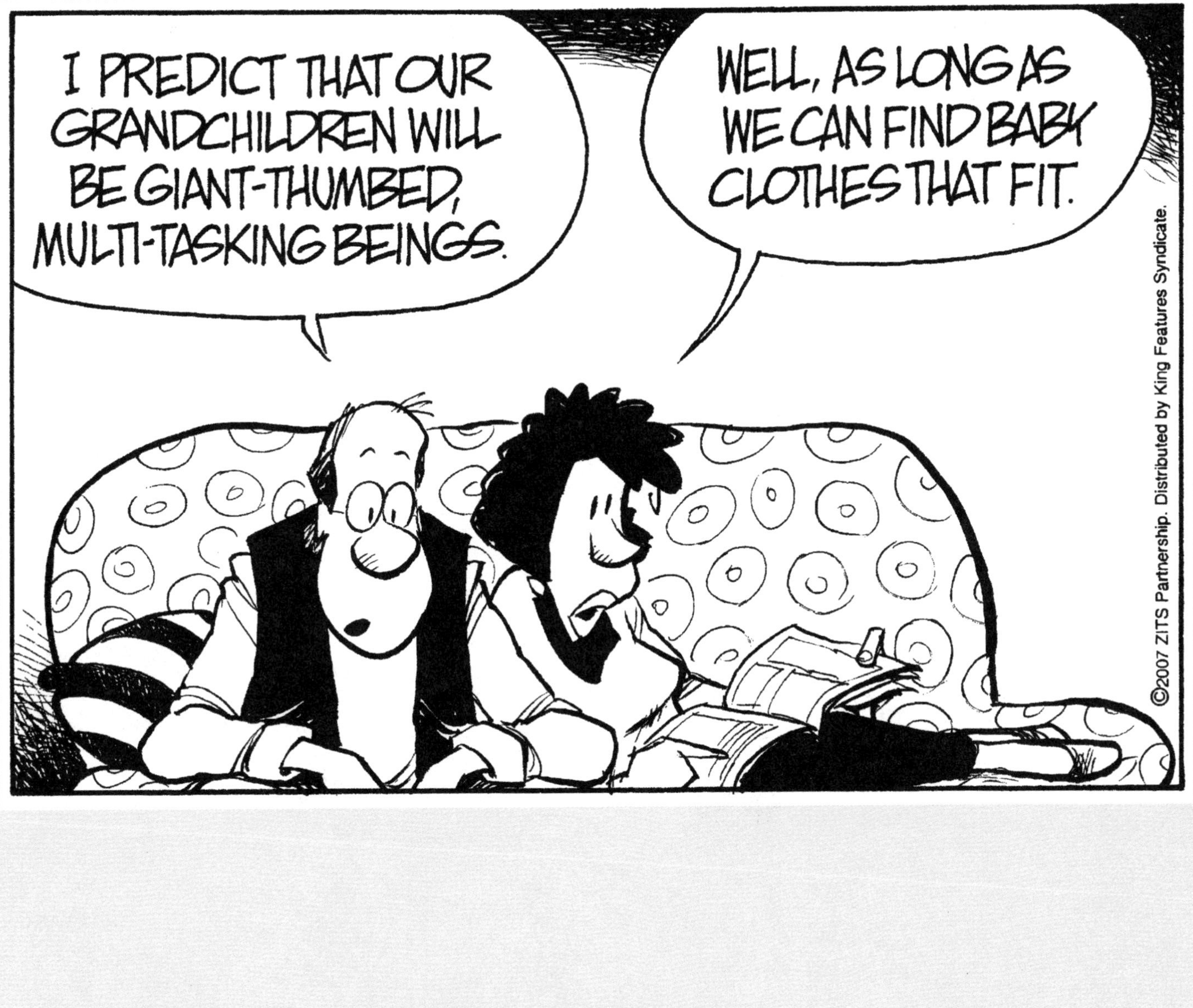
I PREDICT THAT OUR GRANDCHILDREN WILL BE GIANT-THUMBED, MULTI-TASKING BEINGS.
WELL, AS LONG AS WE CAN FIND BABY CLOTHES THAT FIT.
©2007 ZITS Partnership. Distributed by King Features Syndicate.

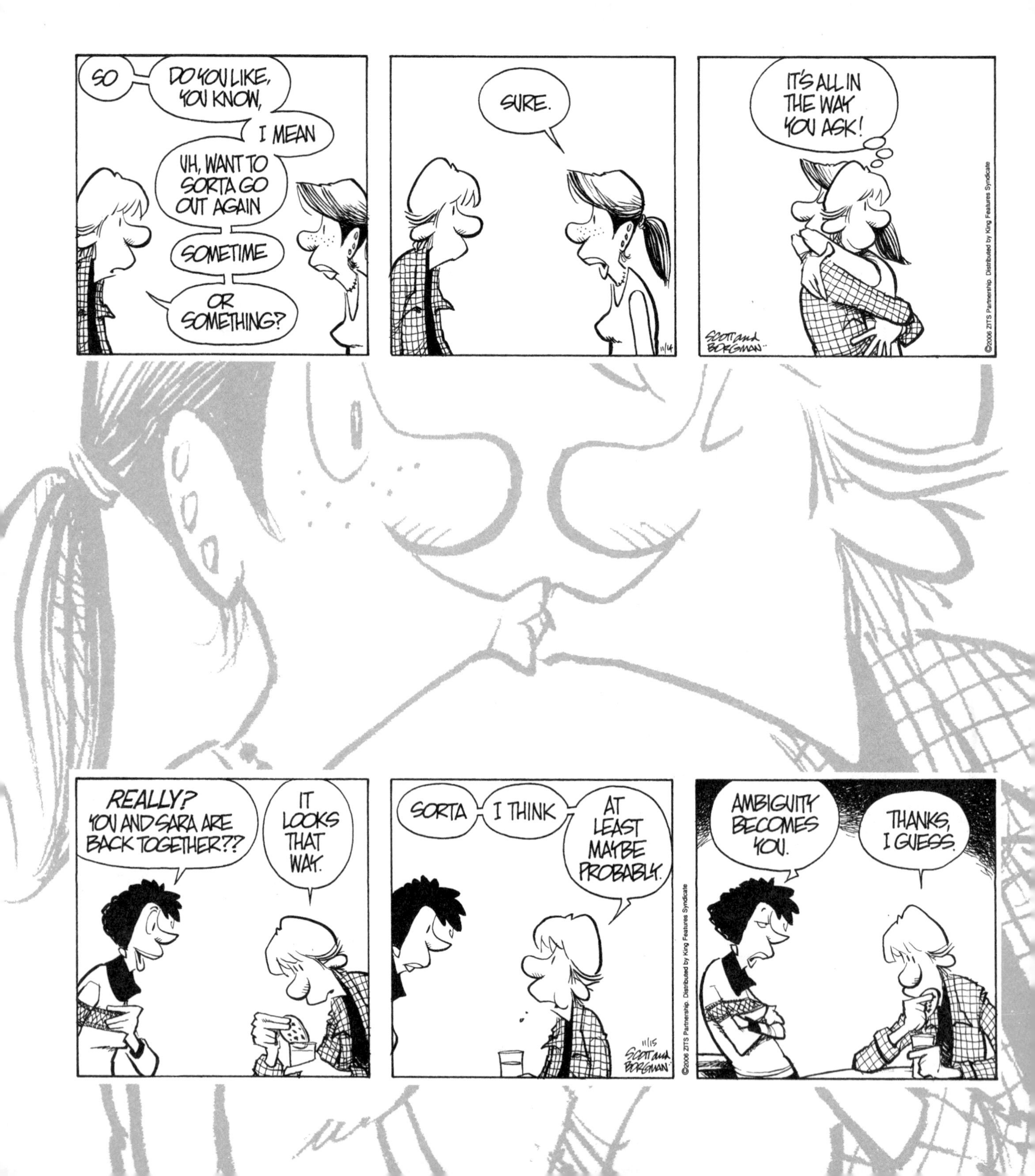

SO
DO YOU LIKE, YOU KNOW,
I MEAN
UH, WANT TO SORTA GO OUT AGAIN
SOMETIME
OR SOMETHING?
SURE.
11/14
IT'S ALL IN THE WAY YOU ASK!
SCOTT and BORGMAN
©2006 ZITS Partnership. Distributed by King Features Syndicate
REALLY? YOU AND SARA ARE BACK TOGETHER??
IT LOOKS THAT WAY.
SORTA
I THINK
AT LEAST MAYBE PROBABLY.
11/15
SCOTT and BORGMAN
©2006 ZITS Partnership. Distributed by King Features Syndicate
AMBIGUITY BECOMES YOU.
THANKS, I GUESS.

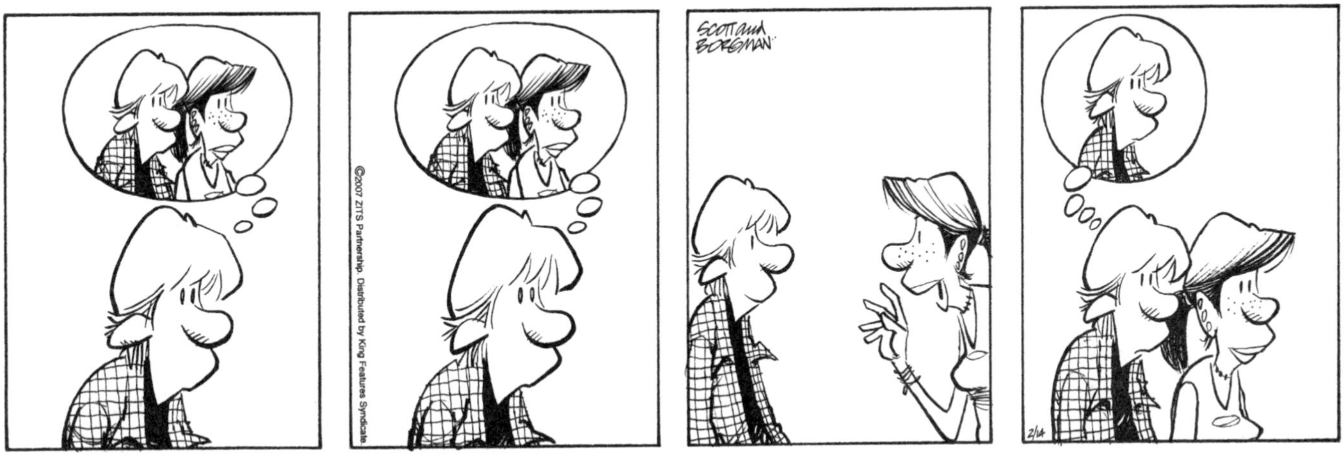
©2007 ZITS Partnership. Distributed by King Features Syndicate
2/14

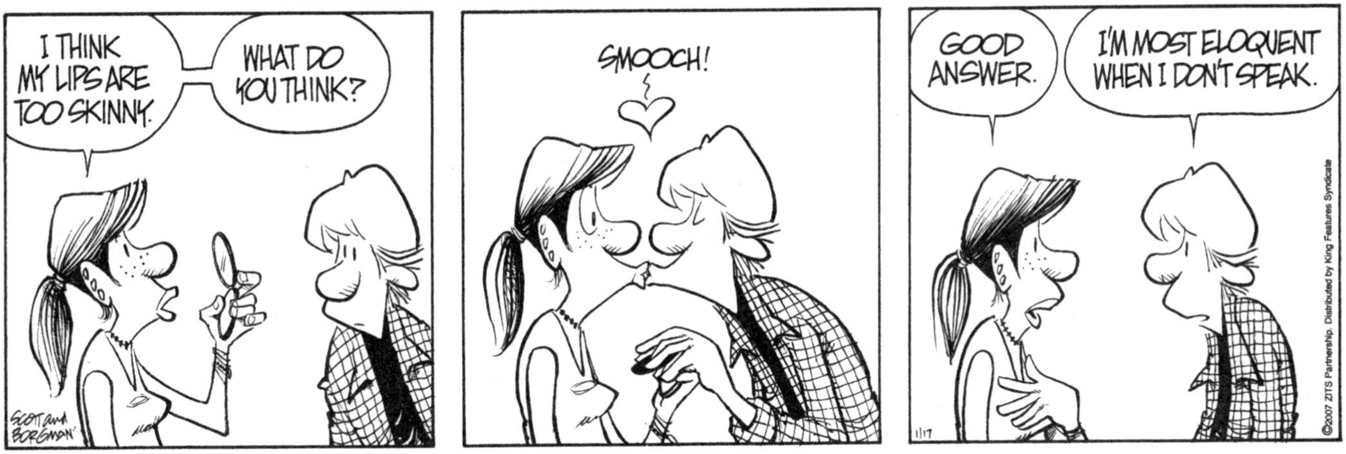
I THINK MY LIPS ARE TOO SKINNY.
WHAT DO YOU THINK?
SMOOCH!
GOOD ANSWER.
I'M MOST ELOQUENT WHEN I DON'T SPEAK.
1/17
©2007 ZITS Partnership. Distributed by King Features Syndicate

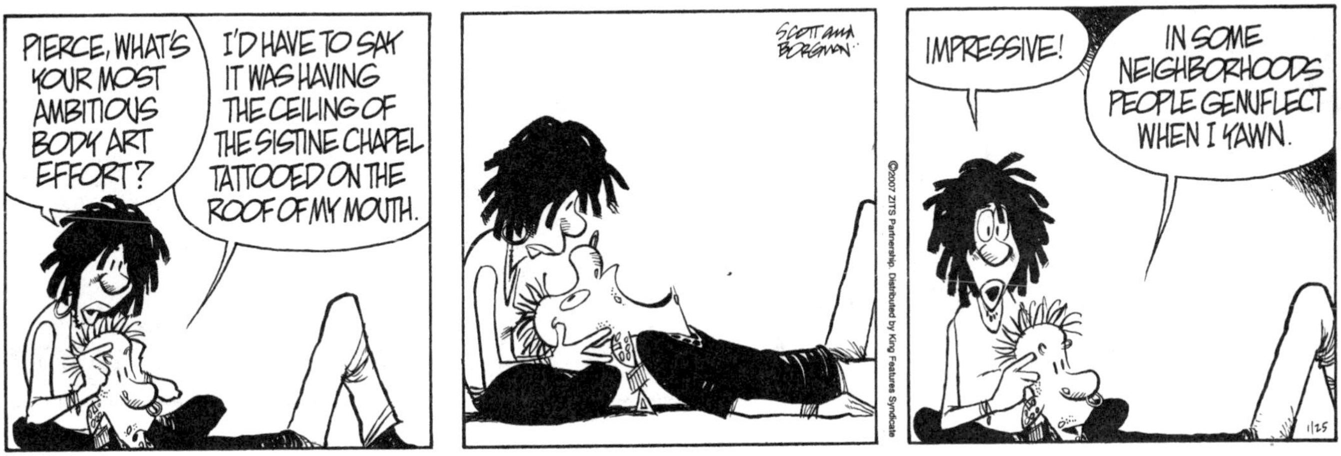
PIERCE, WHAT'S YOUR MOST AMBITIOUS BODY ART EFFORT?
I'D HAVE TO SAY IT WAS HAVING THE CEILING OF THE SISTINE CHAPEL TATTOOED ON THE ROOF OF MY MOUTH.
©2007 ZITS Partnership. Distributed by King Features Syndicate
IMPRESSIVE!
IN SOME NEIGHBORHOODS PEOPLE GENUFLECT WHEN I YAWN.
1/25

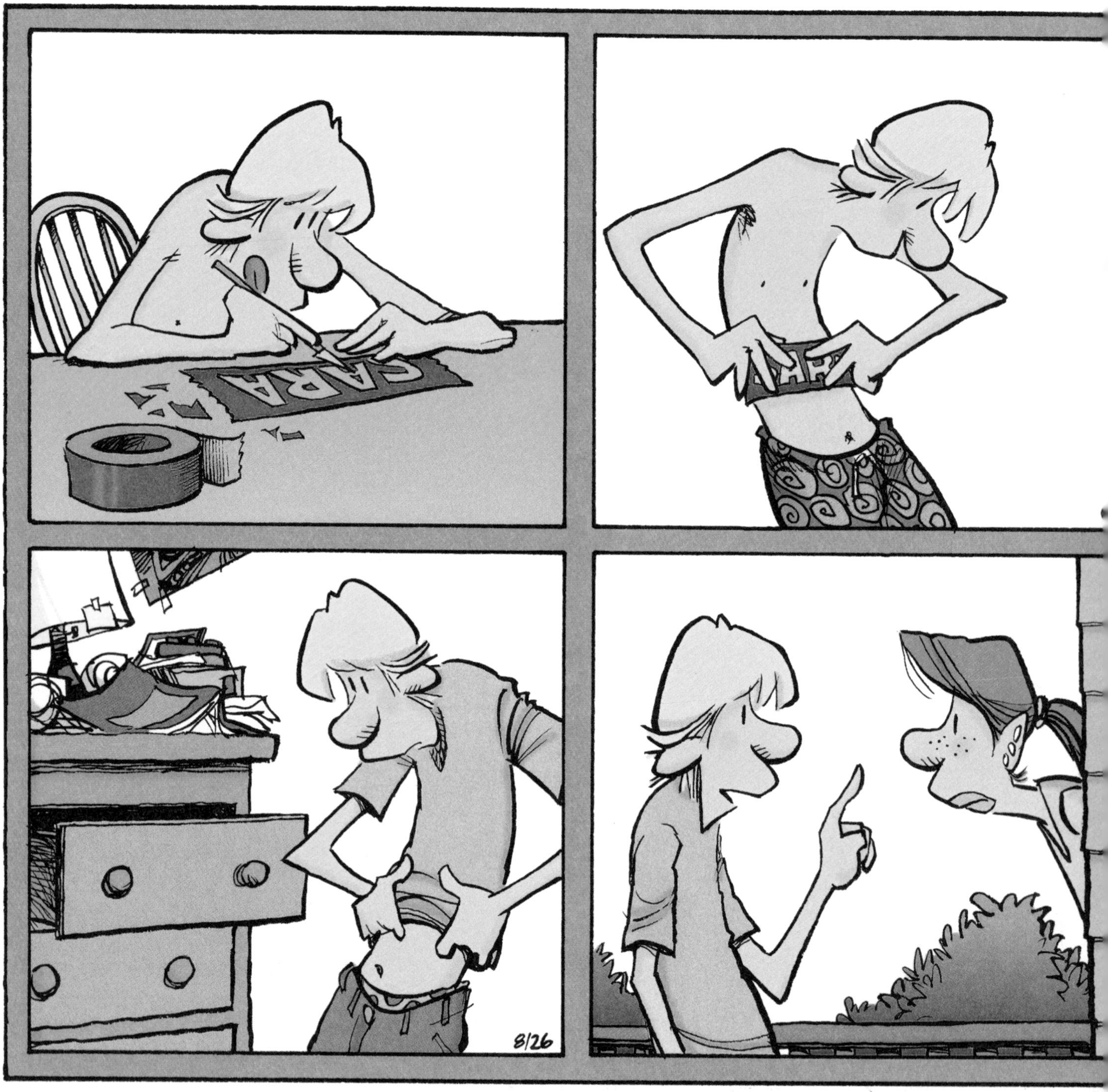
CARA
8/26

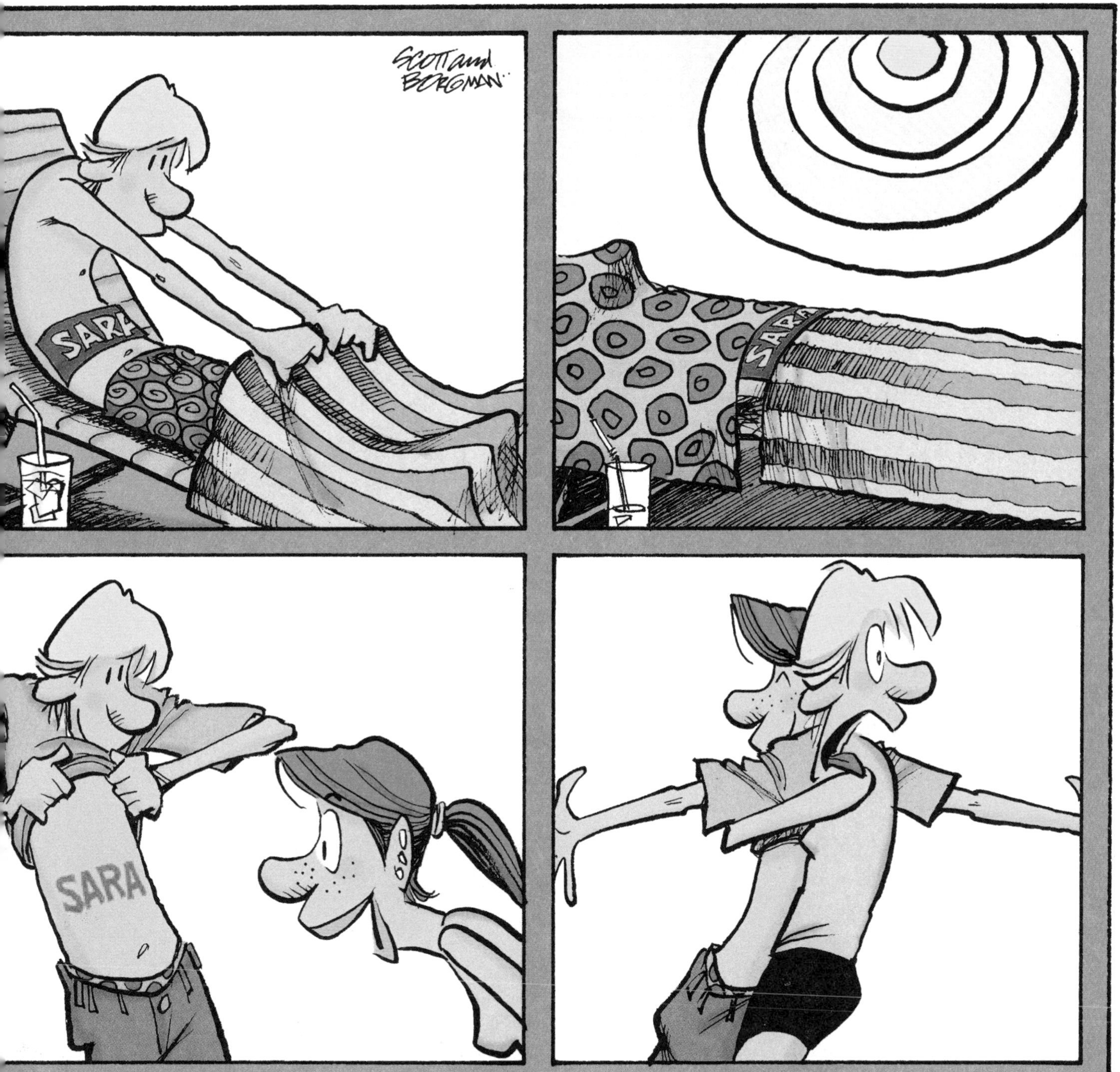
SCOTT and BORGMAN
SARA
SARA
SARA

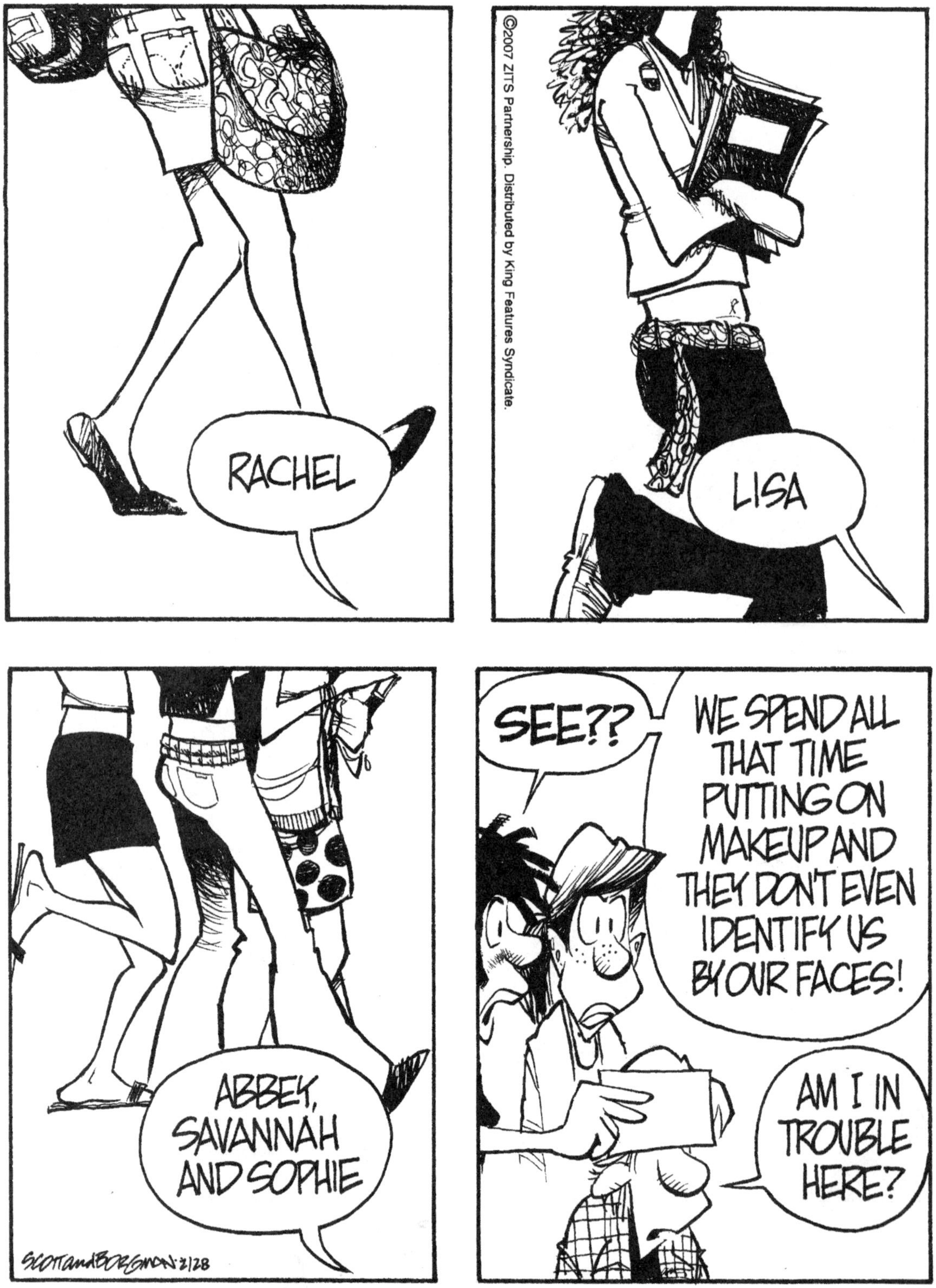
RACHEL
©2007 ZITS Partnership. Distributed by King Features Syndicate.
LISA
ABBEY, SAVANNAH AND SOPHIE
SCOTT and BORGMAN 2/28
SEE??
WE SPEND ALL THAT TIME PUTTING ON MAKEUP AND THEY DON'T EVEN IDENTIFY US BY OUR FACES!
AM I IN TROUBLE HERE?

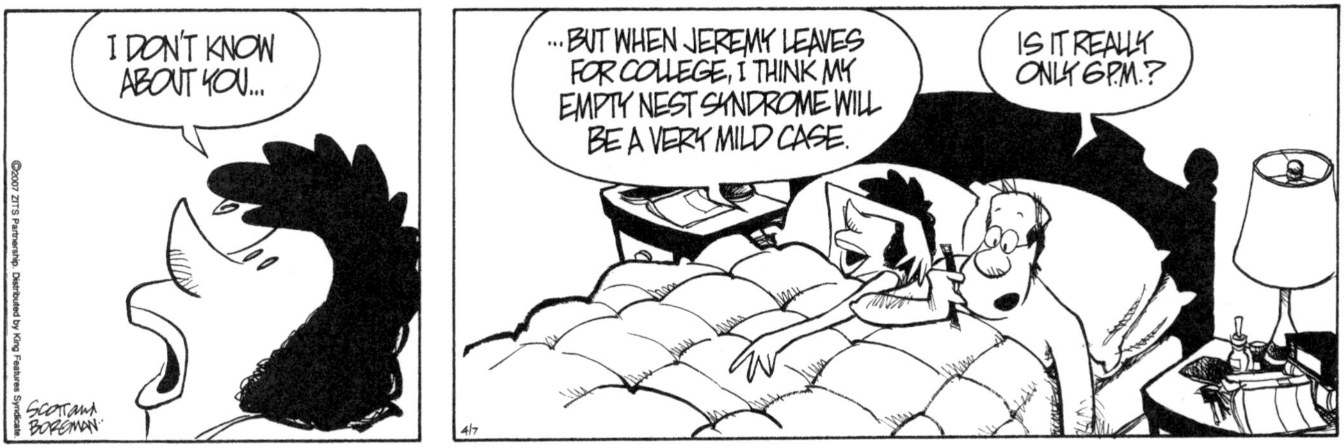
I DON'T KNOW ABOUT YOU...
©2007 ZITS Partnership. Distributed by King Features Syndicate.
...BUT WHEN JEREMY LEAVES FOR COLLEGE, I THINK MY EMPTY NEST SYNDROME WILL BE A VERY MILD CASE.
IS IT REALLY ONLY 6 P.M.?

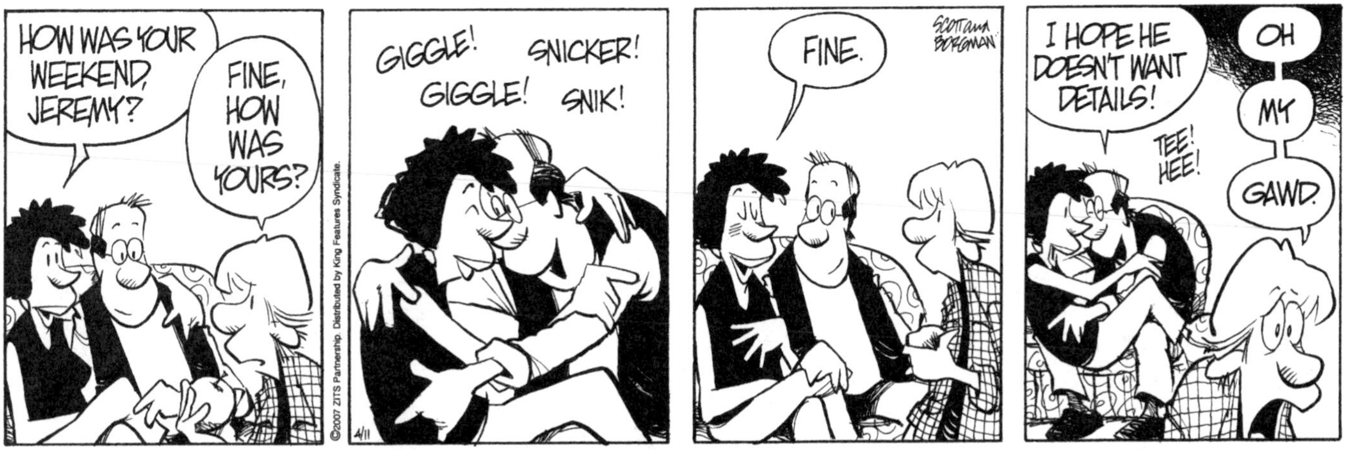
HOW WAS YOUR WEEKEND, JEREMY?
FINE, HOW WAS YOURS?
©2007 ZITS Partnership. Distributed by King Features Syndicate.
GIGGLE! SNICKER!
GIGGLE! SNIK!
FINE.
I HOPE HE DOESN'T WANT DETAILS!
TEE! HEE!
OH
MY
GAWD.

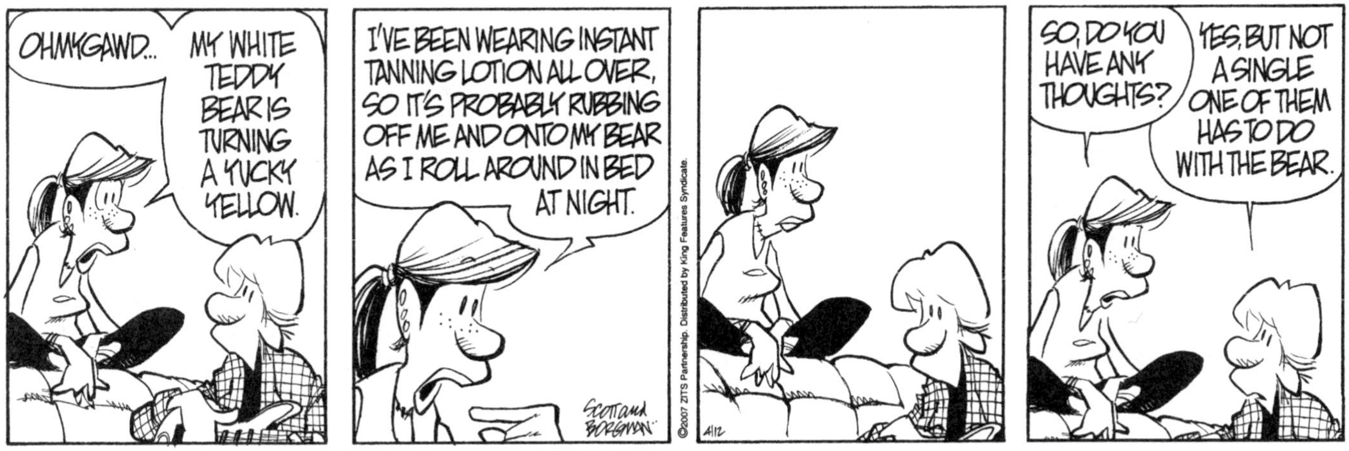
OHMYGAWD...
MY WHITE TEDDY BEAR IS TURNING A YUCKY YELLOW.
I'VE BEEN WEARING INSTANT TANNING LOTION ALL OVER, SO IT'S PROBABLY RUBBING OFF ME AND ONTO MY BEAR AS I ROLL AROUND IN BED AT NIGHT.
©2007 ZITS Partnership. Distributed by King Features Syndicate.
SO, DO YOU HAVE ANY THOUGHTS?
YES, BUT NOT A SINGLE ONE OF THEM HAS TO DO WITH THE BEAR.

Zits
by
JERRY SCOTT and
JIM BORGMAN

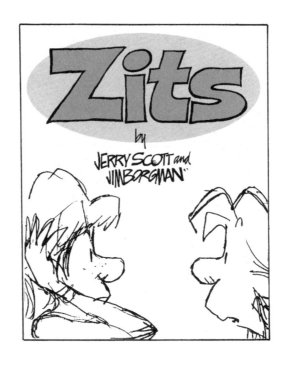

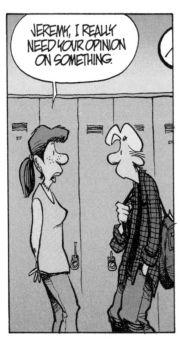

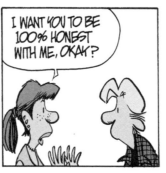

JEREMY, I REALLY NEED YOUR OPINION ON SOMETHING.
I WANT YOU TO BE 100% HONEST WITH ME, OKAY?
I'M NOT LOOKING FOR MORAL SUPPORT, JUST HONESTY.
COMPLETE
TOTAL
HONESTY.
OKAY
HERE GOES
DOES MY HAIR LOOK BETTER UP, OR DOWN?
I DON'T KNOW. I HARDLY EVER LOOK AT YOU ABOVE THE NECK.
THERE'S HONESTY AND THEN THERE'S TRANSPARENCY
©2003 ZITS Partnership. Distributed by King Features Syndicate.

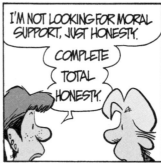

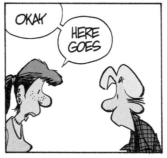

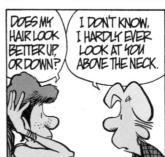

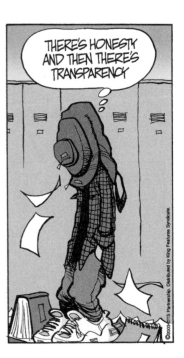

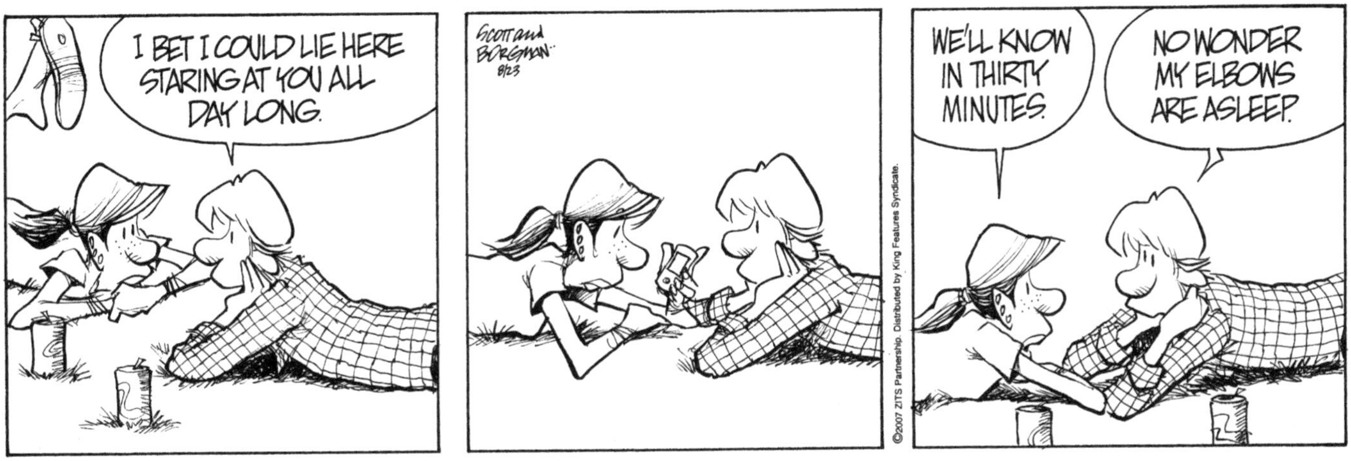
I BET I COULD LIE HERE STARING AT YOU ALL DAY LONG.
SCOTT and BORGMAN 8/23
WE'LL KNOW IN THIRTY MINUTES.
NO WONDER MY ELBOWS ARE ASLEEP.
©2007 ZITS Partnership. Distributed by King Features Syndicate.

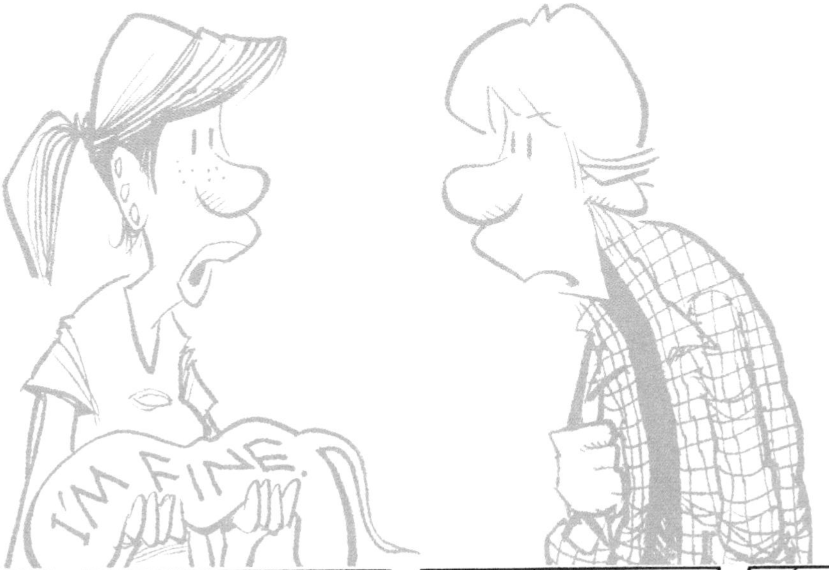
I'M FINE.

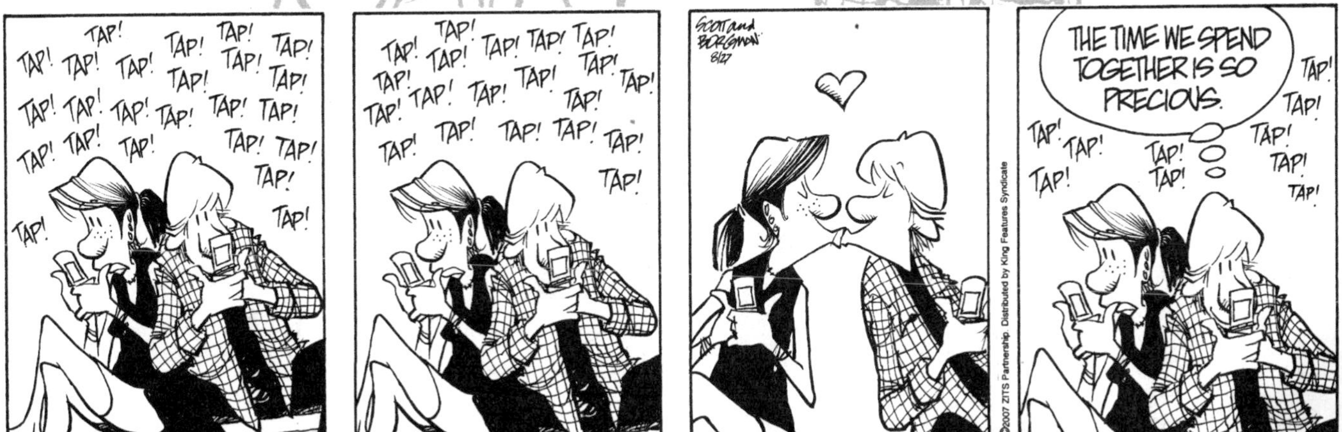
TAP! TAP! TAP! TAP! TAP! TAP! TAP! TAP! TAP! TAP! TAP! TAP! TAP! TAP! TAP! TAP! TAP! TAP! TAP! TAP! TAP! TAP! TAP! TAP!
TAP! TAP! TAP! TAP! TAP! TAP! TAP! TAP! TAP! TAP! TAP! TAP! TAP! TAP! TAP! TAP! TAP! TAP! TAP! TAP! TAP!
SCOTT and BORGMAN 8/27
THE TIME WE SPEND TOGETHER IS SO PRECIOUS.
TAP! TAP! TAP! TAP! TAP! TAP! TAP! TAP! TAP! TAP!
©2007 ZITS Partnership. Distributed by King Features Syndicate

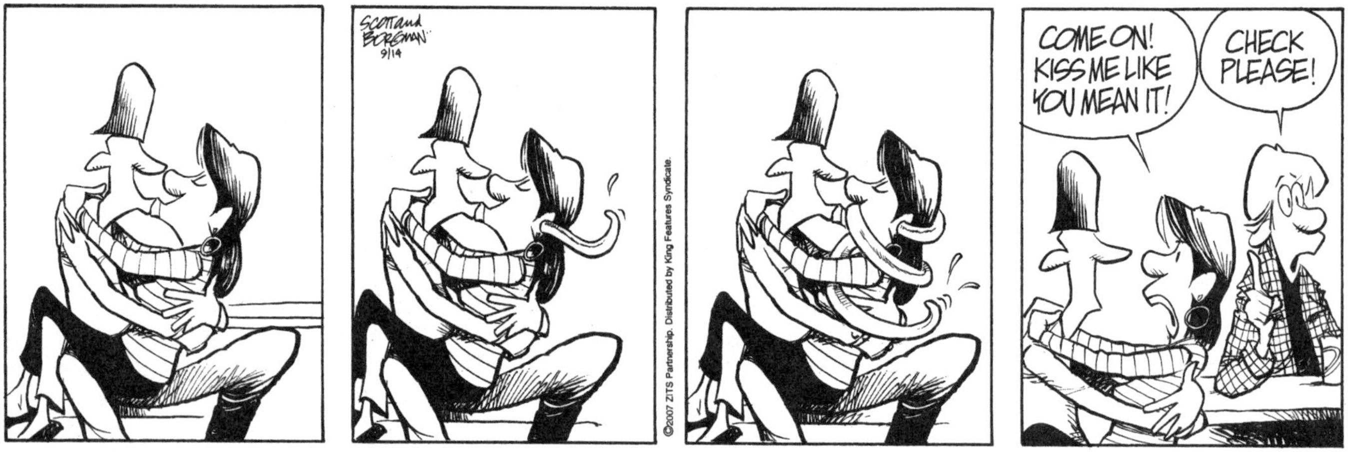
SCOTT and BORGMAN
9/14
©2007 ZITS Partnership. Distributed by King Features Syndicate.
COME ON! KISS ME LIKE YOU MEAN IT!
CHECK PLEASE!

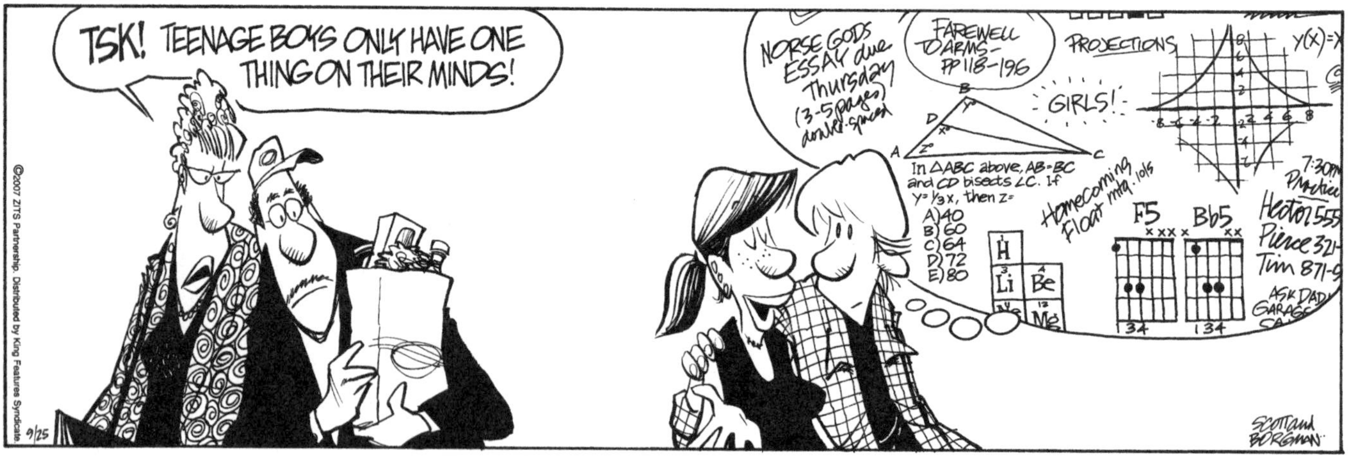
TSK! TEENAGE BOYS ONLY HAVE ONE THING ON THEIR MINDS!
NORSE GODS ESSAY due Thursday (3-5 pages) double-spaced
FAREWELL TO ARMS - PP 118-196
PROJECTIONS
GIRLS!
Homecoming Float mtg. 10:15
F5
Bb5
7:30PM Practice
Hector 555
Pierce 321
Tim 871
ASK DAD GARAGE
©2007 ZITS Partnership. Distributed by King Features Syndicate.
9/25
SCOTT and BORGMAN

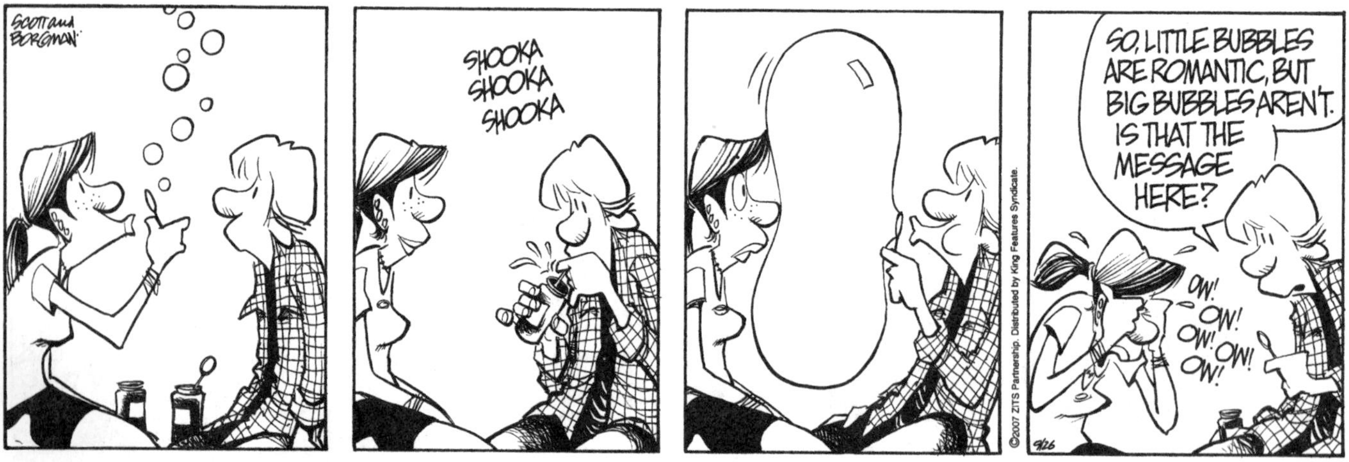
SCOTT and BORGMAN
SHOOKA SHOOKA SHOOKA
©2007 ZITS Partnership. Distributed by King Features Syndicate.
SO, LITTLE BUBBLES ARE ROMANTIC, BUT BIG BUBBLES AREN'T. IS THAT THE MESSAGE HERE?
OW! OW! OW! OW! OW!
9/26

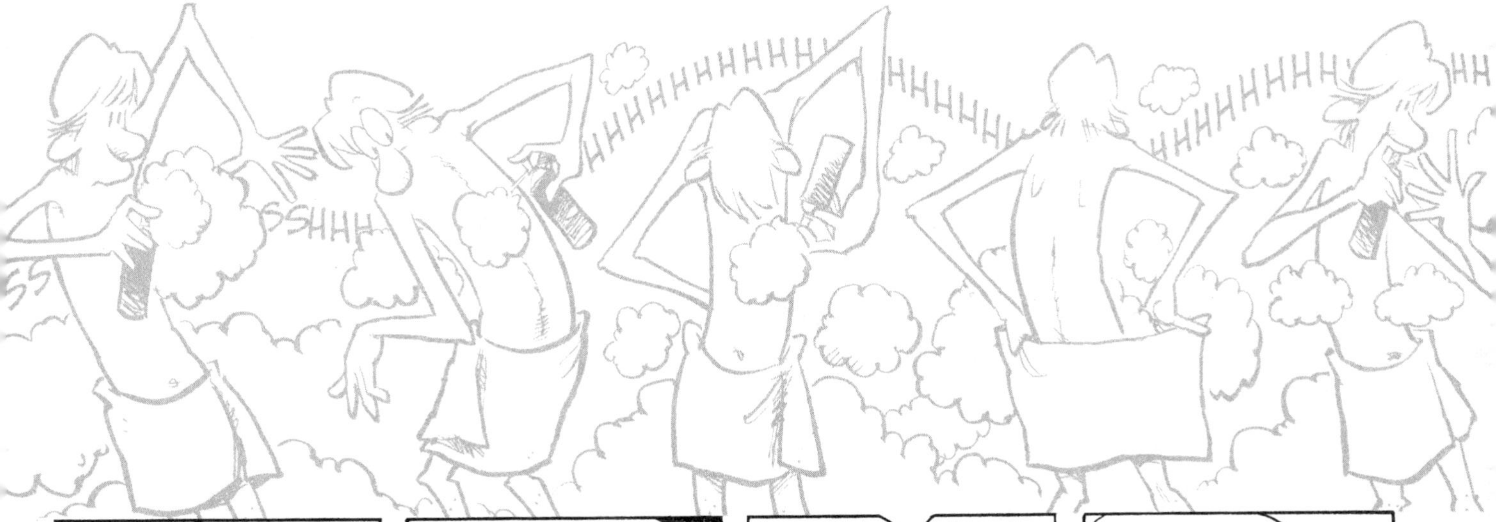

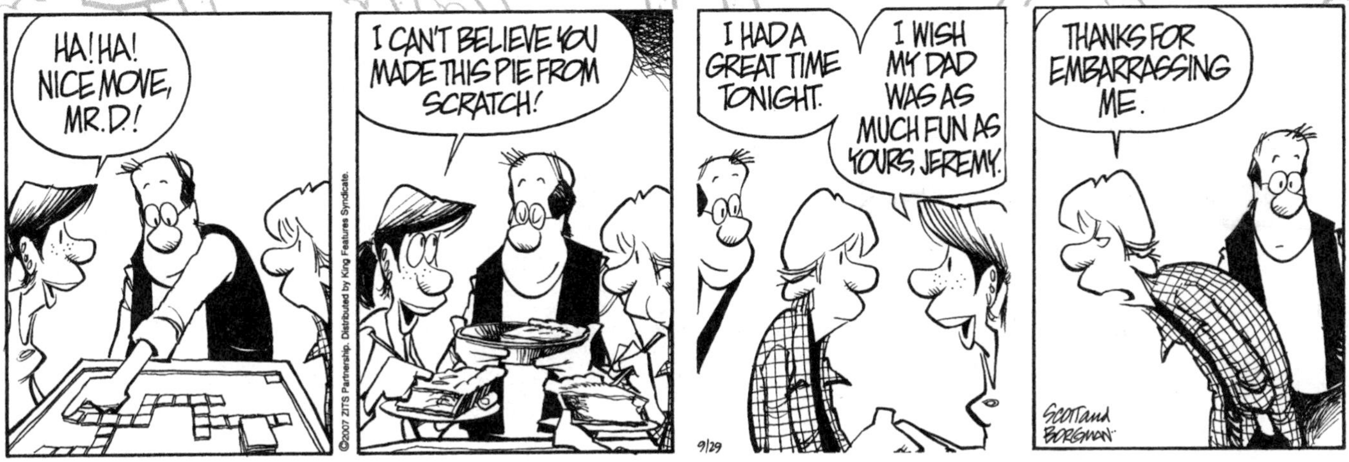
HA! HA! NICE MOVE, MR. D.!
©2007 ZITS Partnership. Distributed by King Features Syndicate.
I CAN'T BELIEVE YOU MADE THIS PIE FROM SCRATCH!
I HAD A GREAT TIME TONIGHT.
I WISH MY DAD WAS AS MUCH FUN AS YOURS, JEREMY.
9/29
THANKS FOR EMBARRASSING ME.
SCOTT and BORGMAN

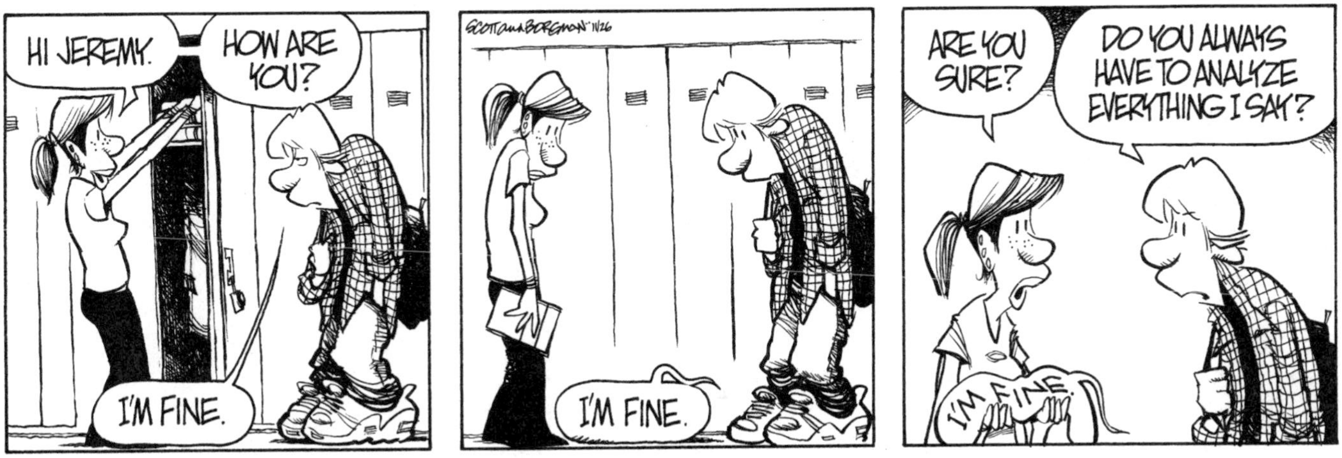
HI JEREMY.
HOW ARE YOU?
I'M FINE.
SCOTT and BORGMAN 11/26
I'M FINE.
ARE YOU SURE?
DO YOU ALWAYS HAVE TO ANALYZE EVERYTHING I SAY?
I'M FINE.

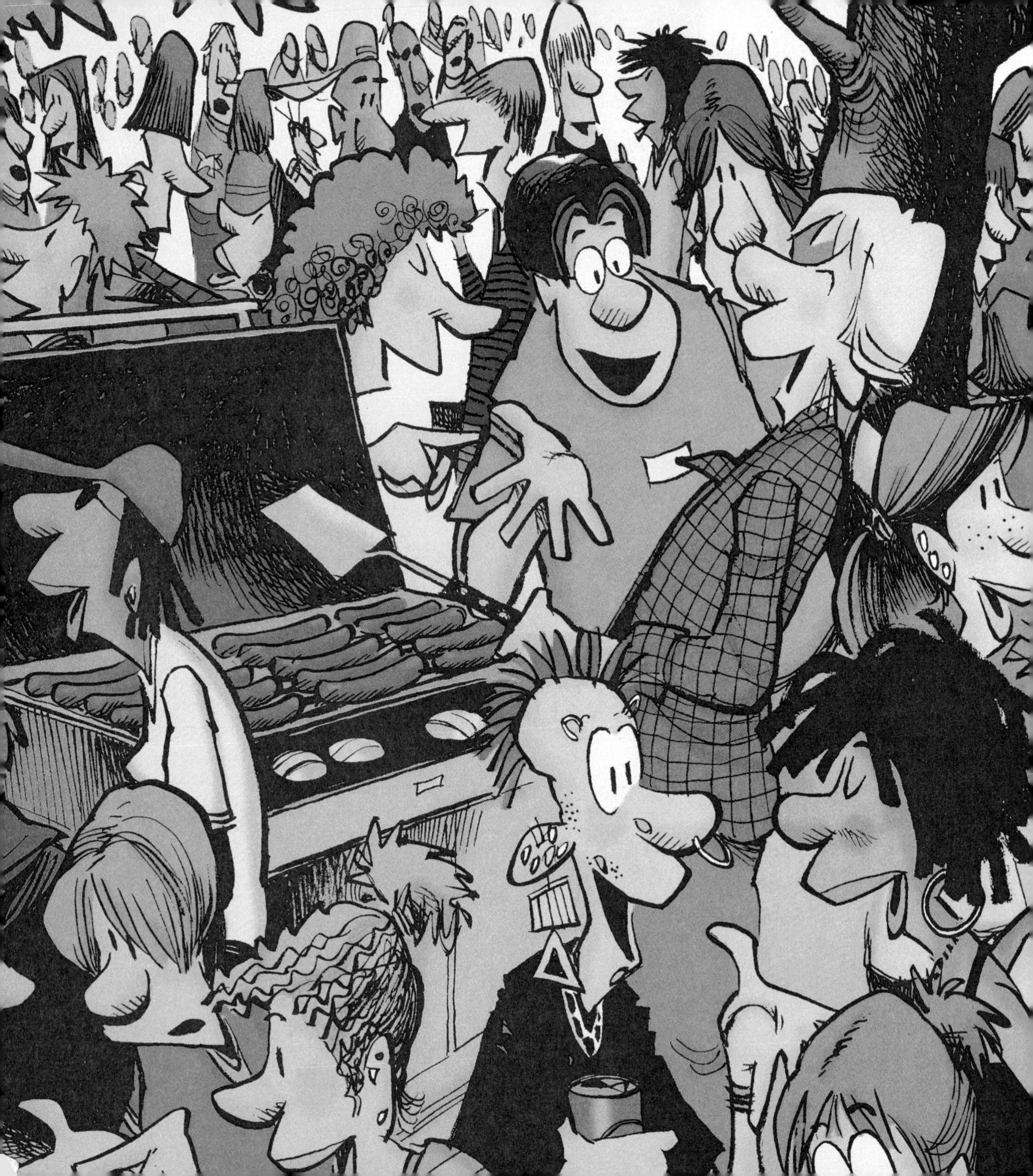

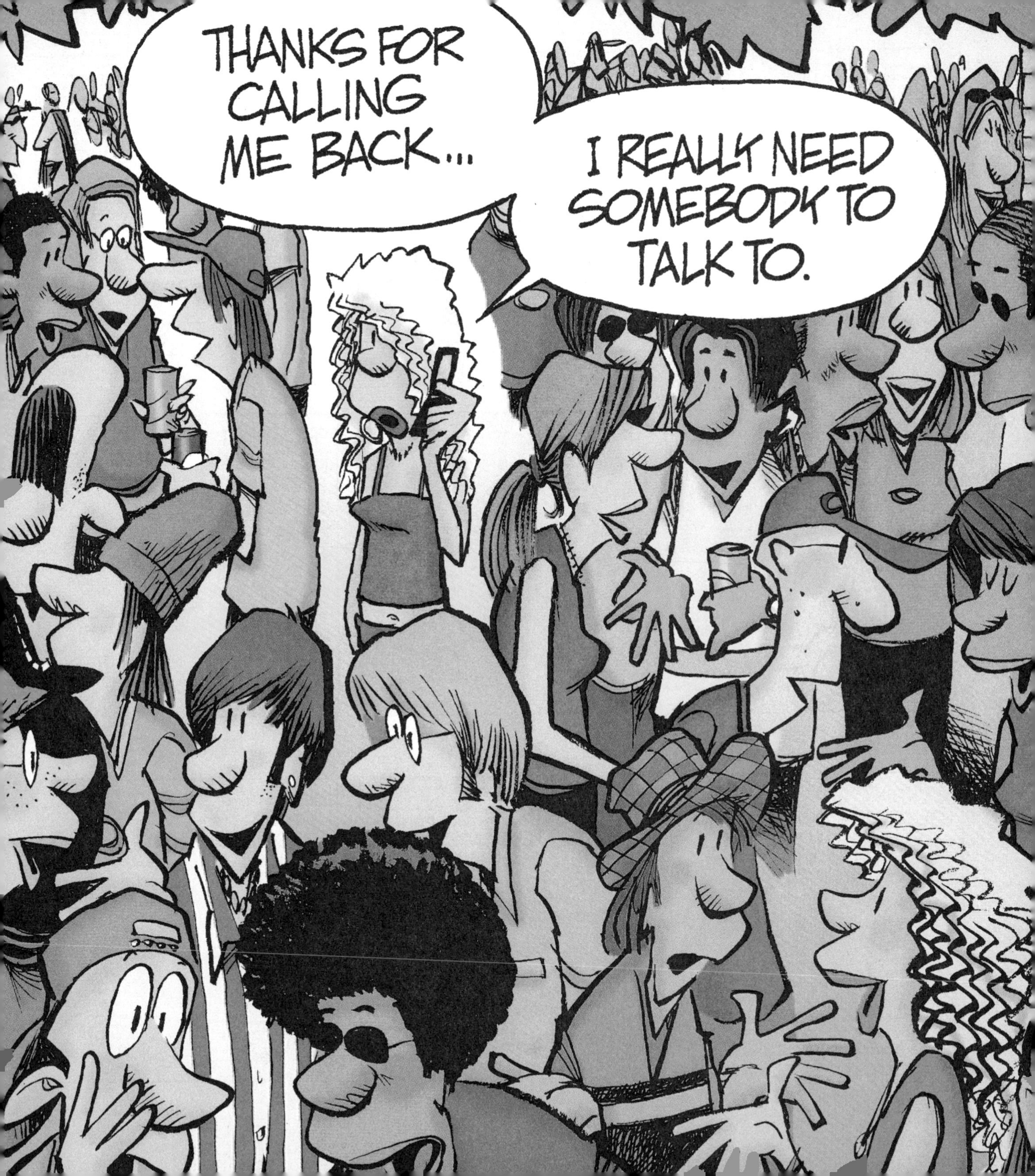
THANKS FOR CALLING ME BACK...
I REALLY NEED SOMEBODY TO TALK TO.

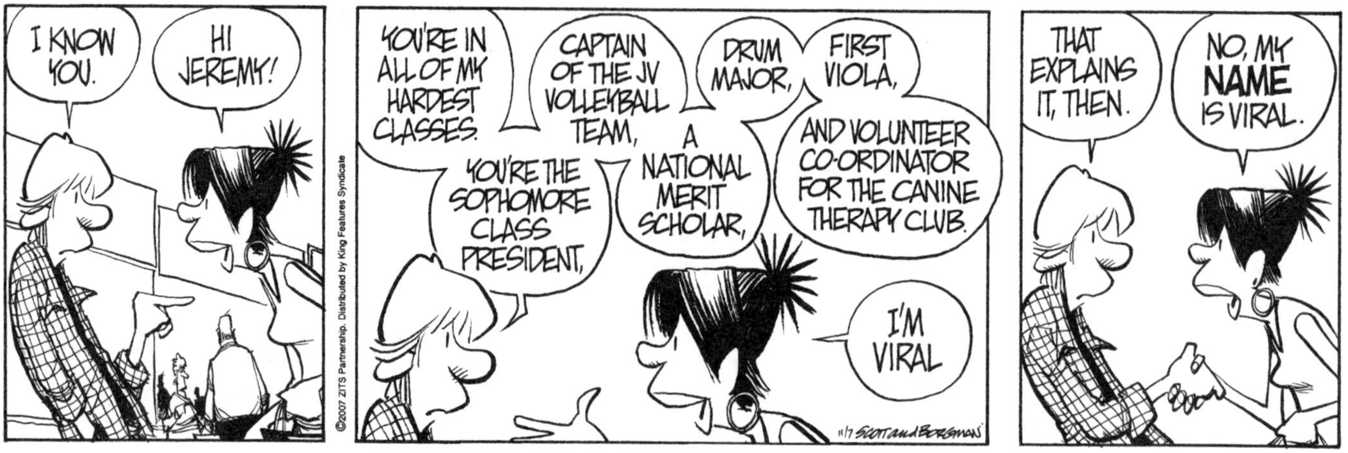
I KNOW YOU.
HI JEREMY!
YOU'RE IN ALL OF MY HARDEST CLASSES.
CAPTAIN OF THE JV VOLLEYBALL TEAM,
DRUM MAJOR,
FIRST VIOLA,
YOU'RE THE SOPHOMORE CLASS PRESIDENT,
A NATIONAL MERIT SCHOLAR,
AND VOLUNTEER CO-ORDINATOR FOR THE CANINE THERAPY CLUB.
I'M VIRAL
©2007 ZITS Partnership. Distributed by King Features Syndicate
11/7 SCOTT and BORGMAN
THAT EXPLAINS IT, THEN.
NO, MY NAME IS VIRAL.

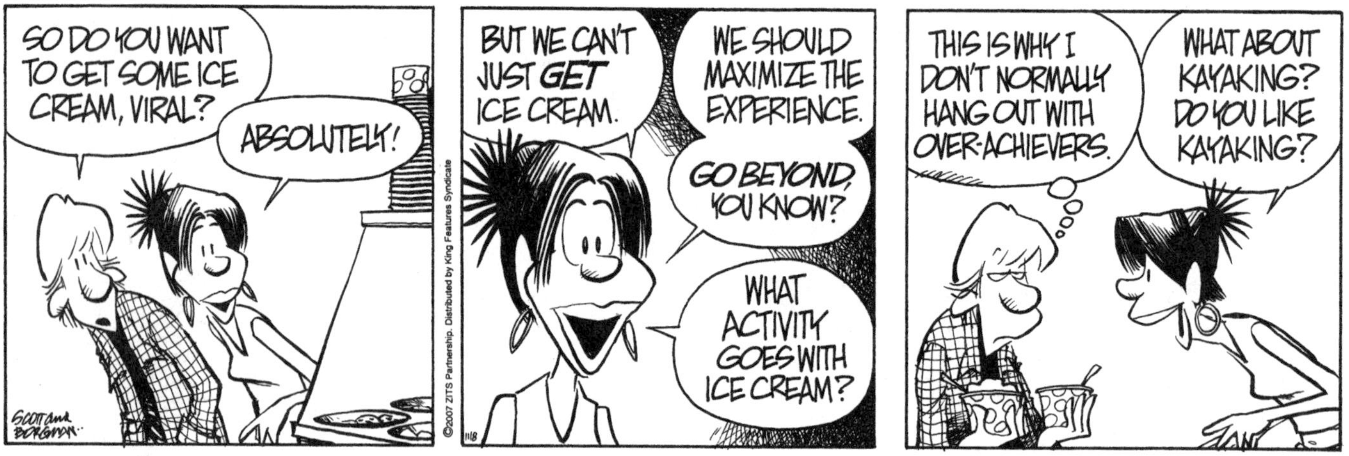
SO DO YOU WANT TO GET SOME ICE CREAM, VIRAL?
ABSOLUTELY!
SCOTT and BORGMAN
BUT WE CAN'T JUST GET ICE CREAM.
WE SHOULD MAXIMIZE THE EXPERIENCE.
GO BEYOND, YOU KNOW?
WHAT ACTIVITY GOES WITH ICE CREAM?
©2007 ZITS Partnership. Distributed by King Features Syndicate
11/8
THIS IS WHY I DON'T NORMALLY HANG OUT WITH OVER-ACHIEVERS.
WHAT ABOUT KAYAKING? DO YOU LIKE KAYAKING?

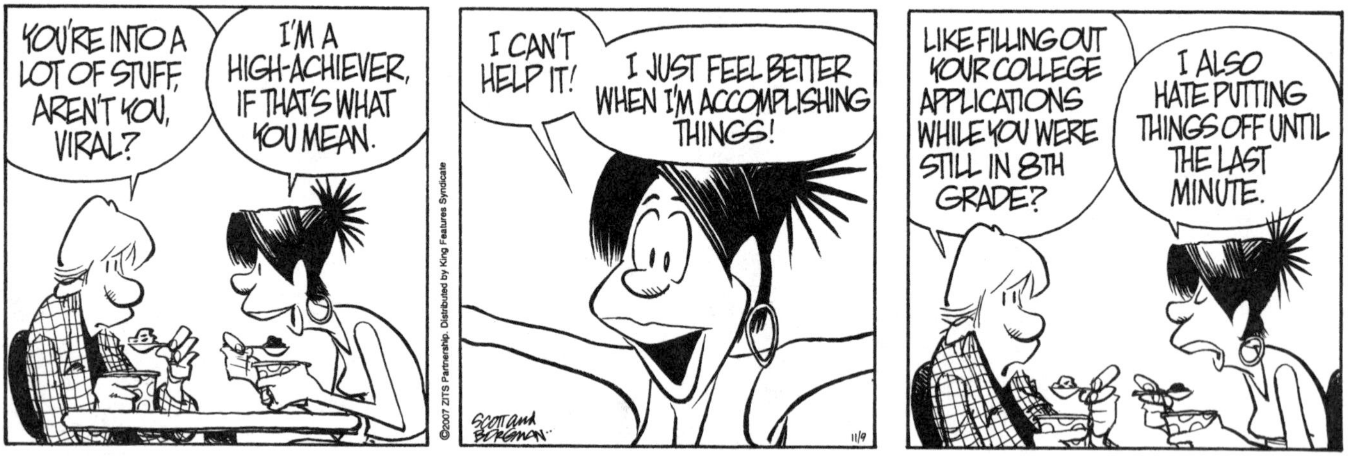
YOU'RE INTO A LOT OF STUFF, AREN'T YOU, VIRAL?
I'M A HIGH-ACHIEVER, IF THAT'S WHAT YOU MEAN.
©2007 ZITS Partnership. Distributed by King Features Syndicate
I CAN'T HELP IT!
I JUST FEEL BETTER WHEN I'M ACCOMPLISHING THINGS!
SCOTT and BORGMAN
11/9
LIKE FILLING OUT YOUR COLLEGE APPLICATIONS WHILE YOU WERE STILL IN 8TH GRADE?
I ALSO HATE PUTTING THINGS OFF UNTIL THE LAST MINUTE.

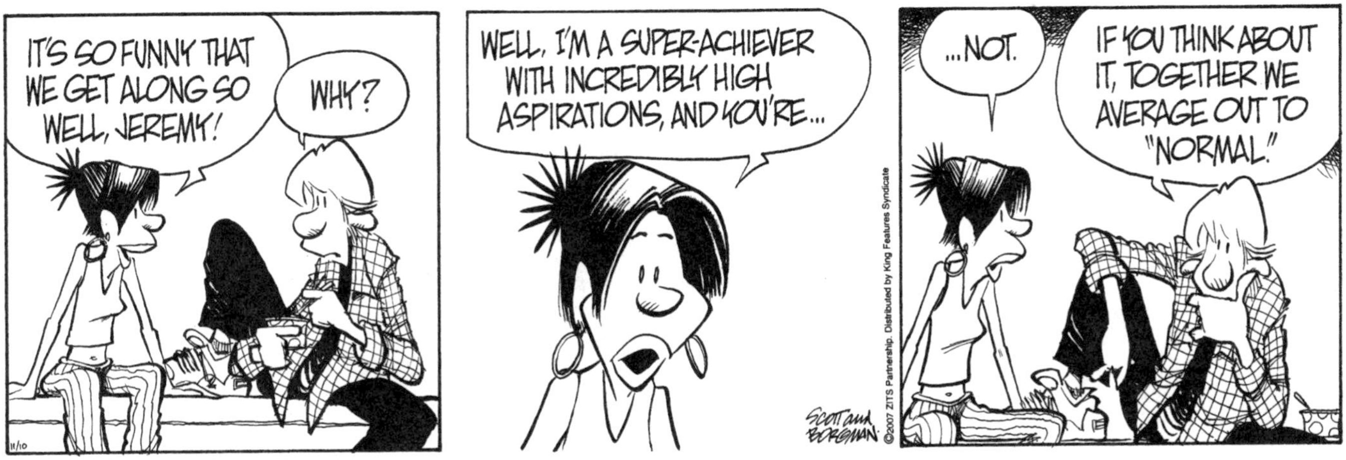
IT'S SO FUNNY THAT WE GET ALONG SO WELL, JEREMY!
WHY?
WELL, I'M A SUPER-ACHIEVER WITH INCREDIBLY HIGH ASPIRATIONS, AND YOU'RE...
...NOT.
IF YOU THINK ABOUT IT, TOGETHER WE AVERAGE OUT TO "NORMAL."
SCOTT and BORGMAN
©2007 ZITS Partnership. Distributed by King Features Syndicate

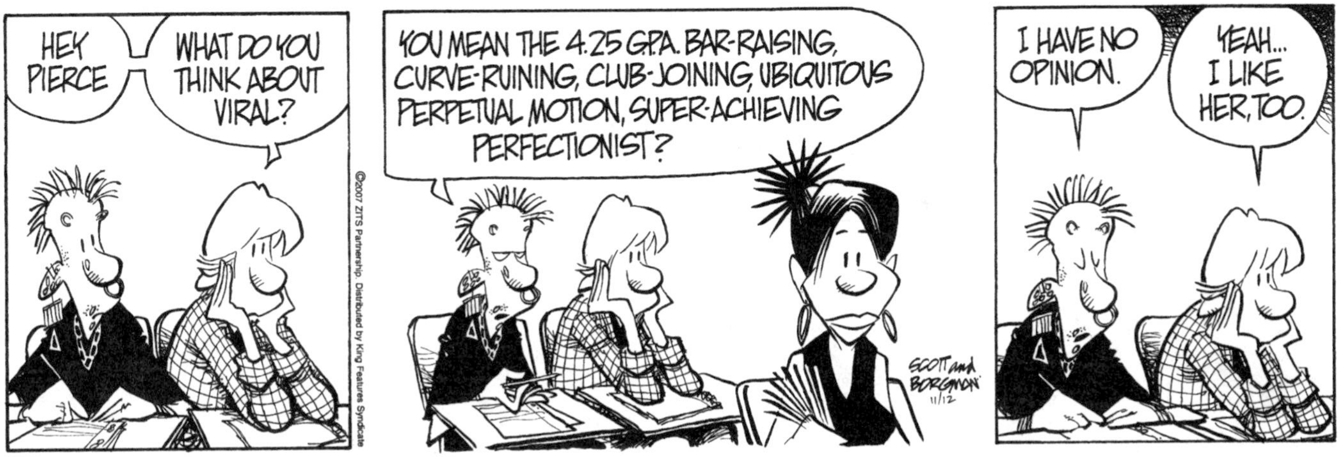
HEY PIERCE
WHAT DO YOU THINK ABOUT VIRAL?
YOU MEAN THE 4.25 G.P.A. BAR-RAISING, CURVE-RUINING, CLUB-JOINING, UBIQUITOUS PERPETUAL MOTION, SUPER-ACHIEVING PERFECTIONIST?
I HAVE NO OPINION.
YEAH... I LIKE HER, TOO.
SCOTT and BORGMAN
©2007 ZITS Partnership. Distributed by King Features Syndicate

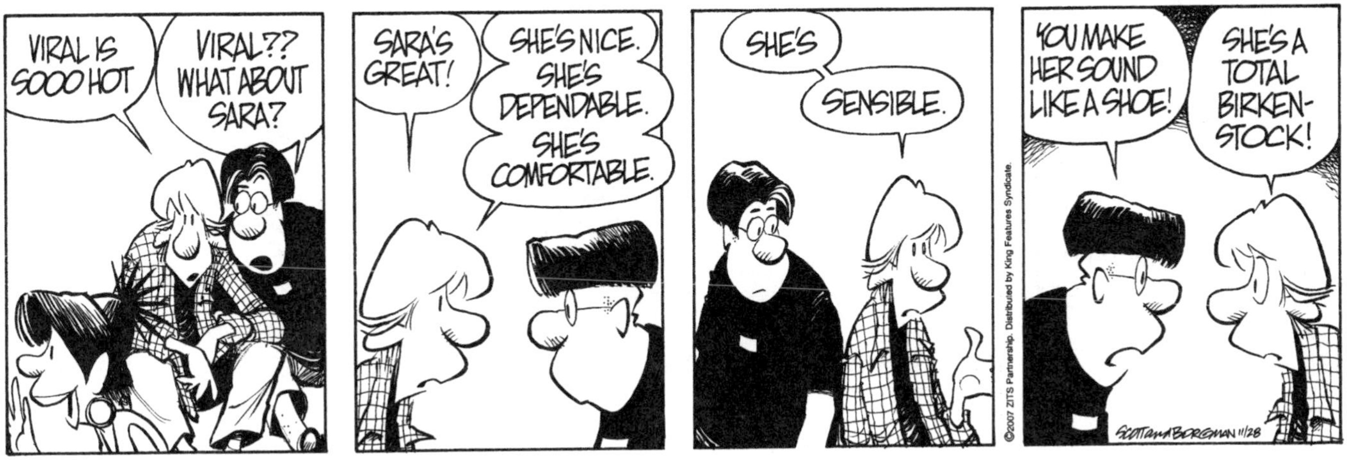
VIRAL IS SOOO HOT
VIRAL?? WHAT ABOUT SARA?
SARA'S GREAT!
SHE'S NICE. SHE'S DEPENDABLE. SHE'S COMFORTABLE.
SHE'S
SENSIBLE.
YOU MAKE HER SOUND LIKE A SHOE!
SHE'S A TOTAL BIRKEN-STOCK!
SCOTT and BORGMAN
©2007 ZITS Partnership. Distributed by King Features Syndicate.

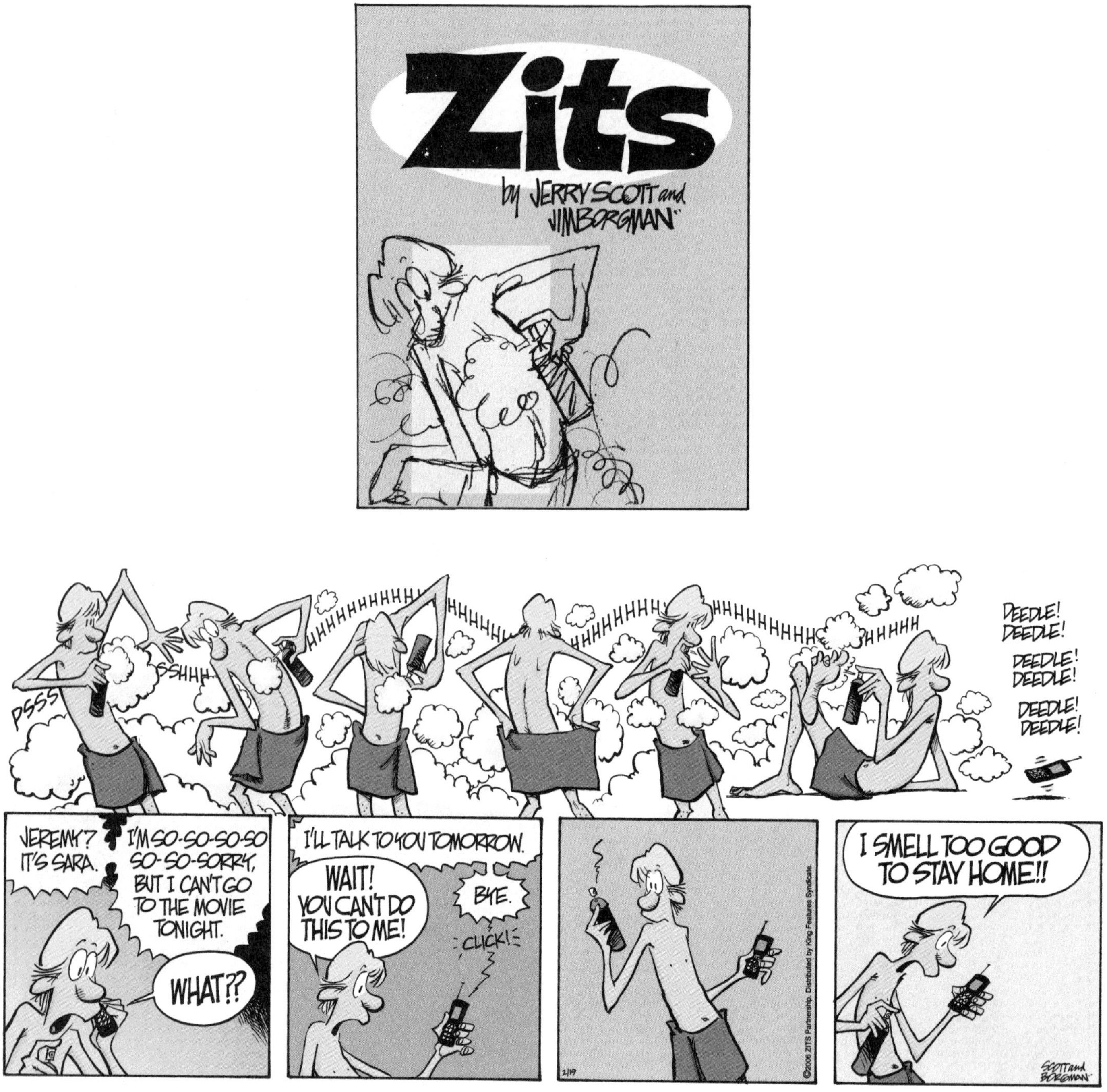

Zits
by JERRY SCOTT and JIM BORGMAN
PSSS
SSHHH
HHHHHHHHHHHHHHHHHHHHHHHHHHHHHHHHHHHHHHHHHHHH
DEEDLE! DEEDLE!
DEEDLE! DEEDLE!
DEEDLE! DEEDLE!
JEREMY? IT'S SARA.
I'M SO-SO-SO-SO SO-SO-SORRY, BUT I CAN'T GO TO THE MOVIE TONIGHT.
WHAT??
I'LL TALK TO YOU TOMORROW.
WAIT! YOU CAN'T DO THIS TO ME!
BYE.
CLICK!
I SMELL TOO GOOD TO STAY HOME!!
SCOTT and BORGMAN

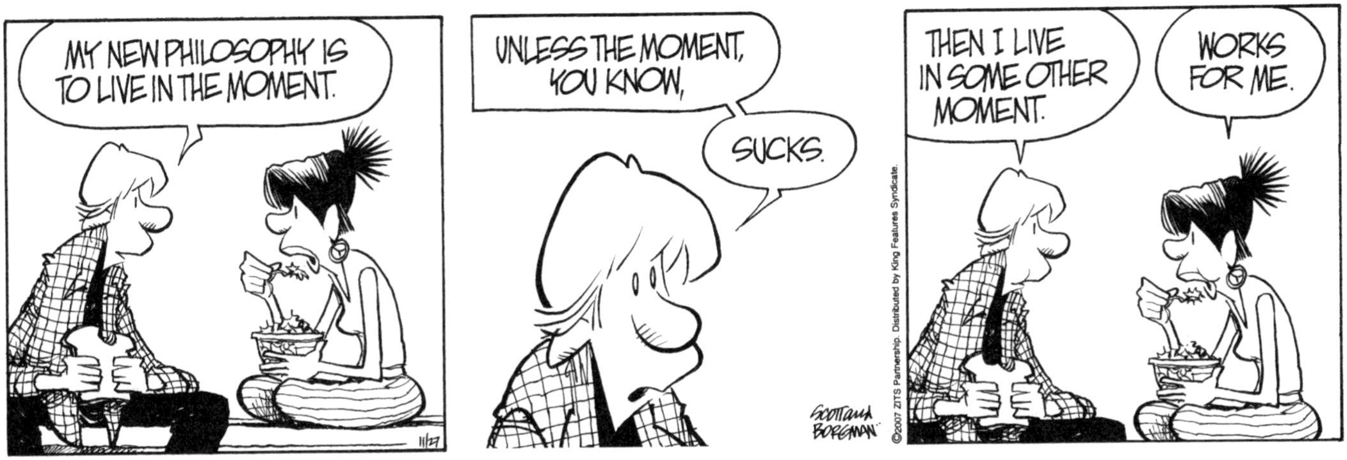
MY NEW PHILOSOPHY IS TO LIVE IN THE MOMENT.
UNLESS THE MOMENT, YOU KNOW,
SUCKS.
THEN I LIVE IN SOME OTHER MOMENT.
WORKS FOR ME.
11/27
SCOTT and BORGMAN
©2007 ZITS Partnership. Distributed by King Features Syndicate.

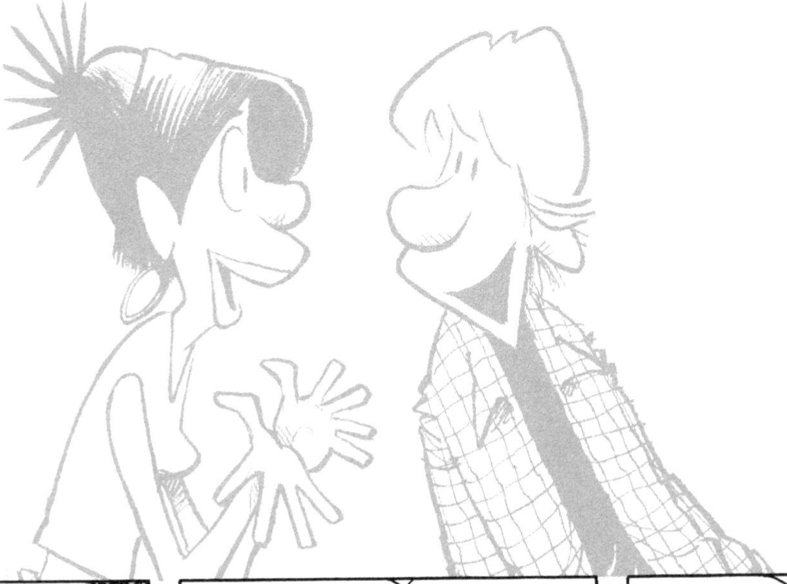

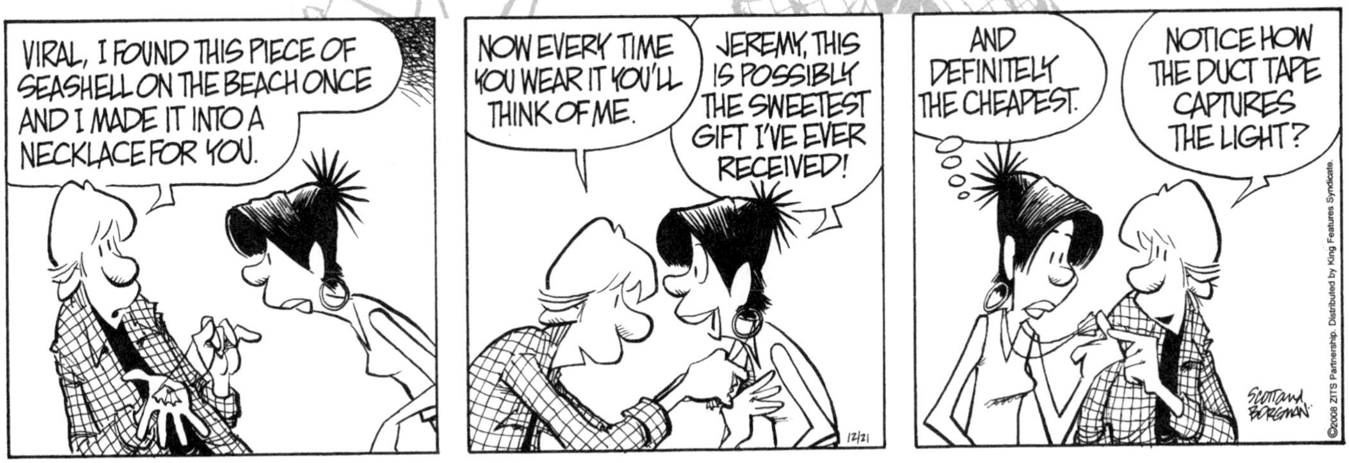
VIRAL, I FOUND THIS PIECE OF SEASHELL ON THE BEACH ONCE AND I MADE IT INTO A NECKLACE FOR YOU.
NOW EVERY TIME YOU WEAR IT YOU'LL THINK OF ME.
JEREMY, THIS IS POSSIBLY THE SWEETEST GIFT I'VE EVER RECEIVED!
12/21
AND DEFINITELY THE CHEAPEST.
NOTICE HOW THE DUCT TAPE CAPTURES THE LIGHT?
SCOTT and BORGMAN
©2008 ZITS Partnership. Distributed by King Features Syndicate.

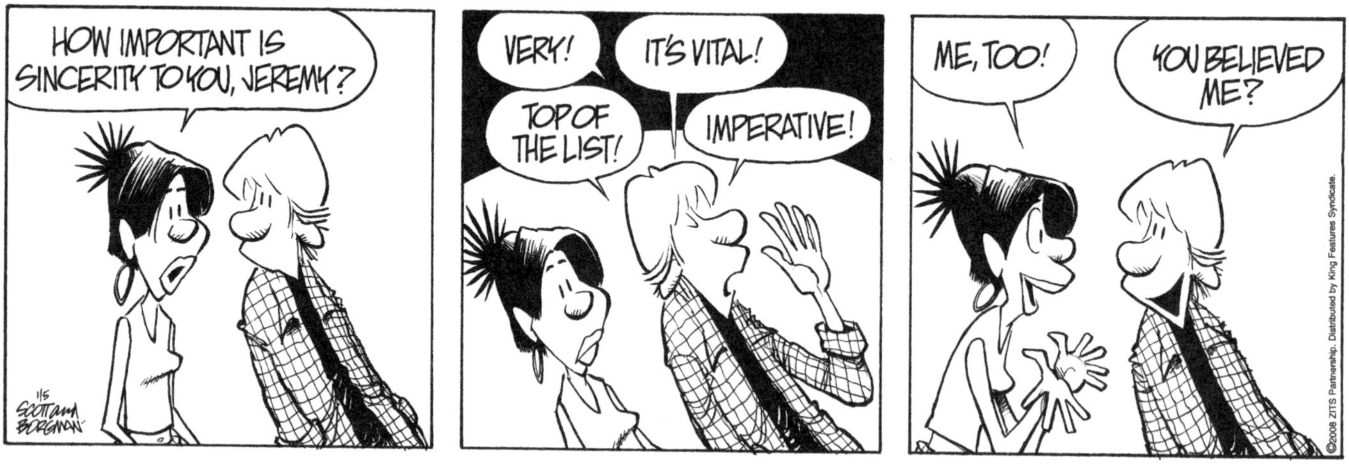
HOW IMPORTANT IS SINCERITY TO YOU, JEREMY?
VERY!
IT'S VITAL!
TOP OF THE LIST!
IMPERATIVE!
ME, TOO!
YOU BELIEVED ME?
©2008 ZITS Partnership. Distributed by King Features Syndicate.

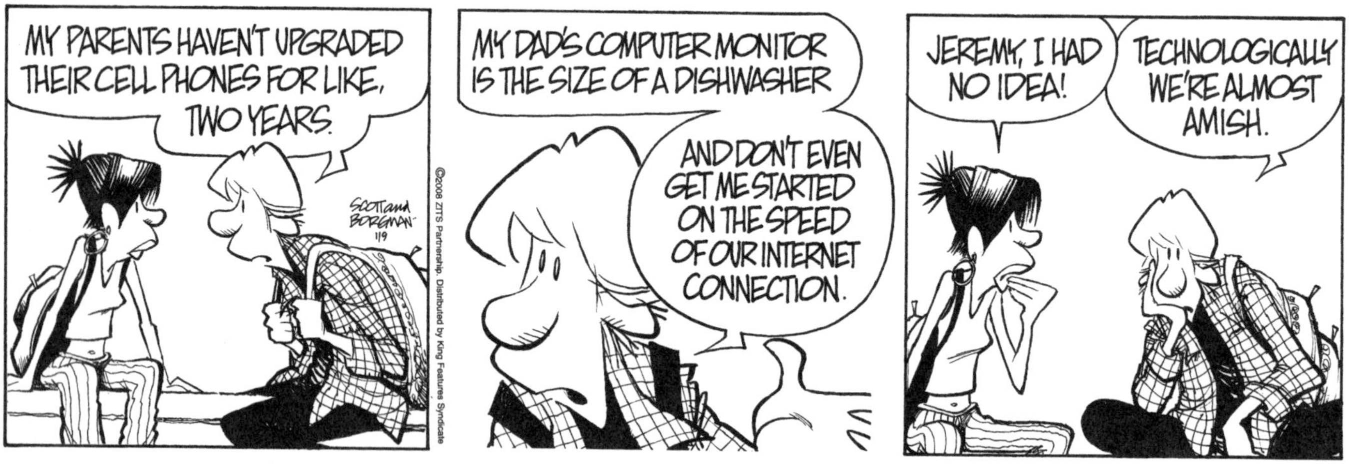
MY PARENTS HAVEN'T UPGRADED THEIR CELL PHONES FOR LIKE, TWO YEARS.
©2008 ZITS Partnership. Distributed by King Features Syndicate.
MY DAD'S COMPUTER MONITOR IS THE SIZE OF A DISHWASHER
AND DON'T EVEN GET ME STARTED ON THE SPEED OF OUR INTERNET CONNECTION.
JEREMY, I HAD NO IDEA!
TECHNOLOGICALLY WE'RE ALMOST AMISH.

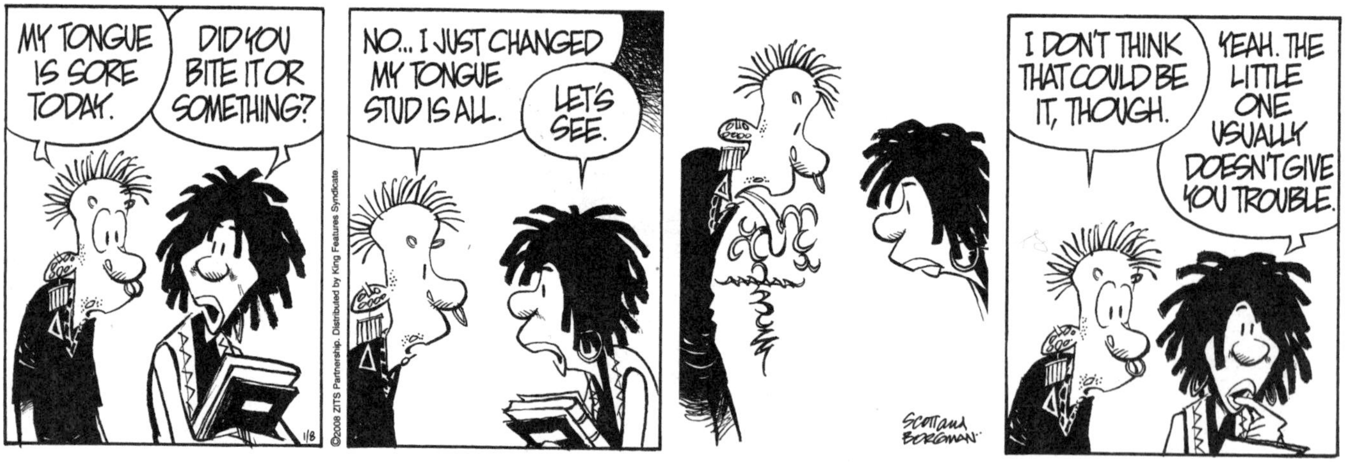
MY TONGUE IS SORE TODAY.
DID YOU BITE IT OR SOMETHING?
©2008 ZITS Partnership. Distributed by King Features Syndicate.
NO... I JUST CHANGED MY TONGUE STUD IS ALL.
LET'S SEE.
I DON'T THINK THAT COULD BE IT, THOUGH.
YEAH. THE LITTLE ONE USUALLY DOESN'T GIVE YOU TROUBLE.

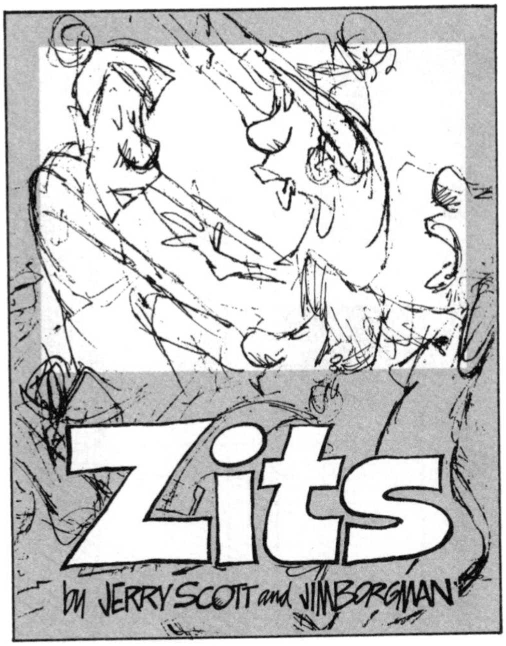
Zits
by JERRY SCOTT and JIM BORGMAN

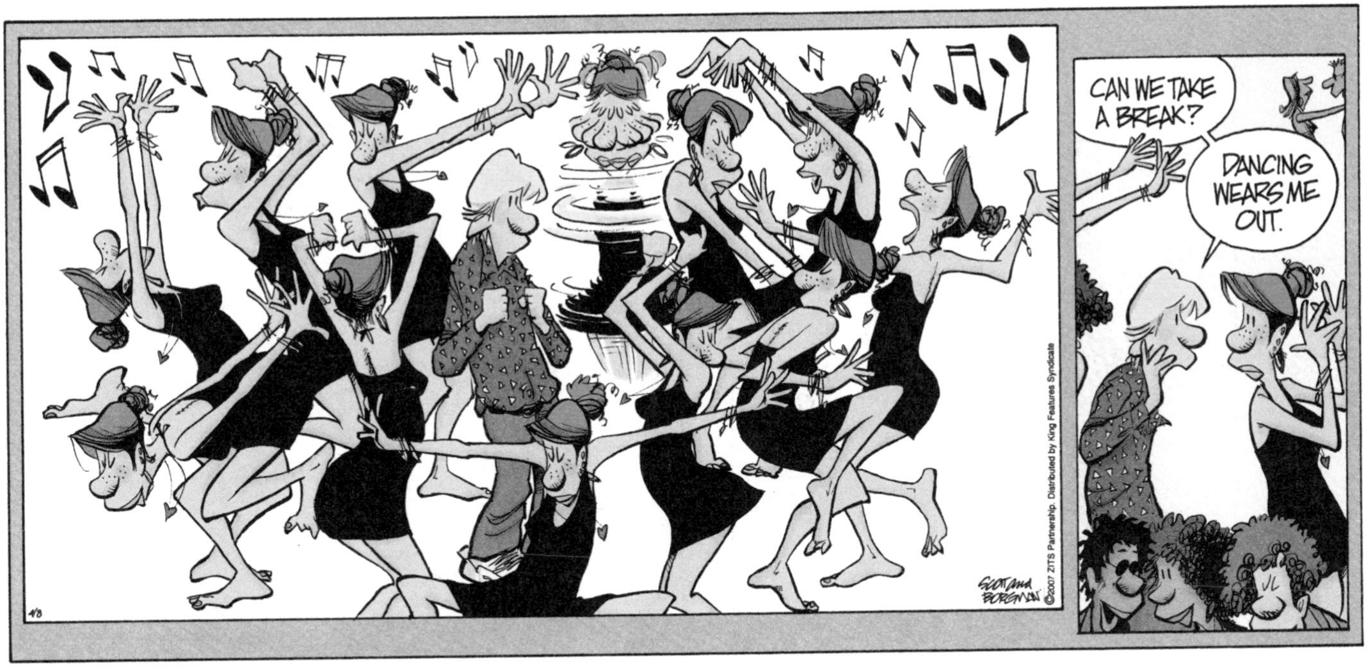
CAN WE TAKE A BREAK?
DANCING WEARS ME OUT.
SCOTT and BORGMAN
©2007 ZITS Partnership. Distributed by King Features Syndicate

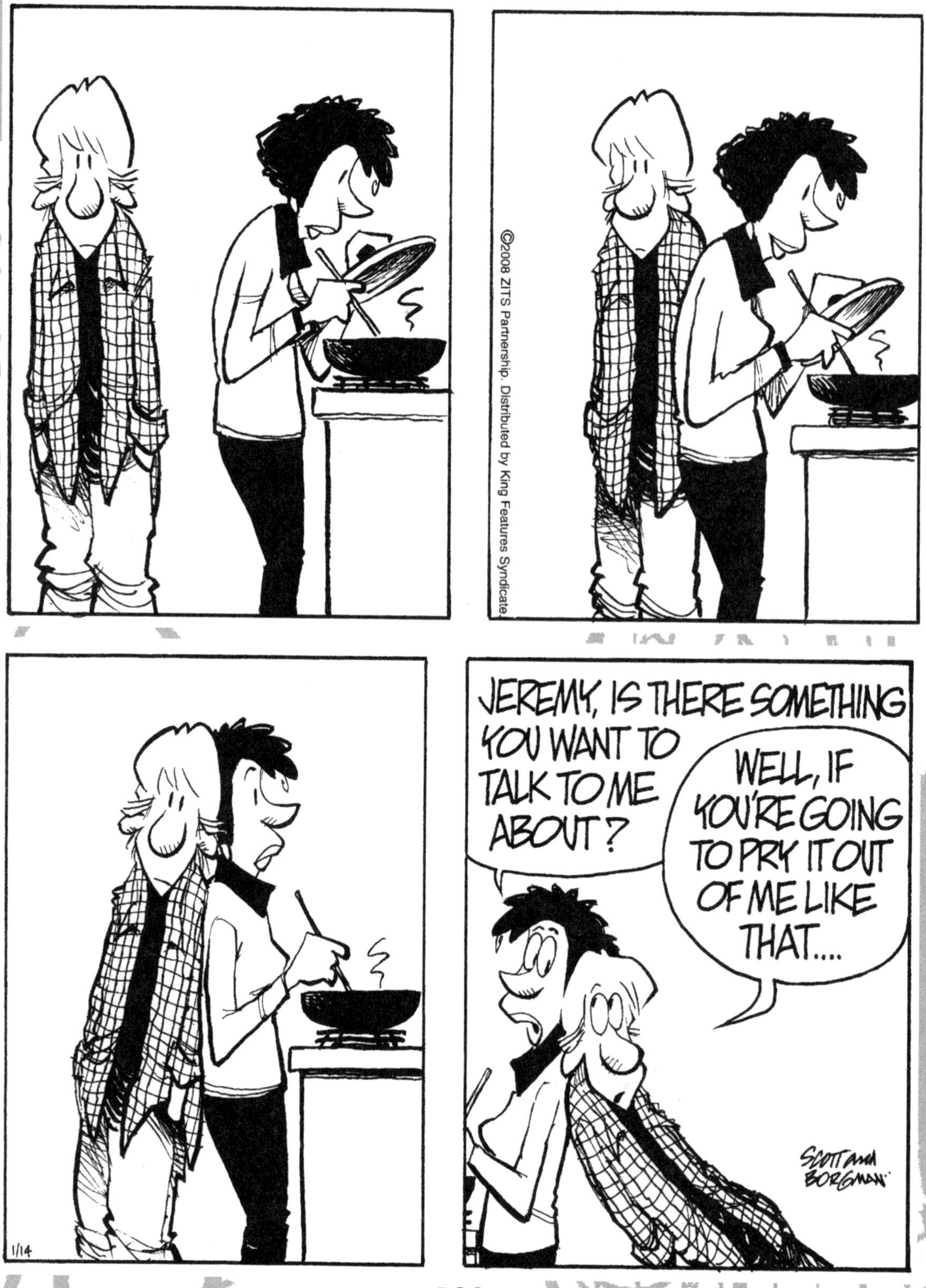
©2008 ZITS Partnership. Distributed by King Features Syndicate.
1/14
JEREMY, IS THERE SOMETHING YOU WANT TO TALK TO ME ABOUT?
WELL, IF YOU'RE GOING TO PRY IT OUT OF ME LIKE THAT....
SCOTT AND BORGMAN

Panel 1: OKAY, THE PROBLEM IS THAT I THINK I DON'T WANT TO GO OUT WITH SARA EXCLUSIVELY ANYMORE.

SCOTT and BORGMAN

Panel 2: AND YOU WANT TO KNOW HOW TO TELL SARA?

NO. I ALREADY TOLD HER.

1/15

Panel 3: SO YOU WANT TO KNOW HOW TO MAKE HER FEEL BETTER?

NO. SHE TOOK IT REALLY WELL. NO BIGGIE.

Panel 4: THEN I DON'T UNDERSTAND WHAT THE PROBLEM—

I WAS HOPING SHE'D BE A LITTLE MORE DEVASTATED.

©2008 ZITS Partnership. Distributed by King Features Syndicate.

Panel 5: SCOTT and BORGMAN 1/17

Panel 6:

Panel 7:

Panel 8: HEY, THIS WAS FUN.

YEAH! WE SHOULD HAVE COFFEE TOGETHER MORE OFTEN!

©2008 ZITS Partnership. Distributed by King Features Syndicate.

Panel 9: I HAD THE MOST RELAXING MORNING!

SCOTT and BORGMAN

Panel 10: I TOOK A RUN, WATCHED THE SUN COME UP, WENT TO YOGA CLASS, AND MEDITATED!

1/18

Panel 11:

©2008 ZITS Partnership. Distributed by King Features Syndicate

Panel 12: OH! AND I RESCUED AN ENDANGERED WETLAND.

NEVER SIT NEXT TO AN OVER-ACHIEVER BEFORE NOON.

Zits
by
JERRY SCOTT and
JIM BORGMAN

YANK!
SCOTT and BORGMAN
©2007 ZITS Partnership. Distributed by King Features Syndicate.
DID YOU HAVE FUN TONIGHT?
CAN WE TALK ABOUT THIS CURFEW THING?

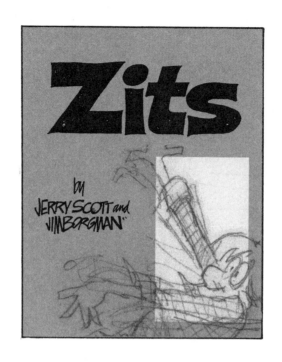

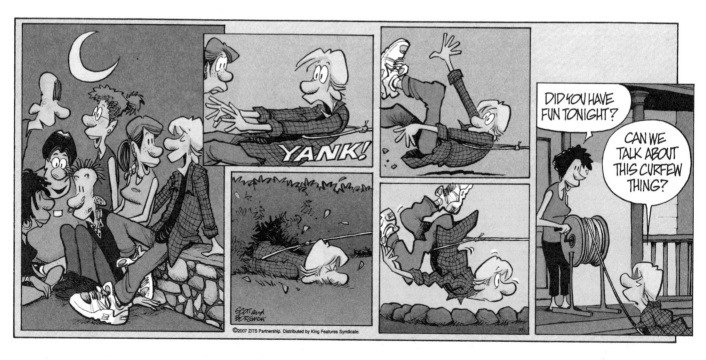

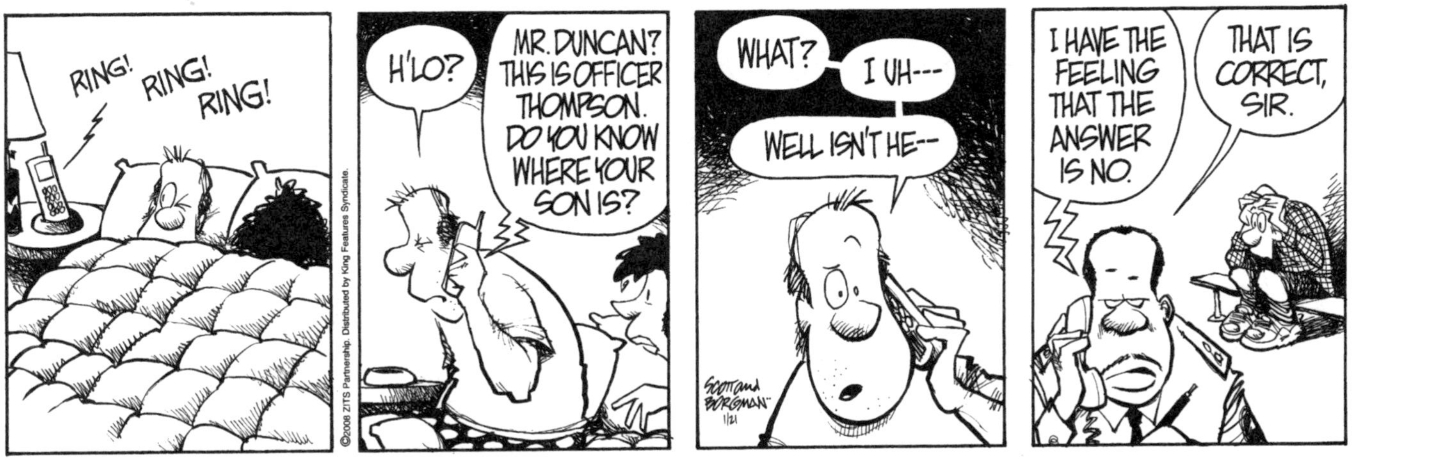
RING! RING! RING!
H'LO?
MR. DUNCAN? THIS IS OFFICER THOMPSON. DO YOU KNOW WHERE YOUR SON IS?
WHAT?
I UH---
WELL ISN'T HE--
I HAVE THE FEELING THAT THE ANSWER IS NO.
THAT IS CORRECT, SIR.

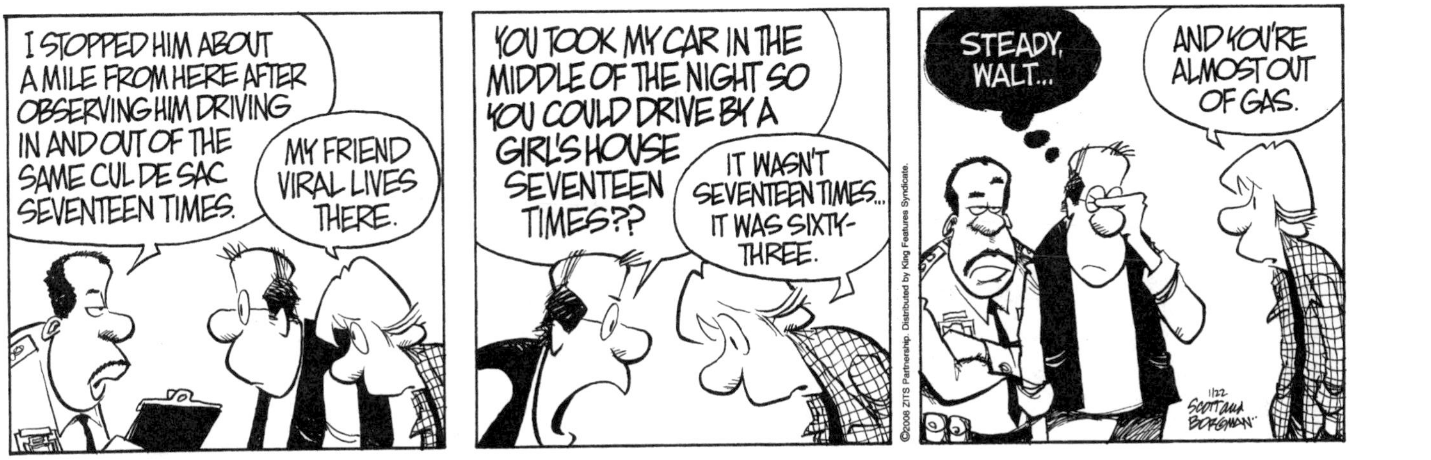
I STOPPED HIM ABOUT A MILE FROM HERE AFTER OBSERVING HIM DRIVING IN AND OUT OF THE SAME CUL DE SAC SEVENTEEN TIMES.
MY FRIEND VIRAL LIVES THERE.
YOU TOOK MY CAR IN THE MIDDLE OF THE NIGHT SO YOU COULD DRIVE BY A GIRL'S HOUSE SEVENTEEN TIMES??
IT WASN'T SEVENTEEN TIMES... IT WAS SIXTY-THREE.
STEADY, WALT...
AND YOU'RE ALMOST OUT OF GAS.

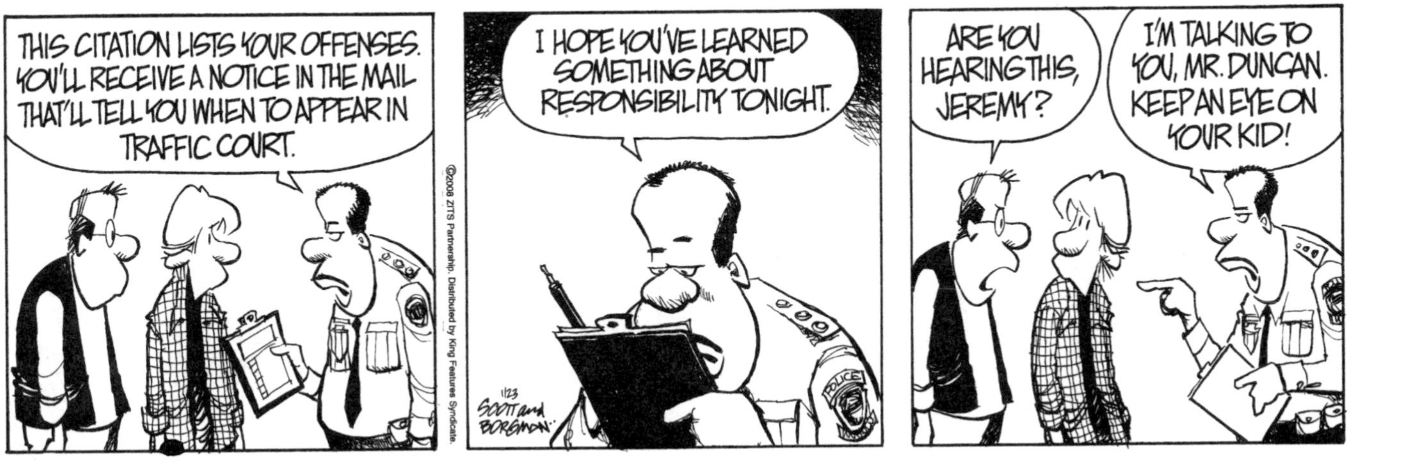
THIS CITATION LISTS YOUR OFFENSES. YOU'LL RECEIVE A NOTICE IN THE MAIL THAT'LL TELL YOU WHEN TO APPEAR IN TRAFFIC COURT.
I HOPE YOU'VE LEARNED SOMETHING ABOUT RESPONSIBILITY TONIGHT.
ARE YOU HEARING THIS, JEREMY?
I'M TALKING TO YOU, MR. DUNCAN. KEEP AN EYE ON YOUR KID!

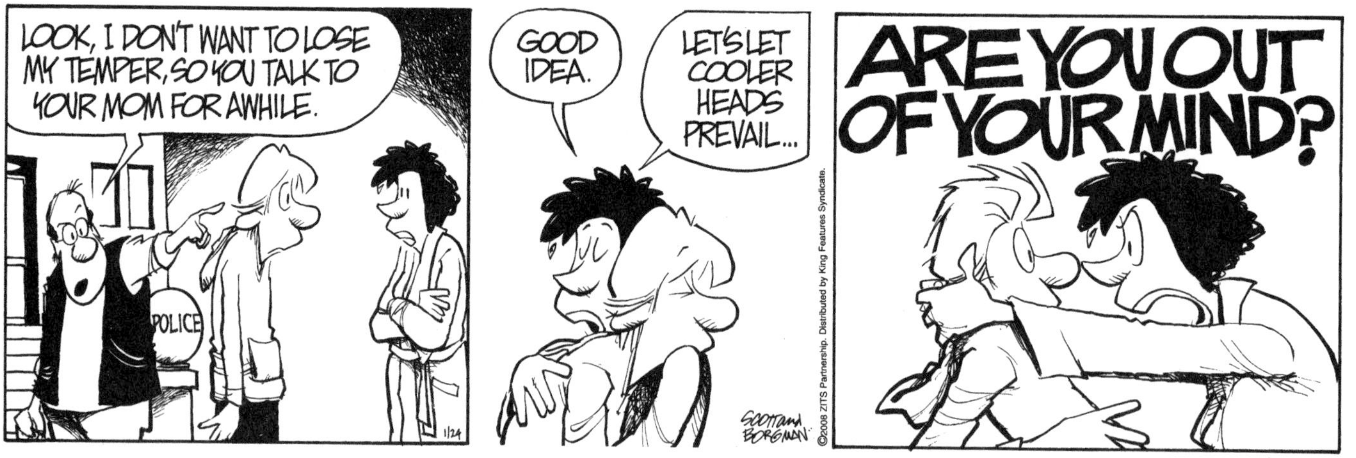
LOOK, I DON'T WANT TO LOSE MY TEMPER, SO YOU TALK TO YOUR MOM FOR AWHILE.
POLICE
GOOD IDEA.
LET'S LET COOLER HEADS PREVAIL...
©2008 ZITS Partnership. Distributed by King Features Syndicate.
ARE YOU OUT OF YOUR MIND?

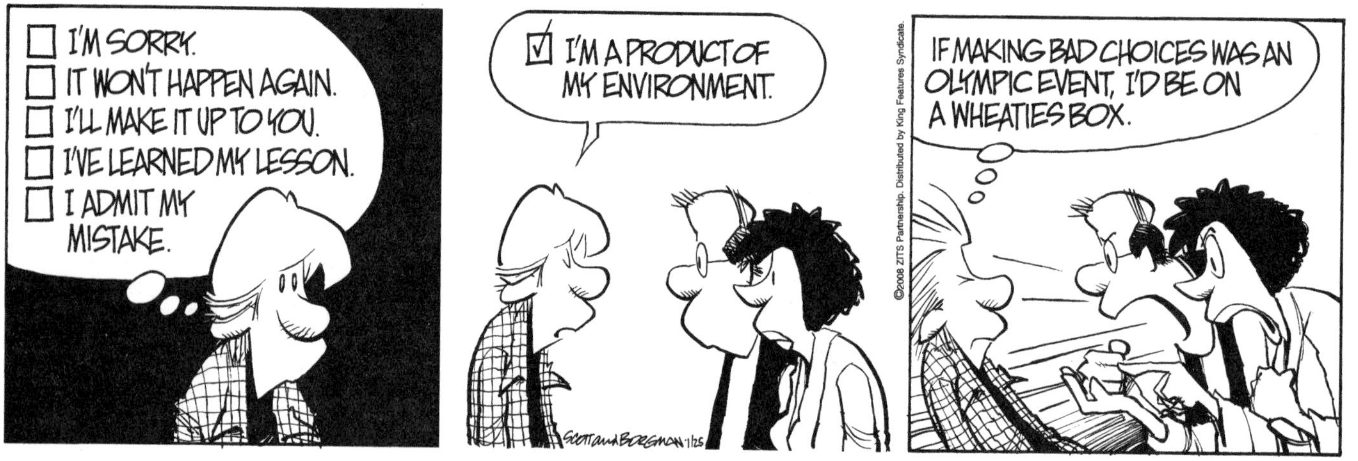
I'M SORRY.
IT WON'T HAPPEN AGAIN.
I'LL MAKE IT UP TO YOU.
I'VE LEARNED MY LESSON.
I ADMIT MY MISTAKE.
I'M A PRODUCT OF MY ENVIRONMENT.
©2008 ZITS Partnership. Distributed by King Features Syndicate.
IF MAKING BAD CHOICES WAS AN OLYMPIC EVENT, I'D BE ON A WHEATIES BOX.

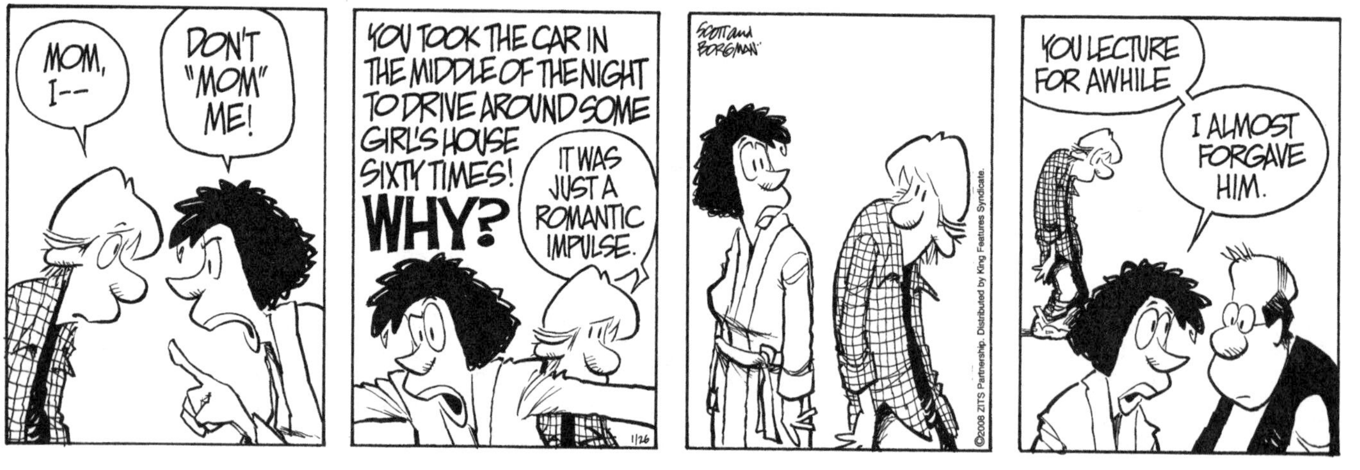
MOM, I--
DON'T "MOM" ME!
YOU TOOK THE CAR IN THE MIDDLE OF THE NIGHT TO DRIVE AROUND SOME GIRL'S HOUSE SIXTY TIMES! WHY?
IT WAS JUST A ROMANTIC IMPULSE.
©2008 ZITS Partnership. Distributed by King Features Syndicate.
YOU LECTURE FOR AWHILE
I ALMOST FORGAVE HIM.

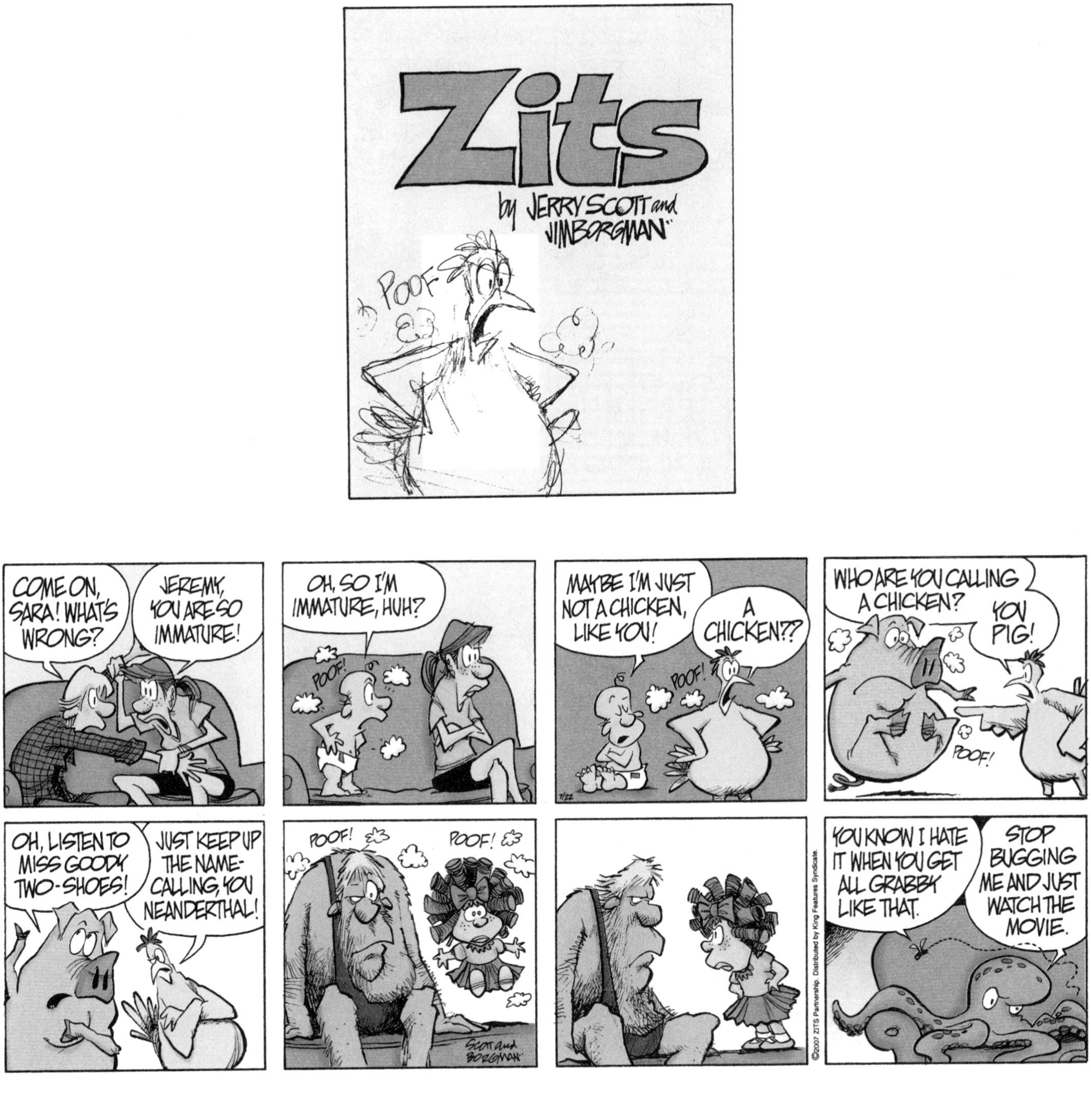
Zits
by JERRY SCOTT and JIM BORGMAN
POOF
COME ON, SARA! WHAT'S WRONG?
JEREMY, YOU ARE SO IMMATURE!
OH, SO I'M IMMATURE, HUH?
POOF!
MAYBE I'M JUST NOT A CHICKEN, LIKE YOU!
POOF!
A CHICKEN??
7/22
WHO ARE YOU CALLING A CHICKEN?
YOU PIG!
POOF!
OH, LISTEN TO MISS GOODY TWO-SHOES!
JUST KEEP UP THE NAME-CALLING, YOU NEANDERTHAL!
POOF!
POOF!
SCOTT and BORGMAN
YOU KNOW I HATE IT WHEN YOU GET ALL GRABBY LIKE THAT.
STOP BUGGING ME AND JUST WATCH THE MOVIE.

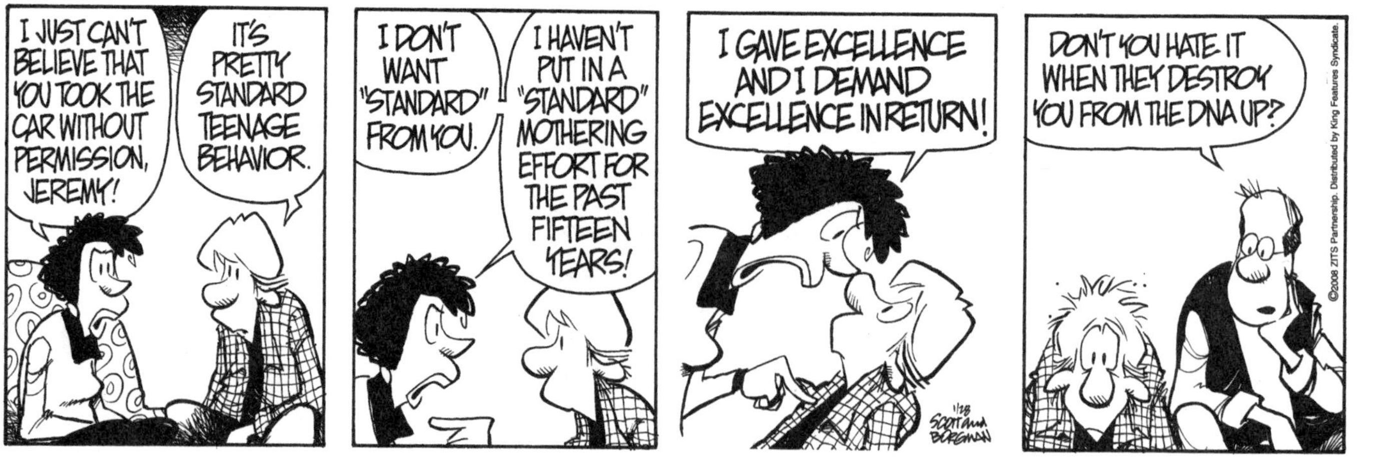
I JUST CAN'T BELIEVE THAT YOU TOOK THE CAR WITHOUT PERMISSION, JEREMY!
IT'S PRETTY STANDARD TEENAGE BEHAVIOR.
I DON'T WANT "STANDARD" FROM YOU.
I HAVEN'T PUT IN A "STANDARD" MOTHERING EFFORT FOR THE PAST FIFTEEN YEARS!
I GAVE EXCELLENCE AND I DEMAND EXCELLENCE IN RETURN!
DON'T YOU HATE IT WHEN THEY DESTROY YOU FROM THE DNA UP?
©2008 ZITS Partnership. Distributed by King Features Syndicate.

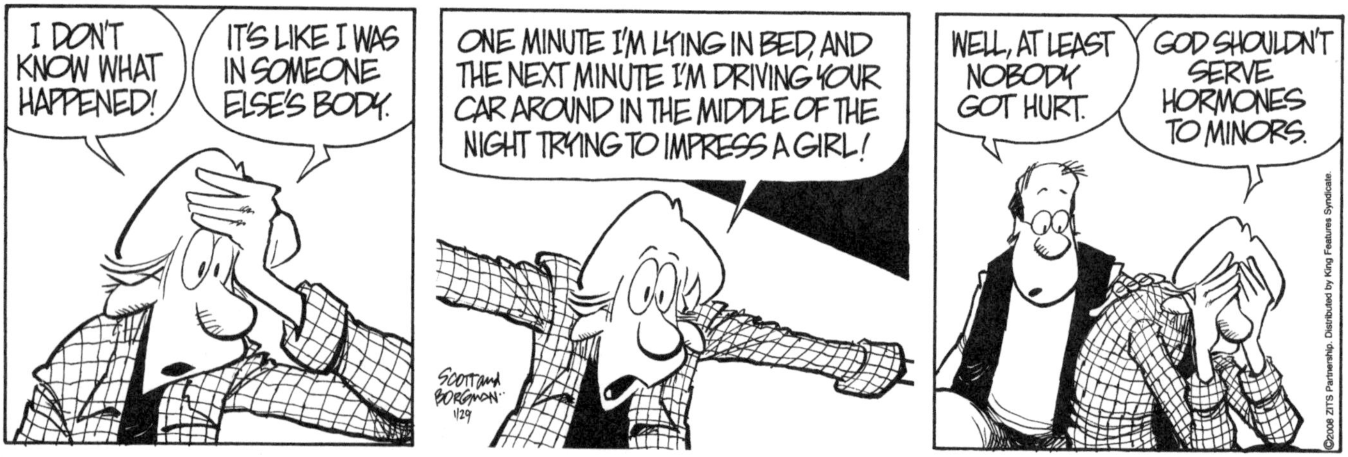
I DON'T KNOW WHAT HAPPENED!
IT'S LIKE I WAS IN SOMEONE ELSE'S BODY.
ONE MINUTE I'M LYING IN BED, AND THE NEXT MINUTE I'M DRIVING YOUR CAR AROUND IN THE MIDDLE OF THE NIGHT TRYING TO IMPRESS A GIRL!
WELL, AT LEAST NOBODY GOT HURT.
GOD SHOULDN'T SERVE HORMONES TO MINORS.
©2008 ZITS Partnership. Distributed by King Features Syndicate.

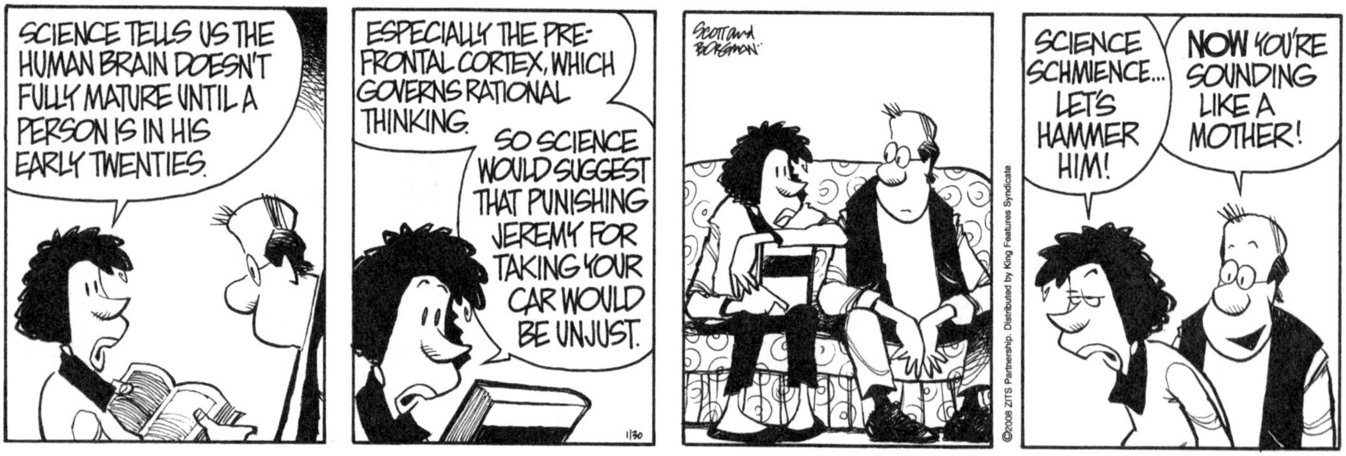
SCIENCE TELLS US THE HUMAN BRAIN DOESN'T FULLY MATURE UNTIL A PERSON IS IN HIS EARLY TWENTIES.
ESPECIALLY THE PRE-FRONTAL CORTEX, WHICH GOVERNS RATIONAL THINKING.
SO SCIENCE WOULD SUGGEST THAT PUNISHING JEREMY FOR TAKING YOUR CAR WOULD BE UNJUST.
©2008 ZITS Partnership. Distributed by King Features Syndicate.
SCIENCE SCHMIENCE... LET'S HAMMER HIM!
NOW YOU'RE SOUNDING LIKE A MOTHER!

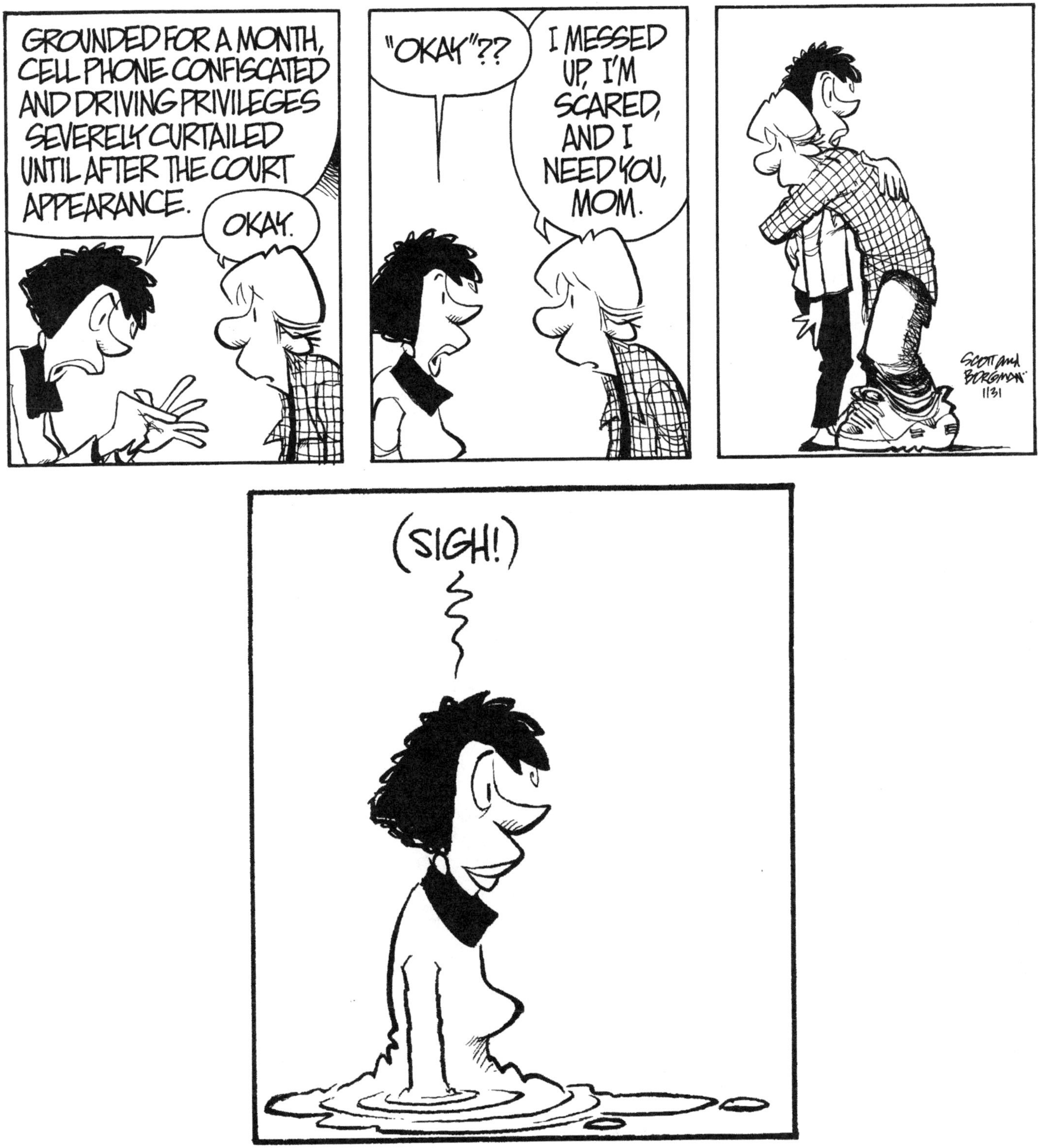
GROUNDED FOR A MONTH, CELL PHONE CONFISCATED AND DRIVING PRIVILEGES SEVERELY CURTAILED UNTIL AFTER THE COURT APPEARANCE.
OKAY.
"OKAY"??
I MESSED UP, I'M SCARED, AND I NEED YOU, MOM.
SCOTT and BORGMAN 1/31
(SIGH!)

Zits
by JERRY SCOTT and JIM BORGMAN

©2008 ZITS Partnership. Distributed by King Features Syndicate.
SCOTT and BORGMAN 5/11
SO, HAVE YOU THOUGHT ABOUT ASKING ANY-BODY TO THE PROM?
AAAAAAAAAGGHH!
I JUST ASKED A QUESTION, JEREMY. DON'T ACT SO TORTURED!
IS THAT IT? CAN I GO NOW?

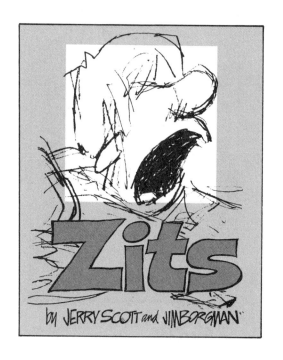

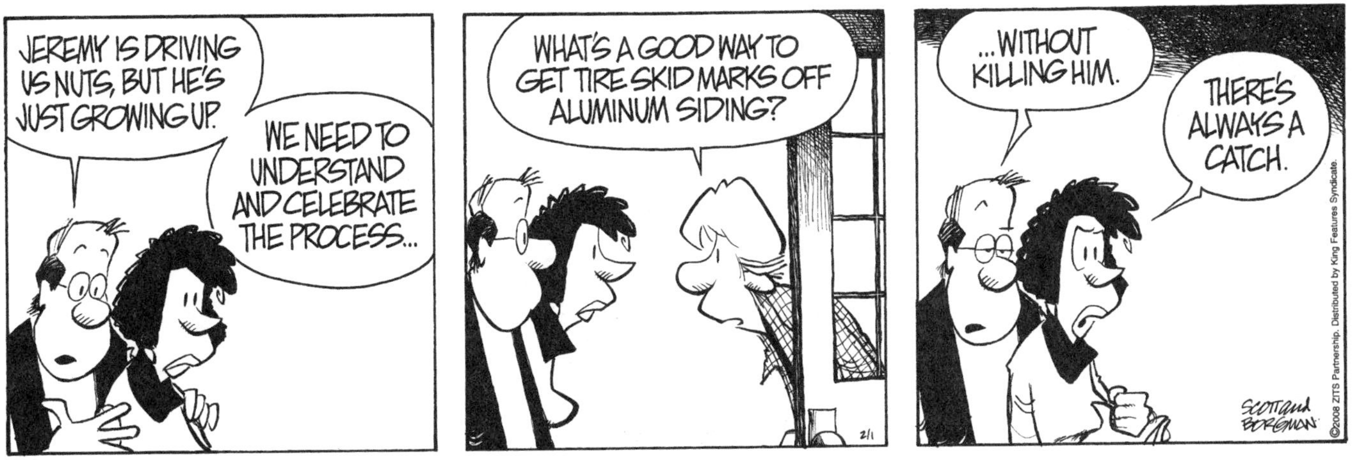
JEREMY IS DRIVING US NUTS, BUT HE'S JUST GROWING UP.
WE NEED TO UNDERSTAND AND CELEBRATE THE PROCESS...
WHAT'S A GOOD WAY TO GET TIRE SKID MARKS OFF ALUMINUM SIDING?
2/1
...WITHOUT KILLING HIM.
THERE'S ALWAYS A CATCH.
SCOTT and BORGMAN
©2008 ZITS Partnership. Distributed by King Features Syndicate.

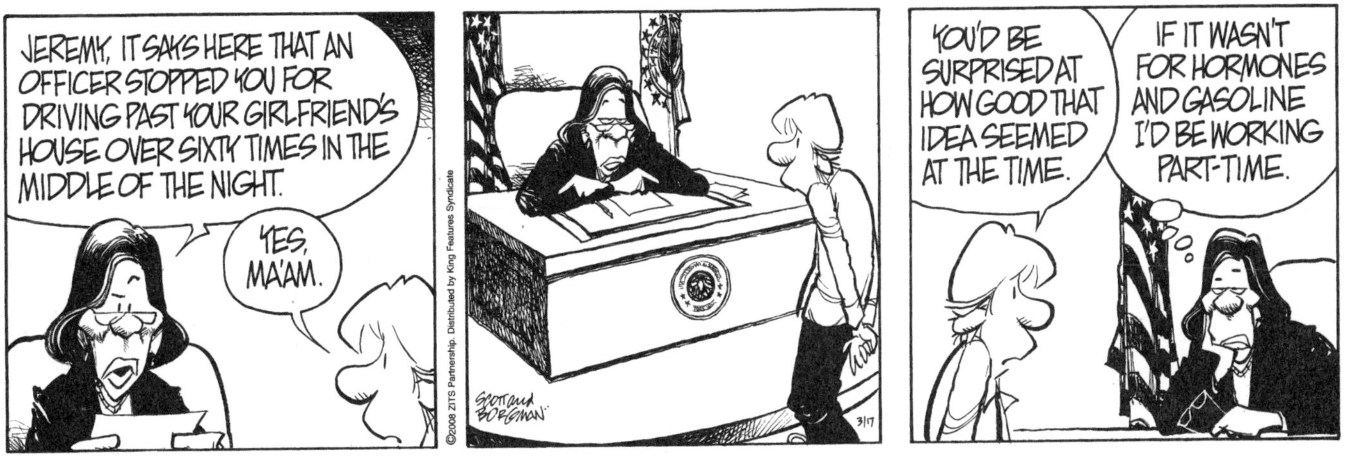
JEREMY, IT SAYS HERE THAT AN OFFICER STOPPED YOU FOR DRIVING PAST YOUR GIRLFRIEND'S HOUSE OVER SIXTY TIMES IN THE MIDDLE OF THE NIGHT.
YES, MA'AM.
©2008 ZITS Partnership. Distributed by King Features Syndicate
SCOTT and BORGMAN
3/17
YOU'D BE SURPRISED AT HOW GOOD THAT IDEA SEEMED AT THE TIME.
IF IT WASN'T FOR HORMONES AND GASOLINE I'D BE WORKING PART-TIME.

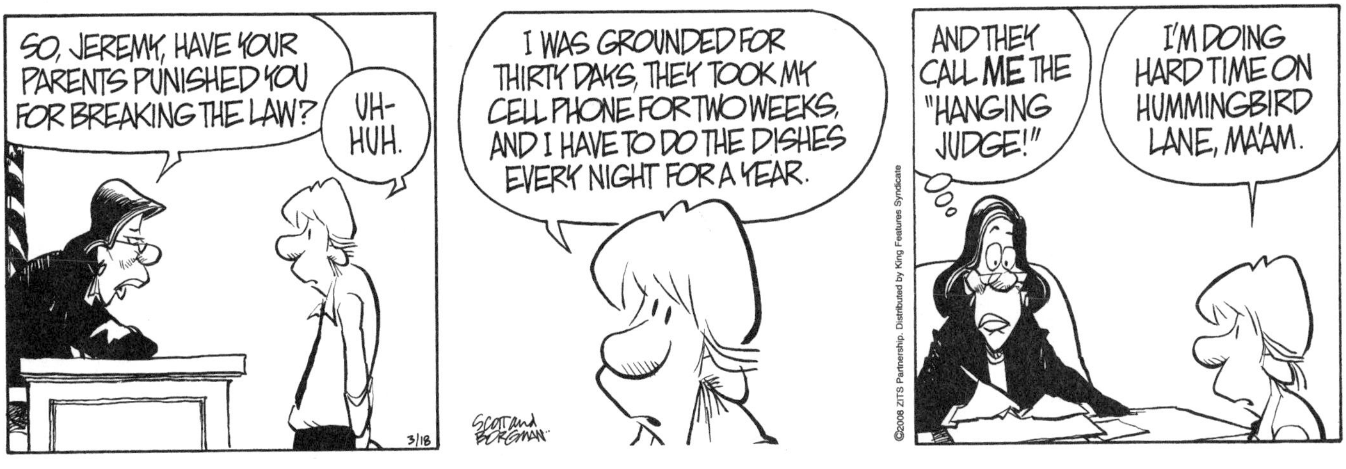
SO, JEREMY, HAVE YOUR PARENTS PUNISHED YOU FOR BREAKING THE LAW?
UH-HUH.
3/18
I WAS GROUNDED FOR THIRTY DAYS, THEY TOOK MY CELL PHONE FOR TWO WEEKS, AND I HAVE TO DO THE DISHES EVERY NIGHT FOR A YEAR.
SCOTT and BORGMAN
©2008 ZITS Partnership. Distributed by King Features Syndicate
AND THEY CALL ME THE "HANGING JUDGE!"
I'M DOING HARD TIME ON HUMMINGBIRD LANE, MA'AM.

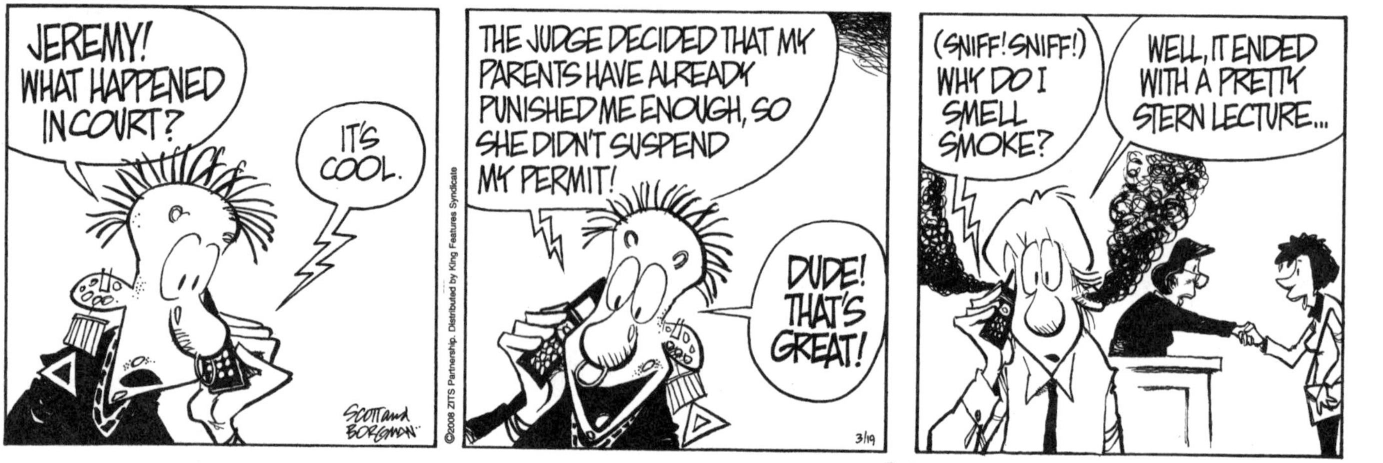
JEREMY! WHAT HAPPENED IN COURT?
IT'S COOL.
THE JUDGE DECIDED THAT MY PARENTS HAVE ALREADY PUNISHED ME ENOUGH, SO SHE DIDN'T SUSPEND MY PERMIT!
DUDE! THAT'S GREAT!
(SNIFF! SNIFF!) WHY DO I SMELL SMOKE?
WELL, IT ENDED WITH A PRETTY STERN LECTURE...
SCOTT and BORGMAN
©2008 ZITS Partnership. Distributed by King Features Syndicate
3/19

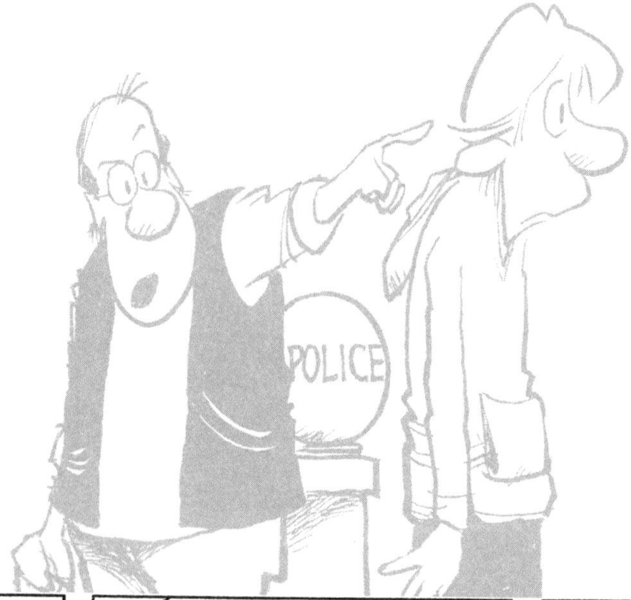
POLICE

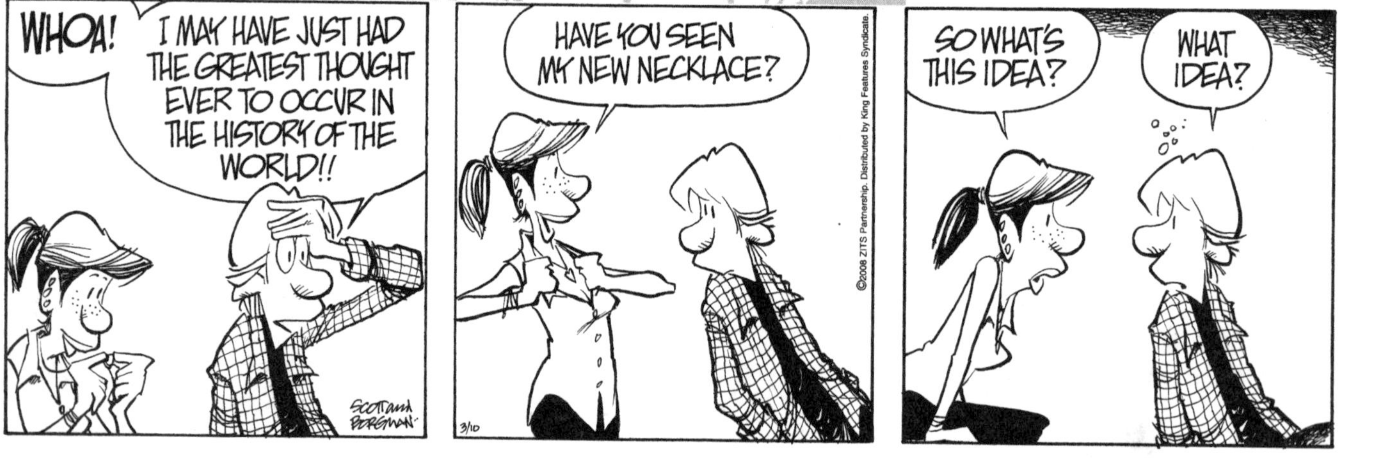
WHOA!
I MAY HAVE JUST HAD THE GREATEST THOUGHT EVER TO OCCUR IN THE HISTORY OF THE WORLD!!
SCOTT and BORGMAN
HAVE YOU SEEN MY NEW NECKLACE?
3/10
©2008 ZITS Partnership. Distributed by King Features Syndicate.
SO WHAT'S THIS IDEA?
WHAT IDEA?

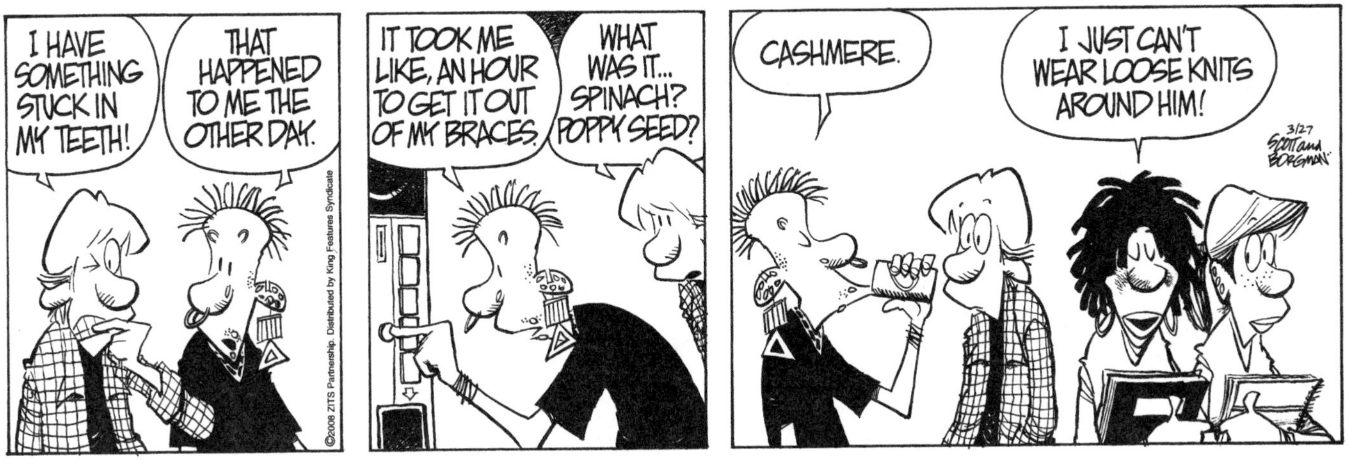
I HAVE SOMETHING STUCK IN MY TEETH!
THAT HAPPENED TO ME THE OTHER DAY.
©2008 ZITS Partnership. Distributed by King Features Syndicate
IT TOOK ME LIKE, AN HOUR TO GET IT OUT OF MY BRACES.
WHAT WAS IT... SPINACH? POPPY SEED?
CASHMERE.
I JUST CAN'T WEAR LOOSE KNITS AROUND HIM!
3/27
SCOTT and BORGMAN

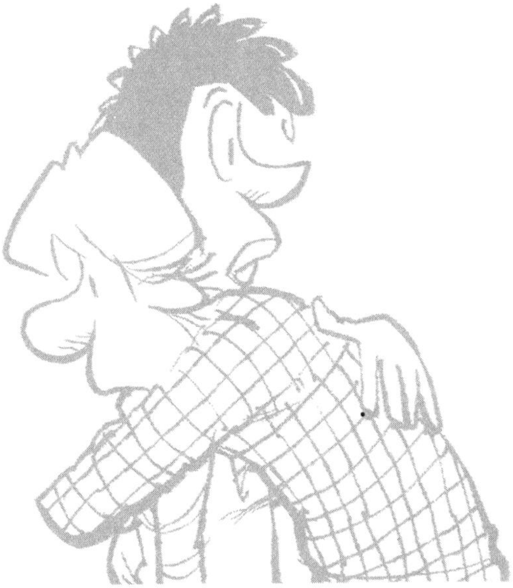

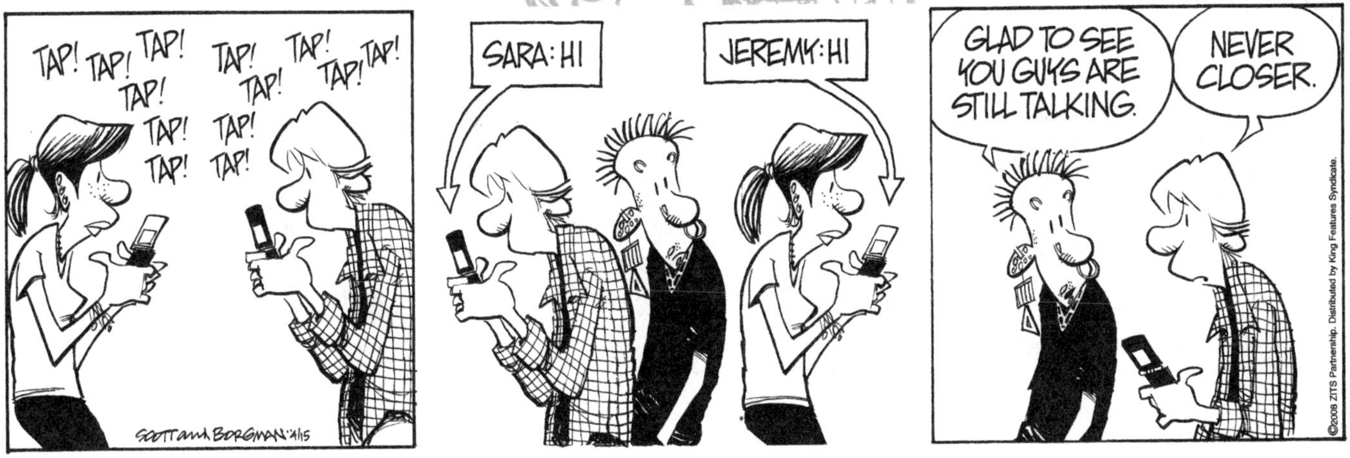
TAP! TAP! TAP! TAP! TAP! TAP!
TAP! TAP! TAP! TAP! TAP! TAP! TAP!
SCOTT and BORGMAN 4/15
SARA: HI
JEREMY: HI
GLAD TO SEE YOU GUYS ARE STILL TALKING.
NEVER CLOSER.
©2008 ZITS Partnership. Distributed by King Features Syndicate.

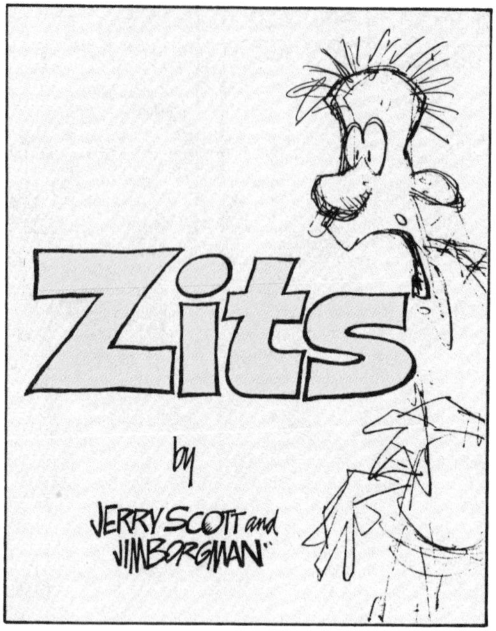
Zits
by
JERRY SCOTT and
JIM BORGMAN

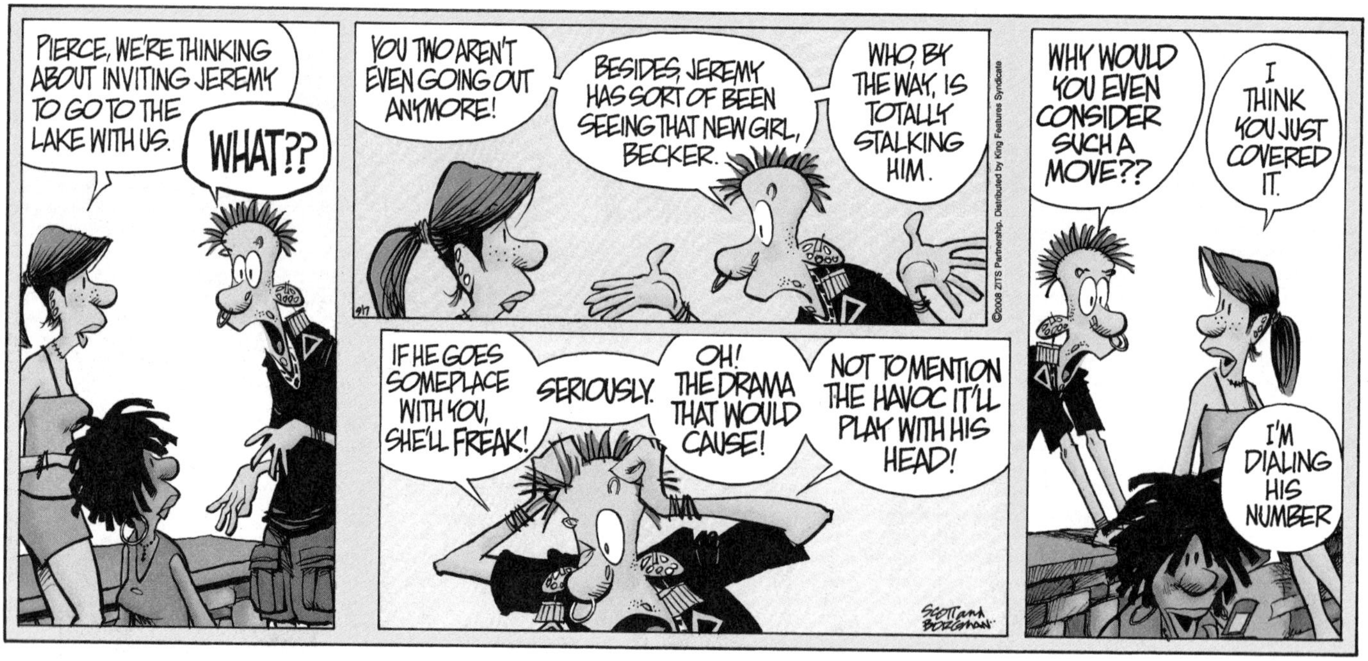
PIERCE, WE'RE THINKING ABOUT INVITING JEREMY TO GO TO THE LAKE WITH US.
WHAT??
YOU TWO AREN'T EVEN GOING OUT ANYMORE!
BESIDES, JEREMY HAS SORT OF BEEN SEEING THAT NEW GIRL, BECKER.
WHO, BY THE WAY, IS TOTALLY STALKING HIM.
©2008 ZITS Partnership. Distributed by King Features Syndicate
IF HE GOES SOMEPLACE WITH YOU, SHE'LL FREAK!
SERIOUSLY.
OH! THE DRAMA THAT WOULD CAUSE!
NOT TO MENTION THE HAVOC IT'LL PLAY WITH HIS HEAD!
SCOTT and BORGMAN
WHY WOULD YOU EVEN CONSIDER SUCH A MOVE??
I THINK YOU JUST COVERED IT.
I'M DIALING HIS NUMBER

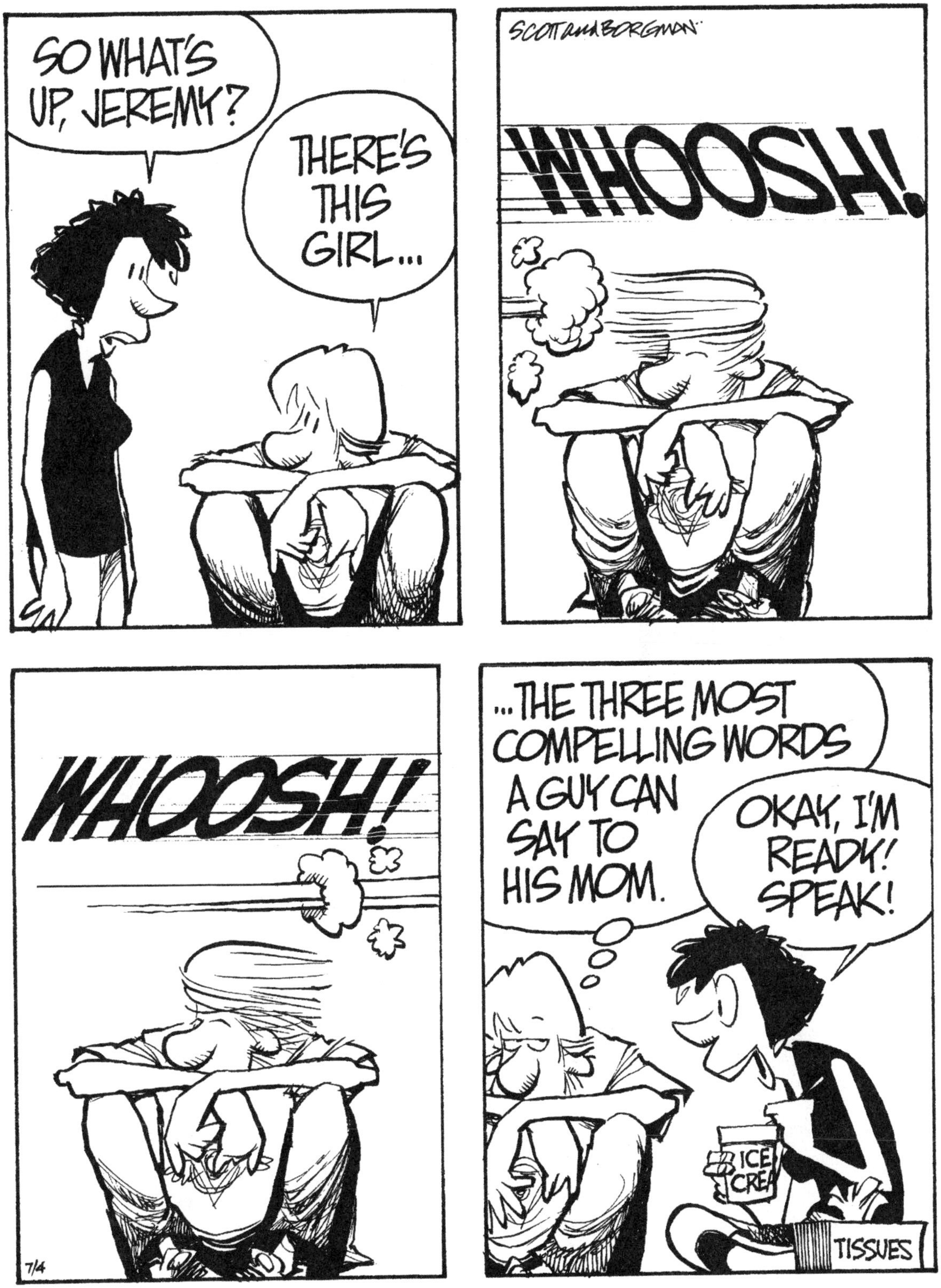
SO WHAT'S UP, JEREMY?
THERE'S THIS GIRL...
SCOTT AND BORGMAN
WHOOSH!
WHOOSH!
...THE THREE MOST COMPELLING WORDS A GUY CAN SAY TO HIS MOM.
OKAY, I'M READY! SPEAK!
ICE CREA
TISSUES
7/4

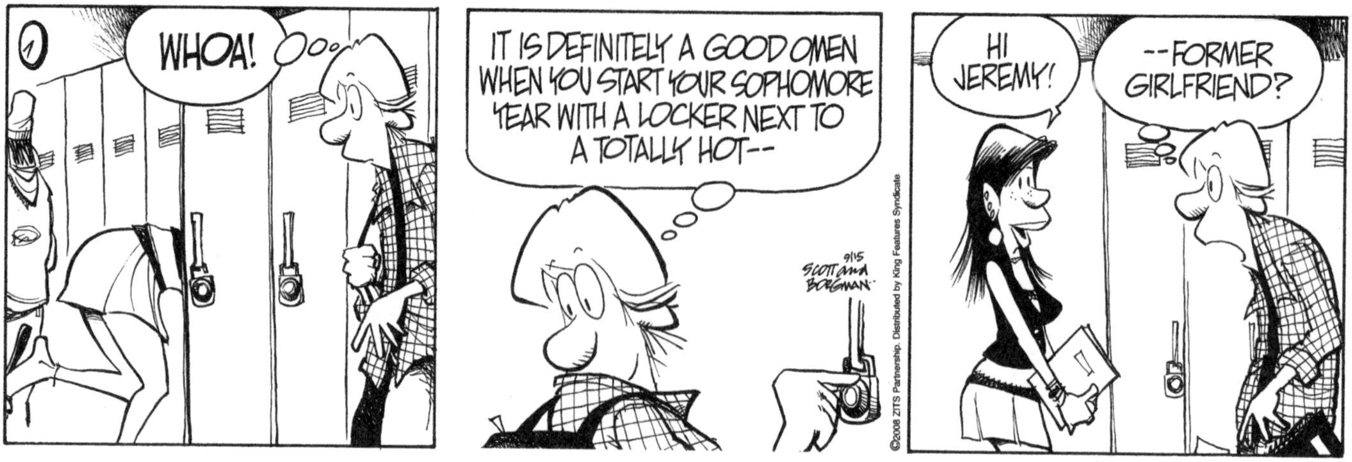
1
WHOA!
IT IS DEFINITELY A GOOD OMEN WHEN YOU START YOUR SOPHOMORE YEAR WITH A LOCKER NEXT TO A TOTALLY HOT--
9/15 SCOTT and BORGMAN
©2008 ZITS Partnership. Distributed by King Features Syndicate
HI JEREMY!
--FORMER GIRLFRIEND?

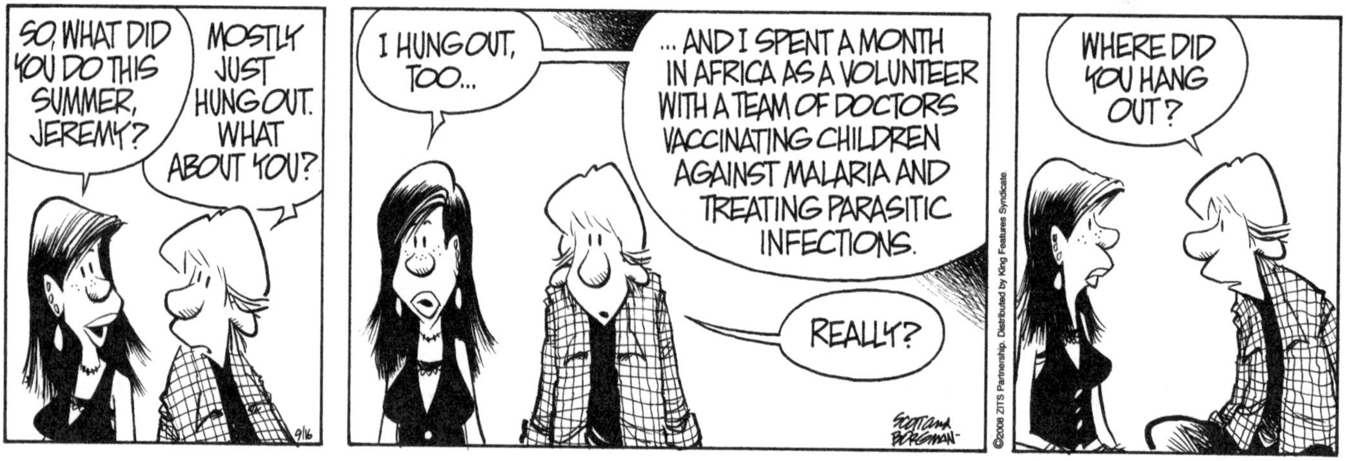
SO, WHAT DID YOU DO THIS SUMMER, JEREMY?
MOSTLY JUST HUNG OUT. WHAT ABOUT YOU?
9/16
I HUNG OUT, TOO...
... AND I SPENT A MONTH IN AFRICA AS A VOLUNTEER WITH A TEAM OF DOCTORS VACCINATING CHILDREN AGAINST MALARIA AND TREATING PARASITIC INFECTIONS.
REALLY?
SCOTT and BORGMAN
©2008 ZITS Partnership. Distributed by King Features Syndicate
WHERE DID YOU HANG OUT?

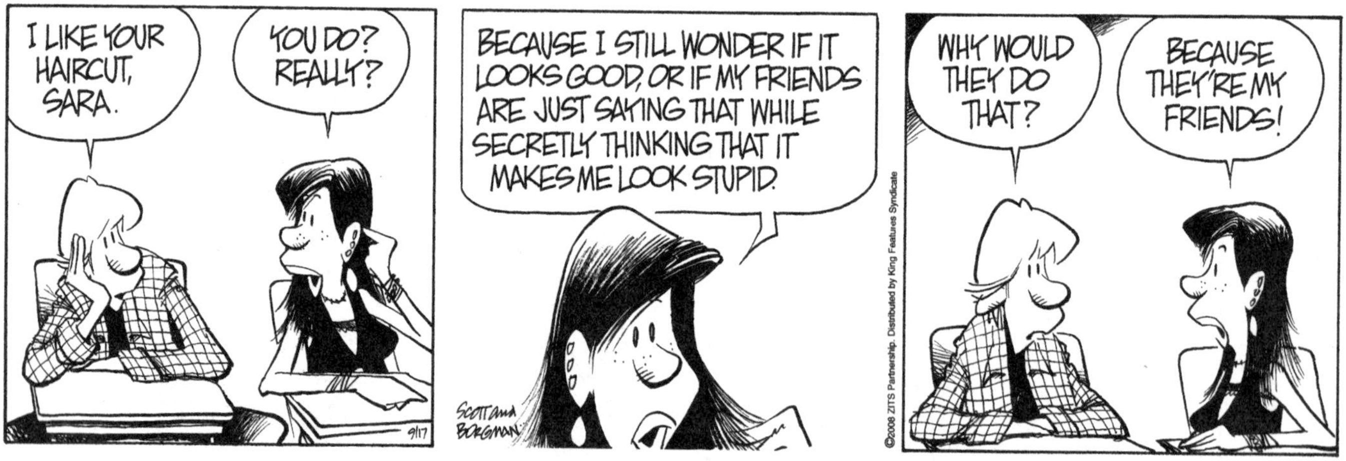
I LIKE YOUR HAIRCUT, SARA.
YOU DO? REALLY?
9/17
SCOTT and BORGMAN
BECAUSE I STILL WONDER IF IT LOOKS GOOD, OR IF MY FRIENDS ARE JUST SAYING THAT WHILE SECRETLY THINKING THAT IT MAKES ME LOOK STUPID.
©2008 ZITS Partnership. Distributed by King Features Syndicate
WHY WOULD THEY DO THAT?
BECAUSE THEY'RE MY FRIENDS!

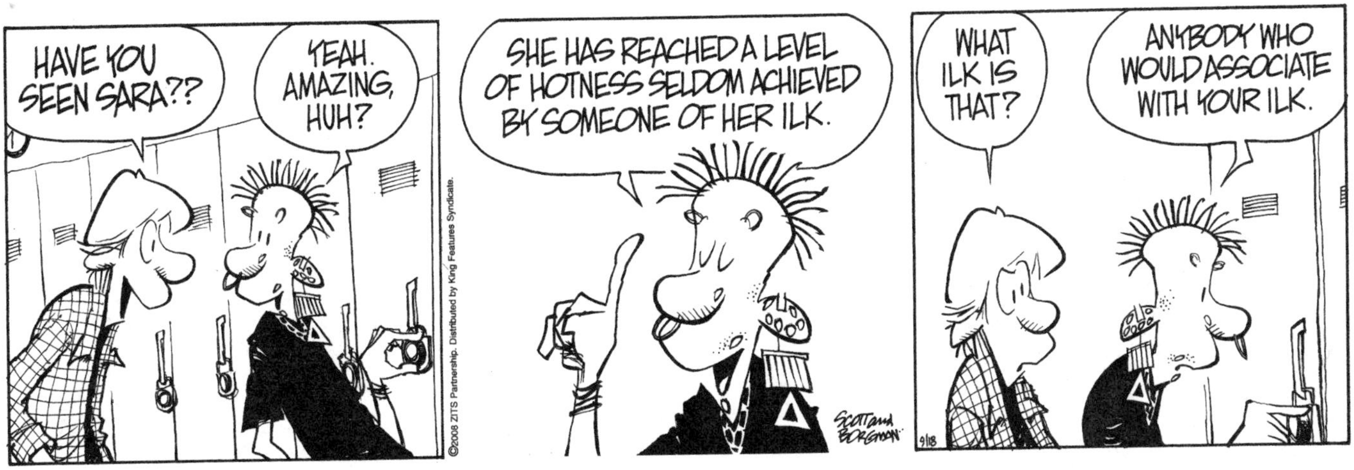
HAVE YOU SEEN SARA??
YEAH. AMAZING, HUH?
©2008 ZITS Partnership. Distributed by King Features Syndicate.
SHE HAS REACHED A LEVEL OF HOTNESS SELDOM ACHIEVED BY SOMEONE OF HER ILK.
SCOTT and BORGMAN
WHAT ILK IS THAT?
ANYBODY WHO WOULD ASSOCIATE WITH YOUR ILK.
9/18

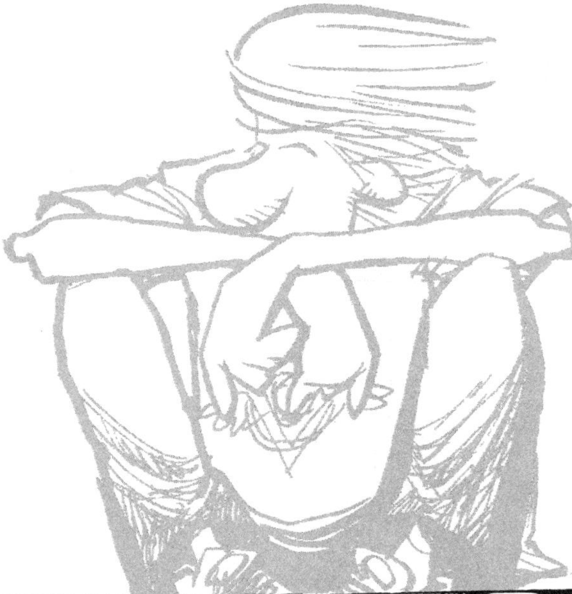

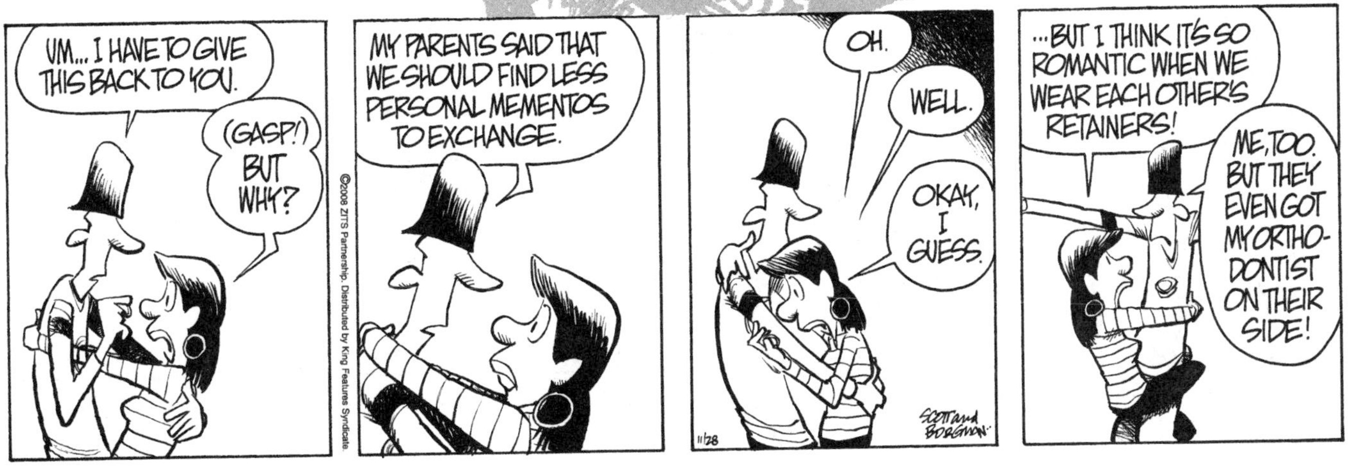
UM... I HAVE TO GIVE THIS BACK TO YOU.
(GASP!) BUT WHY?
©2008 ZITS Partnership. Distributed by King Features Syndicate.
MY PARENTS SAID THAT WE SHOULD FIND LESS PERSONAL MEMENTOS TO EXCHANGE.
OH.
WELL.
OKAY, I GUESS.
11/28
SCOTT and BORGMAN
...BUT I THINK IT'S SO ROMANTIC WHEN WE WEAR EACH OTHER'S RETAINERS!
ME, TOO. BUT THEY EVEN GOT MY ORTHO-DONTIST ON THEIR SIDE!

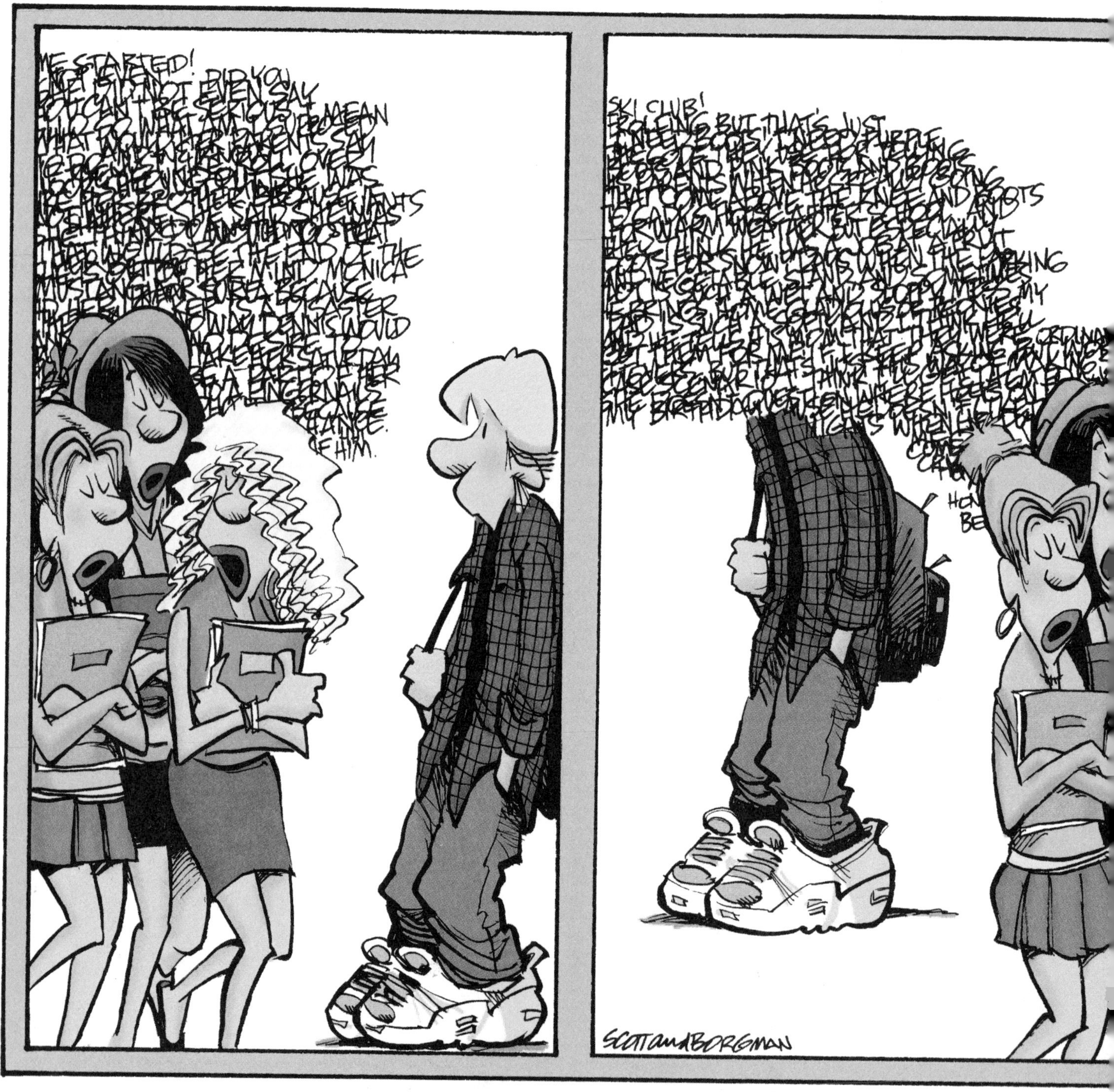
SKI CLUB!
SCOTT and BORGMAN

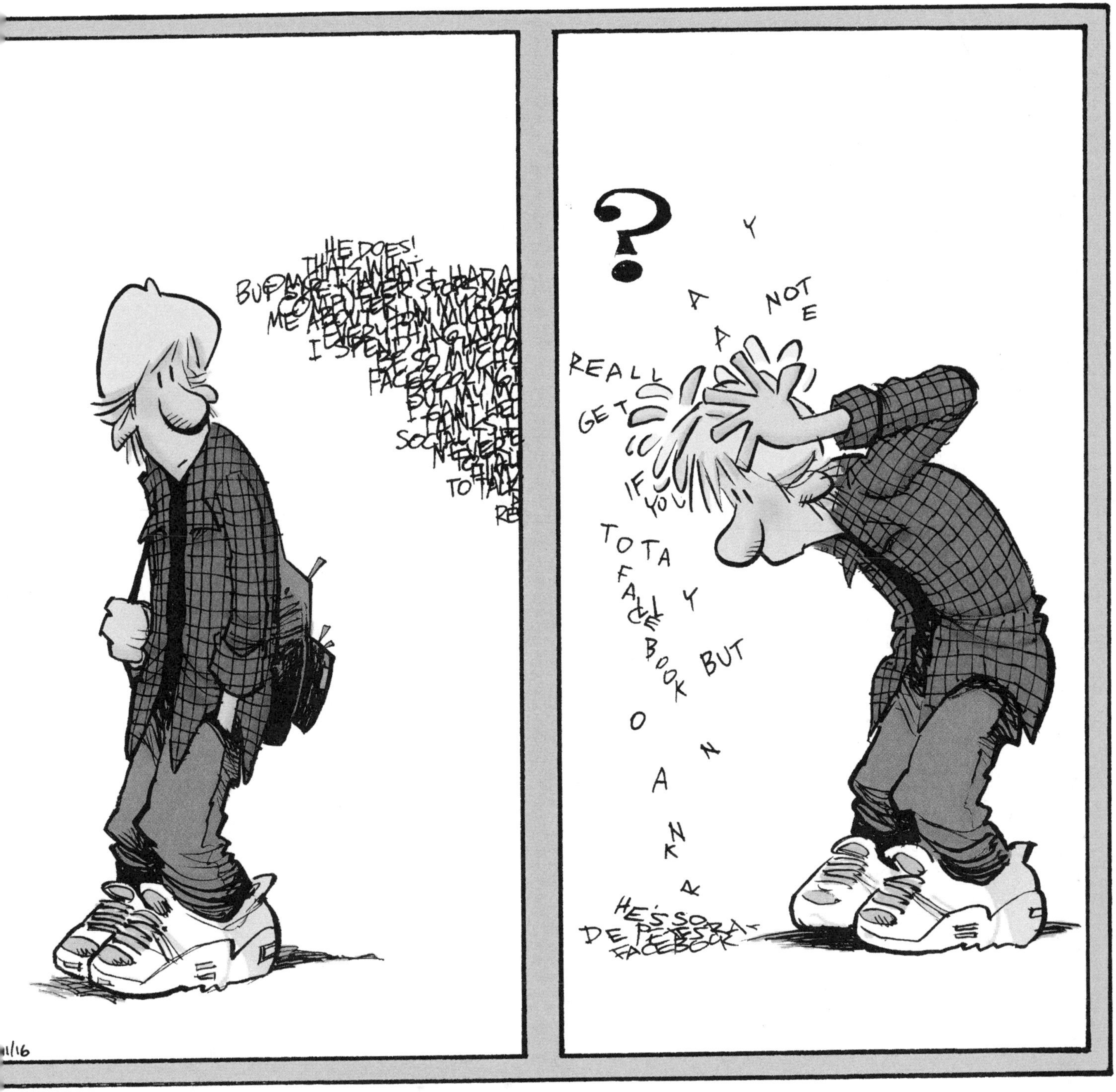
HE DOES!
?
NOT
REALL
GET
IF
YOU
TOTA
BUT
FACEBOOK

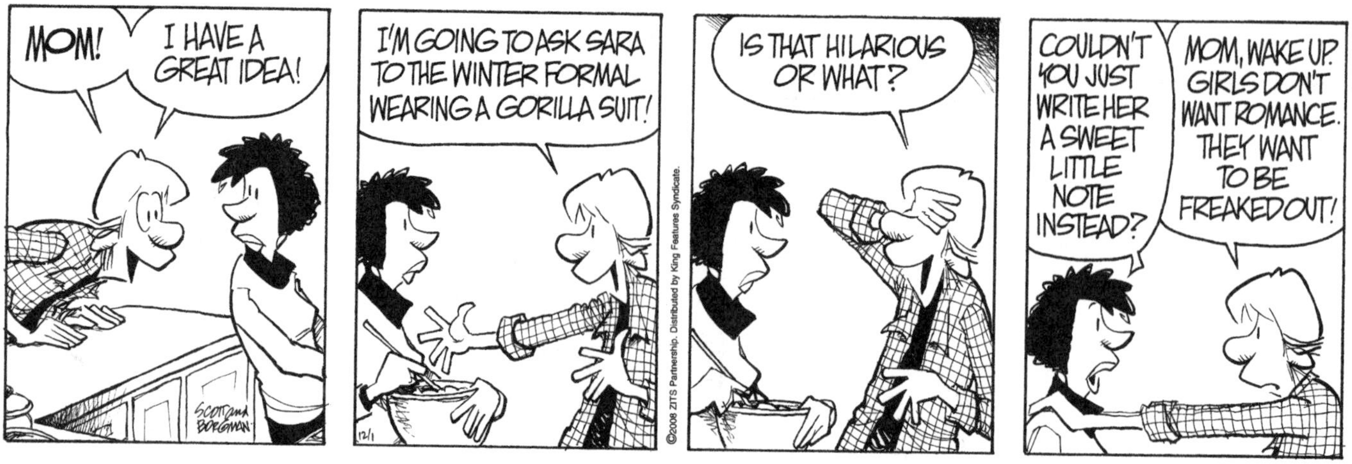
MOM!
I HAVE A GREAT IDEA!
I'M GOING TO ASK SARA TO THE WINTER FORMAL WEARING A GORILLA SUIT!
IS THAT HILARIOUS OR WHAT?
COULDN'T YOU JUST WRITE HER A SWEET LITTLE NOTE INSTEAD?
MOM, WAKE UP. GIRLS DON'T WANT ROMANCE. THEY WANT TO BE FREAKED OUT!
©2008 ZITS Partnership. Distributed by King Features Syndicate.

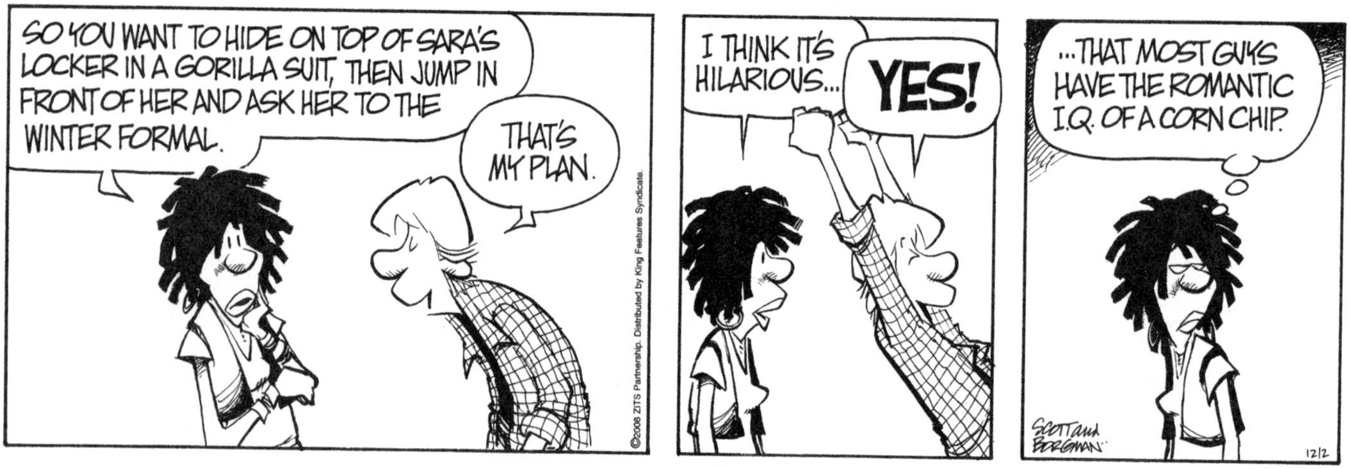
SO YOU WANT TO HIDE ON TOP OF SARA'S LOCKER IN A GORILLA SUIT, THEN JUMP IN FRONT OF HER AND ASK HER TO THE WINTER FORMAL.
THAT'S MY PLAN.
©2008 ZITS Partnership. Distributed by King Features Syndicate.
I THINK IT'S HILARIOUS...
YES!
...THAT MOST GUYS HAVE THE ROMANTIC I.Q. OF A CORN CHIP.

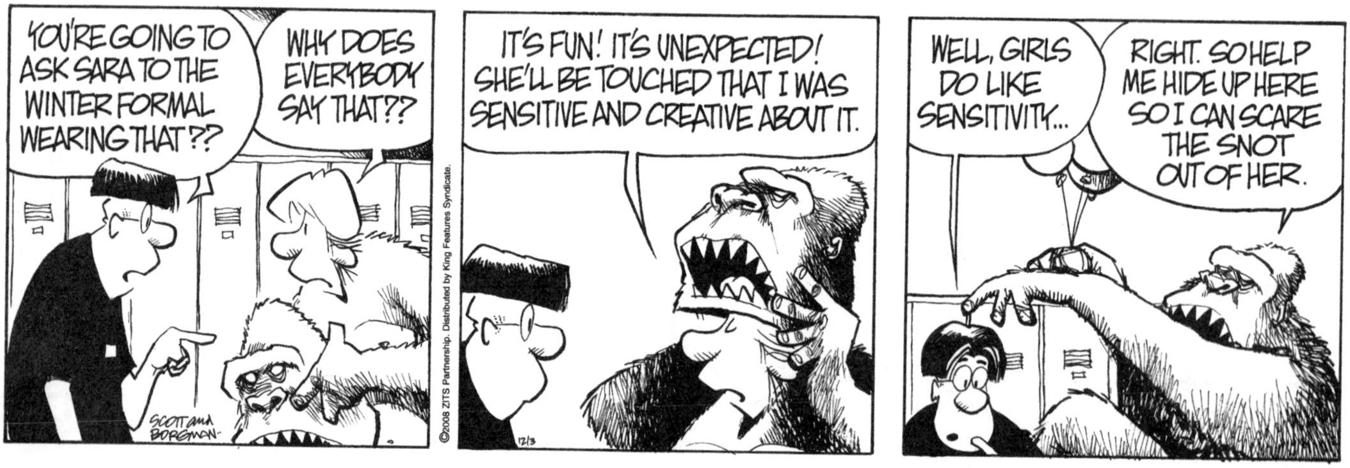
YOU'RE GOING TO ASK SARA TO THE WINTER FORMAL WEARING THAT??
WHY DOES EVERYBODY SAY THAT??
©2008 ZITS Partnership. Distributed by King Features Syndicate.
IT'S FUN! IT'S UNEXPECTED! SHE'LL BE TOUCHED THAT I WAS SENSITIVE AND CREATIVE ABOUT IT.
WELL, GIRLS DO LIKE SENSITIVITY...
RIGHT. SO HELP ME HIDE UP HERE SO I CAN SCARE THE SNOT OUT OF HER.

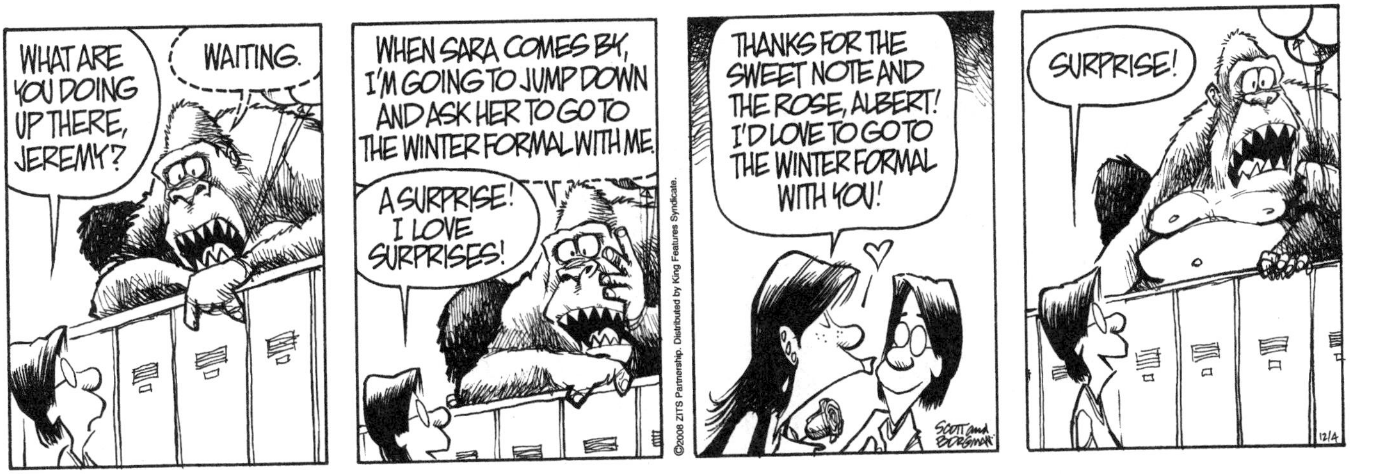
WHAT ARE YOU DOING UP THERE, JEREMY?
WAITING.
WHEN SARA COMES BY, I'M GOING TO JUMP DOWN AND ASK HER TO GO TO THE WINTER FORMAL WITH ME.
A SURPRISE! I LOVE SURPRISES!
©2008 ZITS Partnership. Distributed by King Features Syndicate.
THANKS FOR THE SWEET NOTE AND THE ROSE, ALBERT! I'D LOVE TO GO TO THE WINTER FORMAL WITH YOU!
SCOTT AND BORGMAN
SURPRISE!
12/4

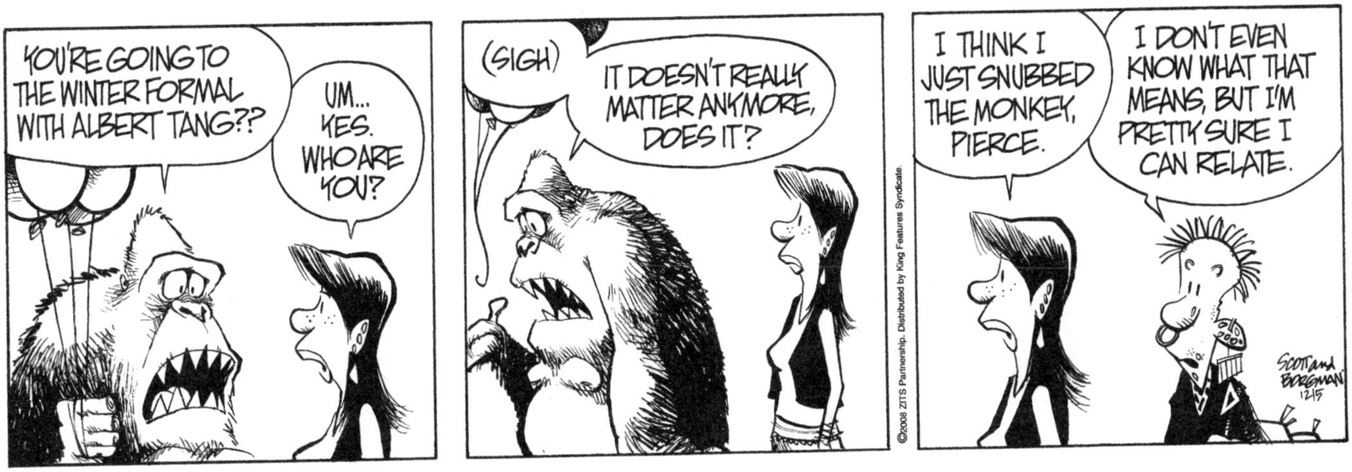
YOU'RE GOING TO THE WINTER FORMAL WITH ALBERT TANG??
UM... YES. WHO ARE YOU?
(SIGH)
IT DOESN'T REALLY MATTER ANYMORE, DOES IT?
©2008 ZITS Partnership. Distributed by King Features Syndicate.
I THINK I JUST SNUBBED THE MONKEY, PIERCE.
I DON'T EVEN KNOW WHAT THAT MEANS, BUT I'M PRETTY SURE I CAN RELATE.
SCOTT AND BORGMAN
12/5

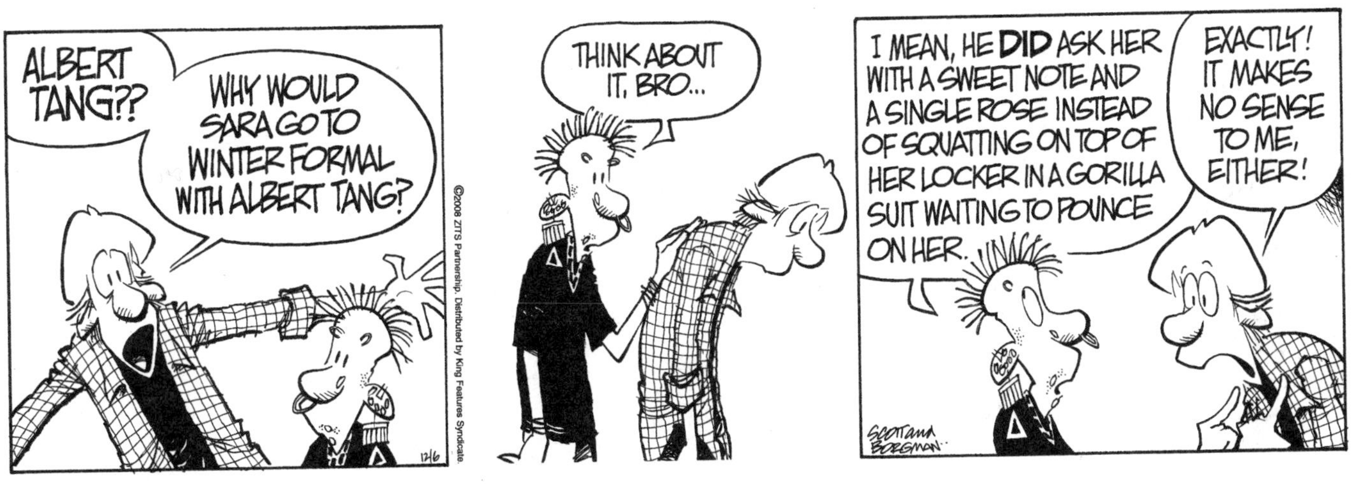
ALBERT TANG??
WHY WOULD SARA GO TO WINTER FORMAL WITH ALBERT TANG?
12/6
©2008 ZITS Partnership. Distributed by King Features Syndicate.
THINK ABOUT IT, BRO...
I MEAN, HE **DID** ASK HER WITH A SWEET NOTE AND A SINGLE ROSE INSTEAD OF SQUATTING ON TOP OF HER LOCKER IN A GORILLA SUIT WAITING TO POUNCE ON HER.
EXACTLY! IT MAKES NO SENSE TO ME, EITHER!
SCOTT AND BORGMAN

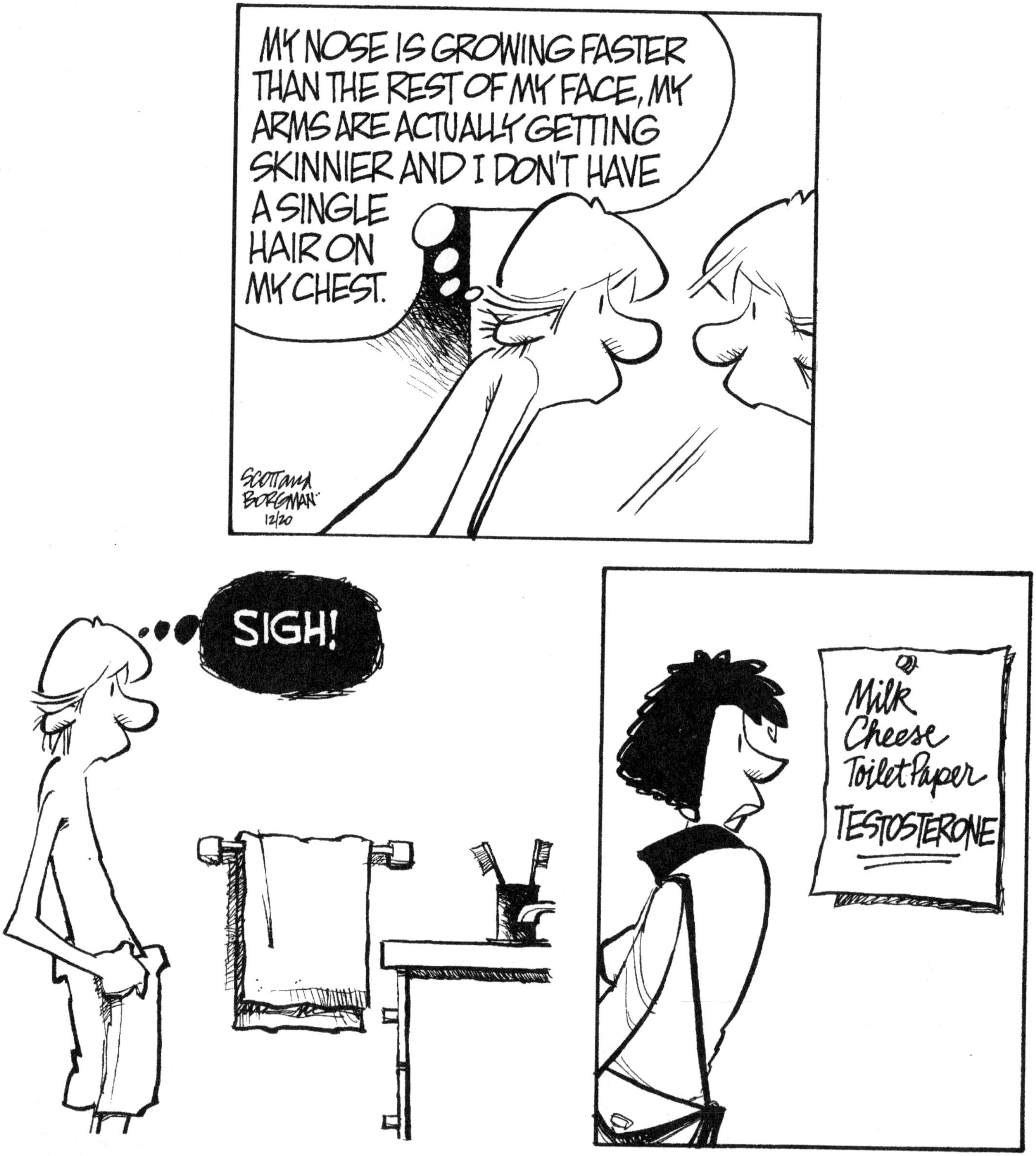
MY NOSE IS GROWING FASTER THAN THE REST OF MY FACE, MY ARMS ARE ACTUALLY GETTING SKINNIER AND I DON'T HAVE A SINGLE HAIR ON MY CHEST.
SIGH!
Milk
Cheese
Toilet Paper
TESTOSTERONE